What people are saying about …

A Practical Guide *to* Culture

"Everyone who works with students and cares about their future needs this guide. It's exactly what the title says: practical. John and Brett have filled this book with clarity, wisdom, and loving advice on the most important issues facing this generation."

Eric Metaxas, author of *Bonhoeffer* and nationally syndicated radio host

"Culture is dynamic and changing—and that change often comes in waves that threaten to overwhelm us. But as Christians, we're able to secure ourselves to solid, unchanging truth in the chaotic ocean of culture. John Stonestreet and Brett Kunkle show us how to navigate the tides and pass those skills on to the next generation."

Jim Daly, president of Focus on the Family

"*A Practical Guide to Culture* is a profound, witty, and forthright manual written by two concerned dads who also happen to be two of the most effective worldview and apologetics experts of our day. Based on their deep experience working with tens of thousands of teenagers, John and Brett show how to stop giving in to a degrading culture that makes kids unhealthy and sad and how to start raising kids who love Jesus and live without fear and regret."

Jeff Myers, PhD, president of Summit Ministries

"I wish John Stonestreet and Brett Kunkle had written *A Practical Guide to Culture* years ago. As a parent and youth pastor, I was often concerned about the impact the culture might have on my children and students, and I wasn't always sure how to address the challenges. John and Brett have written a hopeful, engaging book that will prepare parents, educators, and youth leaders to equip young minds. This isn't just a survey of culture; it's an active, purposeful, and thoughtful action plan. If you want your students and children to represent Christ in a fallen world as they thrive in their Christian walk, *A Practical Guide to Culture* is an essential guide."

J. Warner Wallace, cold-case detective, adjunct professor of apologetics at Biola University, and author of *Cold-Case Christianity, God's Crime Scene*, and *Forensic Faith*

"Will the next generation be defined by the radical cultural shifts taking place, or will the culture be defined by a generation committed to the radical love, redemptive truth, and restorative grace of Jesus? In *A Practical Guide to Culture,* John Stonestreet and Brett Kunkle provide a biblically based roadmap designed to assist a generation's navigation through the difficult currents of relativism, decadence, and apathy, while simultaneously shining the light of Christ."

Rev. Samuel Rodriguez, president of the National Hispanic Christian Leadership Conference

"A wise and accessible guide for Christian parents in these rapidly changing times. Stonestreet and Kunkle do more than scratch the surface; they take us deeper into the underlying worldview issues that give rise to so many conflicts in our culture."

Trevin Wax, Bible and reference publisher for LifeWay Christian Resources and author of several books, including *This Is Our Time*

"*A Practical Guide to Culture* is smart, clear, and incredibly helpful for Christians trying to raise faithful, resilient children in a post-Christian—and increasingly anti-Christian—society. This is a book written by intelligent men who know how to relate big ideas to daily life in terms everyone can understand. When people ask me, 'But what can we Christians do about the collapsing culture?', I will emphatically recommend this book as the place to begin. I'm buying two copies: one for my family's use and one for my pastor's."

Rod Dreher, author of *The Benedict Option*

"*A Practical Guide to Culture* lives up to its name. John and Brett have written an insightful, timely, and easy-to-use book that will help youth influencers guide students through some of the most murky issues of our day. They tackle issues like consumerism, pornography, gender identity, racial tension, and more. And they do it with both clarity and conviction. If you are a parent, teacher, or youth worker, this book is an indispensable guide."

Sean McDowell, PhD, author, speaker, and professor

"Using illustrations, data, and ideas, John and Brett masterfully explain why we're facing the contemporary cultural challenges we are. They uncover what God wants us to understand about them and what we can do. Their explanation of the Bible and the way they consistently frame issues with the Bible story is a refreshing perspective I haven't seen or heard. It's compelling and extremely valuable. You and your children can move from anger to love, despair to hope, apathy to involvement, fear to confidence, ignorance to wisdom, and isolation to collaboration. You'll be empowered and full of hope."

Kathy Koch, PhD, founder and president of Celebrate Kids, Inc.

A Practical Guide *to* Culture

John Stonestreet & Brett Kunkle

A Practical Guide *to* Culture

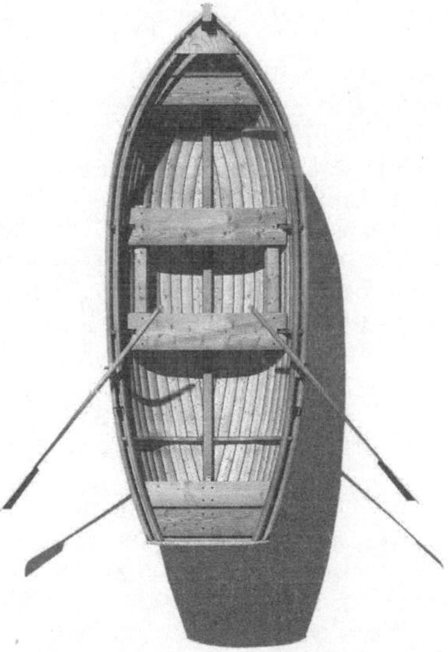

Helping *the* Next Generation Navigate Today's World

DAVID C COOK
transforming lives together

A PRACTICAL GUIDE TO CULTURE
Published by David C Cook
4050 Lee Vance Drive
Colorado Springs, CO 80918 U.S.A.

Integrity Music Limited, a Division of David C Cook
Eastbourne, East Sussex BN23 6NT, England

The graphic circle C logo is a registered trademark of David C Cook.

LCCN 2017931374
ISBN 978-1-4347-1101-4
eISBN 978-1-4347-1178-6

The Team: Tim Peterson, Keith Jones, Amy Konyndyk, Nick Lee,
Jennifer Lonas, Abby DeBenedittis, Susan Murdock
Cover Design: James Hershberger
Cover Photo: Getty Images

Printed in the United States of America
First Edition 2017

5 6 7 8 9 10 11 12 13 14

052318

To Erin and Sarah, the loves of our lives and the mothers of our children, who make us better men, better fathers, and better at what we do.

We outkicked our punt coverage when we found you.

Contents

Part Four: Christian Worldview Essentials

Acknowledgments

Due to the sheer number of topics covered in this book, and given my tendency to be a translator—rather than an originator—of good ideas, there is no way that I will be able to recognize all to whom I am indebted in the writing of this book. Those who have served as my teachers and mentors in person and in print include, but are not limited to, Chuck Colson, Francis Schaeffer, T. M. Moore, Abraham Kuyper, Rod Thompson, C. S. Lewis, Bill Brown, C. Ben Mitchell, Jennifer Marshall, Don Armstrong, Rod Dreher, Kevin Vanhoozer, Eric Metaxas, Ed Stetzer, Joni Eareckson Tada, Ravi Zacharias, Craig M. Gay, J. I. Packer, W. Gary Phillips, Paul Henderson, Timothy George, Roberto Rivera, Os Guinness, Steven Garber, Scott Klusendorf, Jeff Myers, Glenn Stanton, Jeff Ventrella, David Noebel, John Woodbridge, and my parents.

Culture is a big topic and is much more easily theorized about than engaged in. Yet we live in *this* time and place, and not another. I am thankful to Cris Doornbos and Tim Peterson, of David C Cook, for catching the vision of this book and for being so helpful throughout the entire writing and publishing process.

It was a real pleasure to work with Brett Kunkle, a friend and co-conspirator on a number of life-giving and significant projects. I am also grateful to David Carlson and the Colson Center editorial team, with whom I share a constant exchange of argument, insight, and observation about culture that eventually come out in the *BreakPoint* commentaries. Thanks also to the Colson Center board of directors who allowed me to take on this project and to Steve Verleye, who gladly allowed his second career to significantly intensify while my head was buried in researching and writing.

And to my bride Sarah and my three girls—you have been so gracious in allowing me the time and space to write, while still brightening my days with more love, laughter, and happiness than I deserve.

John Stonestreet
Colorado Springs, CO

For me, it starts with my mom and dad. They came to Christ when I was an infant and brought me up in the fear, knowledge, and wisdom of the Lord. Thank you for providing a home where I was not only loved, but where God's Story was proclaimed and lived out.

For eleven years, there were countless young people who were gracious enough to let me work with them when I was a young naive youth pastor. I am indebted to these students. You gave me space and grace to begin working out many of the ideas that have come to fruition in this book.

There are two groups of people who have been formative in the discipleship of my mind and thus have had an important influence on this book. First, I am grateful for the brilliant and godly men who taught and mentored me as I slowly (very slowly!) worked my way through a master's degree in philosophy of religion and ethics at Talbot School of Theology. J. P. Moreland, Scott Rae, Garry DeWeese, Doug Geivett, and David Horner have had a massive impact on my life.

Second, I am grateful to the past and present team at Stand to Reason. In particular, Greg Koukl, Melinda Penner, Alan Shlemon, Amy Hall, and Scott Klusendorf (now the president of Life Training Institute) have helped shape my thinking over the last fourteen years, and I'm thankful for their influence.

John Stonestreet isn't just a coauthor but a true friend and kingdom partner. It has been a joy and pleasure to work with my friend on this project. The team at David C Cook has been phenomenal. A huge thanks to Cris Doornbos, Tim Peterson, Abby DeBenedittis, Michelle Webb, and Annette Brickbealer for their commitment to this book and tremendous patience with its authors. And my good friends Brad and Cindy Heck were incredibly generous to let me escape to their idyllic mountain cabin anytime I needed, where much of my writing was completed.

Finally, and most significantly, there's no adequate way to communicate how the most important people to me—my wife, Erin, and our five kids (Alexis, Micah, Paige, Ella, and Jonah)—have deeply shaped my life and helped me become a better husband, father, and man. Thank you for every big and little sacrifice you made to allow me the time and space to write. After Jesus, my family has been God's greatest gift to me.

Brett Kunkle
Orange County, CA

Introduction

My name is Brett, and I surf. As a surfing dad, I've dreamed of the day when my kids will paddle out to the lineup and catch waves on their own, with me cheering them on. But the ocean can be a punishing place. Pounding waves can give them such a beating, they may never want to go back in the ocean. So there are steps I must take now to protect and prepare my kids for the waves I hope one day they'll ride on their own.

As Christian dads, John and I both dream of the day our kids will wade out into the culture and impact the world for Christ. But like ocean waves, the culture can be a punishing place too. How many kids do you know who have been raised in the church only to be lost to the world after (and sometimes before) they leave home? How many Christian students, who seem to be grounded in the faith, end up making poor decisions that harm themselves and others?

Some Christian parents, oblivious to any danger, send their kids into the culture headfirst. Others think total protection is the answer, prohibiting their kids from ever dipping a toe in the cultural waters until they're out on their own. Most of us vacillate between these extremes, depending on the issue and maybe the child. Neither extreme, however, will bring about the vision of a courageous, new generation of Christ followers, able and willing to not only navigate the cultural waters without drowning but also emerge as leaders in the days ahead.

It's always been rough out there, but the palpable sense of many American Christians—especially parents—is that the cultural currents have shifted and intensified. The past few years have brought a tsunami of change, and not for the better. One issue after another after another hits us like a series of waves at high tide. We wonder if and how our kids can keep their heads above water, much less live the sort of flourishing Christian lives we hope they will. As dads, we wonder how we can too.

John and I have invested much of our lives working with the emerging generation of kids, as well as their parents, teachers, mentors, and church leaders. John has spent the past decade and a half observing culture, following stories and tracking trends, helping Christians understand the world around them, and calling them to engage it. I've spent my entire career in youth ministry, first as a youth pastor and then as the director of student impact for Stand to Reason (www.str.org), an apologetics ministry committed to equipping Christians to be ambassadors of Christ.

We, too, sense that times have changed. In our lifetimes, we have never seen the pressure on Christian conviction greater than it is right now. We try to avoid alarmism, but standing for Christ in our culture is getting harder and harder.

The kids we care about most, however, are our own. Forgive us for being selfish, but between our families, we have nine little image bearers we love more than anything (including a little Stonestreet who will leave the oven sometime before this book is published). Though both of us married out of our leagues, we know even that distinct advantage doesn't guarantee our kids won't struggle. There are no perfect parents, and there are no perfect kids. Still, we'll do everything we can to teach our kids to trust God, read the cultural waters, and ride above the waves without drowning.

We know you care about the next generation of kids too. We wrote this book for all who have a vested interest in their success like we do. The kids of today will build the culture of tomorrow. We've aimed this book at parents, grandparents, mentors, teachers, and pastors who have some little image bearers in their lives, as we have in ours, and who want to see them navigate this cultural moment as champions for Christ.

By now you've likely noticed a metaphor. We chose the imagery of the ocean partly because I am, at heart, a surf bum, but mostly because it's a terrific analogy for culture. Like the ocean, culture is all around us. Just as fish swim in the ocean, culture is the water in which we swim. (We'll present more on this in the next chapter.) Also, like the ocean, culture has both seen and unseen elements. Though cultural undercurrents are invisible, they powerfully pressure us to conform to their collective assumptions about the world. Cultural issues, however, are more like waves: seen, heard, and felt. Understanding both is critically important if we're to keep our heads above water.

Part 1 provides a framework of culture for Christians. In the first chapter, we define culture, both what it is and what it is not.

Culture is a lot of things, but it's not everything. In the second chapter, we put culture in the context of the gospel because, well, that's where it belongs. Too many Christians try to put the gospel in the context of culture, but we think that's getting things exactly backward. In the third chapter, we suggest what success will look like in this cultural moment. What is it we hope our kids will become in this culture? How will we know if they're okay? We hope this chapter helps parents like us who may struggle with the idol of safety.

Once the framework is in place, we'll turn our attention to our current cultural moment. Every culture is made up of both obvious issues and less-than-obvious trends or norms. It's vital to understand both.

Part 2 focuses on those powerful yet subtle undercurrents of our culture that often go unnoticed. For example, chapter 4 examines the significant ramifications of living in the information age, where there's a lot of noise but little truth. Chapter 5 examines the crucial issue of identity or what it means to be human, which is, as many have noted, in crisis in the West today. Kids are given very few societal resources for coming to grips with who they are, but the church has the best story of humanity on the market. Chapter 6 examines how we can help kids navigate a technoculture that threatens their relational capacities. While chapter 5 talks about what it means to be human, this chapter will talk about how to be human together. In chapter 7, we'll discuss the loss of virtue in an age of extended adolescence. If Christian kids can just *grow up*, they'll be way ahead of many of their peers.

Each chapter in part 3 focuses on a singular cultural issue (or "wave"). The first four chapters deal with what our friend Jay Richards has called "the pelvic issues": pornography, casual sex, sexual orientation, and gender identity. Each of these issues has to do with how our culture currently misunderstands sex and sexuality. The remaining chapters deal with the issues of affluence and consumerism, addiction, entertainment, and racial tension. In each chapter, we identify the cultural lies, compare those lies with biblical truth, and offer both practical action points and a vision of hope for overcoming the challenges these issues present.

Parents or mentors facing a particular issue may just want to jump to the appropriate chapter in part 3. That's fine, of course, but don't miss the big-picture teachings in parts 1 and 2. Too many Christians have a tendency to *react* to what is loudest and noisiest in our culture, which often means *overreacting* to what isn't ultimately important and *underreacting* to what is.

Finally, part 4 contains four shorter chapters on topics that, through the writing of this book, repeatedly popped up as essential "tool kit" items. We call these "Christian worldview essentials" for parents and kids. There are other essentials of a Christian worldview, of course, but these are the ones that seem particularly important for the task this book seeks to tackle: empowering parents and mentors to help kids navigate this cultural moment.

Throughout the book, we rely heavily on the insights of others. As students of culture ourselves, John and I want you to be aware of men and women who see the world more clearly than we do. So be sure to check out the endnotes and the books, articles, videos, and other helpful tools we recommend in each chapter. We rely on these resources, but, we should add, they shouldn't be blamed for any mistakes, oversights, or misrepresentations on our part. We'll take the blame for those while hoping and praying this book serves and helps those who are concerned with serving and helping the next generation.

Part One

Why Culture Matters

Chapter One

What Culture Is and What It Does to Us

The problem of leading a Christian life in a non-Christian society is now very present to us.... And as for the Christian who is not conscious of his dilemma—and he is in the majority—he is becoming more and more de-Christianized by all sorts of unconscious pressure: paganism holds all the most valuable advertising space.

T. S. Eliot, *The Idea of a Christian Society*

I (John) once quoted an ancient Chinese proverb to a group of high school students: "If you want to know what water is, don't ask the fish." I then asked, "Why shouldn't you ask the fish?"

A smart-aleck student replied, "Because fish can't talk!"

The correct answer is that fish don't know they're wet. In one sense, of course, there is nothing fish know more than water. But the proverb points to the difficulty of understanding our own environment, the one in which we are completely immersed and take for granted as normal.

Culture is for humans what water is for fish: the environment we live in and think is normal. The main difference is, unlike the fish, we make our own environments. Humans impose themselves on the world in a way animals don't. Animals make habitats in the world, but humans make little worlds within the world. Culture is, in fact, one of the things that makes us different from the animals.

Like fish immersed in water, we become so immersed in ways of thinking and patterns of living that we become unable to recognize them. Think of being unaware of the sheer beauty of a mountain you've always lived near or not recognizing the dysfunction of an abusive family because it was the only one you knew. Culture shapes our perceptions of reality in similar ways, and short of doing the hard, intentional work of examining the culture around us, it won't occur to us that the world should be any different.

That's not to say, of course, that we'll necessarily like the world we live in. People will always find certain aspects of their culture more or less enjoyable, convenient, and attractive than others. We may even find ourselves longing to live elsewhere because we're disgusted by the lifestyles or values reflected in the products, the art, or the neighbors we encounter. But reacting to specific cultural expressions isn't the same thing as being fully aware of the cultural forces impacting our lives.

Those forces, however, demand our attention. Few things shape us like the issues, ideas, habits, and influences of our culture. In fact, some postmodern theorists argue that *nothing but culture* shapes us. When it comes to how we think about gender and the structure of families, arrange our governments, define and pursue success, choose art to create and enjoy, and a million other details, we are—they say—"socially constructed" beings.

Of course, Christians say our truest identity is determined by God, fixed in our humanity. We are, Scripture tells us, the pinnacle of God's creation, made to be His image bearers (Gen. 1:26–28), and we're therefore much more than mere products of our social environments.

Academics have long studied the relationship between individuals and their cultures, but this topic should also matter to the rest of us because of its enormous everyday implications. In fact, as we'll see throughout this book, how humans and human life are understood, valued, and treated are critical indicators of a culture's health. Of all the reasons we must be *intentional* to make sense of culture, this is the most important. The biblical vision of our identity and value as the most precious of God's creation also acknowledges just how much the norms of our time and place shape us.

You may be thinking by now, *When are we going to get to the interesting stuff? Enough of all this theory. I need help navigating my family through same-sex marriage, transgender bathrooms, Snapchat, #BlackLivesMatter, and evolution. Let's get practical already!*

Trust us, we'll get to the practical. The goal of this book is not to merely talk about culture but to help the next generation *live well* in the culture. To be human and to be alive is to deal with a world of ideas, values, issues, artifacts, institutions, and structures. We have no choice but to jump in, make decisions, interact with others, and build lives together as families and citizens while navigating around the land mines that seem to be everywhere.

It's a daunting task. We may be fully aware of the hot topics of our time and yet be oblivious to the many cultural undercurrents shaping how we think and live. Beneath the obvious issues, debates, and controversies (the "waves") that dominate our nation's twenty-four-hour news cycle and our personal social-media feeds are the subtle, often-unseen, yet important norms of culture (the "under-currents"). We'll start with the undercurrents not only because they tend to be outside our critical reflection but also because we must understand them in order to fully grasp the issues discussed later in the book. After all, culture's greatest influence is in what it presents as being *normal.* Clearly, not all that seems normal *ought* to be, but what is left unexamined is also left unchallenged. As C. S. Lewis said, "The most dangerous ideas in a society are not the ones that are being argued, but the ones that are assumed."[1]

For example, it's easy to wonder how anyone could be ambivalent toward, much less support, such a grave evil as genocide. "How could they have done that?" we ask before claiming, "I certainly would have been on the right side of that one!" Smugly, we think ourselves immune to the great evils of the past, confident we see more clearly than our morally unenlightened ancestors, as if we have no blind spots of our own.

However, any illusion of moral superiority over those who lived before us is what C. S. Lewis aptly labeled "chronological snobbery."[2] Each culture has its own blind spots. Thinking otherwise reveals our ignorance not only of the subtle power culture wields over our hearts and minds but also of the universal human condition that infects all people in all times and all places.

For our sake, and especially for the sake of the next generation, we must think clearly about the most important issues of our time, as well as the dehumanizing undercurrents driving those issues. To start, we need to be clear on what culture *is* and what it *is not*. With an accurate and useful definition of *culture*, we can clarify how it works and what it does to us. Along the way, we'll talk about ideas, their consequences, and their champions. We'll also talk about the roles artifacts and institutions play, and the importance of structures and habits. All of this is involved in talking about culture.

What Culture Is (and What It Is Not)[3]

Among Christians, *culture* is a word much used but rarely defined. It comes from the Latin word *cultura*, which means "agriculture." If plowing, tilling, and cultivating come to mind, they should. In its most basic sense, culture refers to what people do with the world: we build, we invent, we imagine, we create, we tear down, we replace, we compose, we design, we emphasize, we dismiss, we embellish, we engineer. As Andy Crouch says, "Culture is what human beings make of the world."[4]

Cultivating is exactly the sort of behavior the Scriptures would have us expect from God's image bearers. After all, He commanded our first parents to "be fruitful and multiply and fill the earth and subdue it" (Gen. 1:28).[5] God made humans with the capacity to do something with His world, and that's exactly what we do. Culture was an integral part of God's plan for us and His world from the very beginning.

Another term found within the word *culture* adds necessary texture to our understanding. Culture, Chuck Colson often said, is a reflection of the belief system, or "cult" of a group of people. "When you have a healthy cult, you have a healthy culture."[6] Colson wasn't referring to a cult in the creepy commune, dress-in-burlap, share-all-of-your-possessions, and distribute-religious-literature sense. Rather, he used the word *cult* to point us to the deeply held religious beliefs of a culture. He was clarifying that humans do more *with* the world than merely trying to survive in it. We have conceptions of God, truth, morality, humanity, and history that shape how we live.

We live life the way we do because of our worldview. Our worldview, whether or not we're consciously aware of it, informs our actions in the world and our interactions with others. It consists of our deeply held beliefs about God, morality, and the nature of reality. As many have noted, humans are incurably religious creatures. (John Calvin even called human nature a "perpetual factory of idols."[7]) The cultures we create reflect our religious commitments.

This is why cultures differ so greatly from one time and place to another. As Christian apologist Ravi Zacharias often says, "In some cultures, people love their neighbors. In other cultures, they eat them." Dramatic differences between cultures reveal dramatic differences of worldview. Dramatic shifts within a culture, like those that have taken place over the past few decades in the West, reveal a dramatic shift in worldview. Understanding worldview is crucial to understanding cultures.

Even so, there's more to culture than worldview. Ken Myers of *Mars Hill Audio* has a great job. He reads good books, interviews their authors, and then sells audio recordings of the interviews to people like us. It's a sweet gig if you can get it. To be fair, Myers has written some excellent books himself, including the cleverly titled *All God's Children and Blue Suede Shoes.* In it, he offers this description of culture:

> It's not a person. It's not even an institution, like the church or the state or the family. It is instead a dynamic pattern, an ever-changing matrix of objects, artifacts, sounds, institutions, philosophies, fashions, enthusiasms, myths, prejudices, relationships, attitudes, tastes, rituals, habits, colors, and loves, all embodied in individual people, in groups and collectives and associations of people (many of whom do not know they are associated), in books, in buildings, in the use of time and space, in wars, in jokes, and in food.[8]

In addition to highlighting things we don't always associate with culture and the interdependence of things we don't always associate with each other, Myers also demonstrates how helpful it can be to describe what culture is *not.*

For example, culture is not the same thing as nature, or creation. There is a world outside ourselves that God created. "In the beginning," says Genesis 1:1, "God created the heavens and the earth." Culture doesn't refer to this created world; rather, it refers to what humans do with it. To clarify a bit further, culture refers not to what humans do by instinct or nature (like circulating blood, eating food, having sex, or sleeping) but to what they do freely (like donating blood for a good cause, garnishing food before serving it, committing to marital monogamy, or sleeping in elaborately decorated beds with more pillows than one could possibly need in a lifetime).

Also, culture doesn't just refer to all the bad stuff humans do. For many Christians, "the culture" is synonymous with the kind of debauched music, alternative lifestyles, liberal education, alcoholic indulgence, social policies, immodest dress, and sexualized movies that tempt young adults to abandon their morals and their faith. It's the bad, worldly stuff "out there" (as opposed to the Christian stuff "in here"), reflected in the statement "The culture is destroying our kids."

As fathers of teens, preteens, and young children, Brett and I fully understand these sentiments. Trust us. We get it. What passes these days as art, education, fashion, progress, and fun makes us angry and worried about the souls of those little image bearers entrusted to our care. It often feels as if "the culture" is out to steal our kids, and in ways far less subtle and more dangerous than when our parents worried about *Three's Company*, Aerosmith, the Soviet Union, and Bill Clinton. Those days seem tame compared to Tinder, Miley Cyrus, ISIS, *Obergefell v. Hodges*, and the indoctrination that passes as sex education in elementary schools.

Certainly every culture consists of bad things, but it's incomplete to think of these things *as* the culture. Culture includes the good, the bad, the morally neutral, and the morally complex.

We also should distinguish between people and culture. People make culture and are, in turn, shaped by culture, but equating them with culture is wrong and can even be dangerous. If we see people as culture and culture as the enemy, we'll likely see people as the enemy and confuse their bad ideas with evil intentions. But culture is not people; culture is what people *do* as people.

Finally, culture isn't fixed, static, or monolithic. In a time and place not so long ago, bell-bottom jeans were considered high fashion, but not anymore. And at one time in our history, most Americans didn't go to an office or company to work; they worked where they lived. This changed more than a century ago. It was also normal to stay married for life, write letters by hand, and answer the telephone *before* knowing who was calling—but no longer. Culture is dynamic. It changes according to human innovations, inventions, fashions, and ideas. What one generation considers normal, the next generation thinks of as odd or funny. In the same way, grandparents shake their heads at the fashions, entertainment choices, values, and lifestyles of the young, and vice versa.

Adding to the dynamic nature of a culture are its subcultures. Though cultural norms span groups of people within a country or society (like interstate highways, Internet access, and a federal government), trends, fashions, and ways of life distinguish some groups of people from others (like farming, hiking, hymn singing, or homeschooling). Especially in the Western world (and nowhere more than in America!), it's more accurate to speak of cultures (plural) than of a singular culture. In the chapters that follow, we'll examine the undercurrents that are shaping our cultural moment and influencing, in different ways, life across most subcultures.

How Culture Works and What It Does to Us

Culture, then, in its most basic sense is what people do with the world. But clearly more needs to be said. After all, not everything we do becomes part of culture. For example, people commit murder, but that behavior is seen as criminal and antisocial. In 2010, entertainer Lady Gaga wore a dress made of meat to the MTV Video Music Awards, but it didn't become a fashion trend. In New York City, you may encounter a hipster hauling an old-timey typewriter to Starbucks, but the *New York Times* is still using computers. To make sense of what does and doesn't affect culture, we need to unpack some sociology.

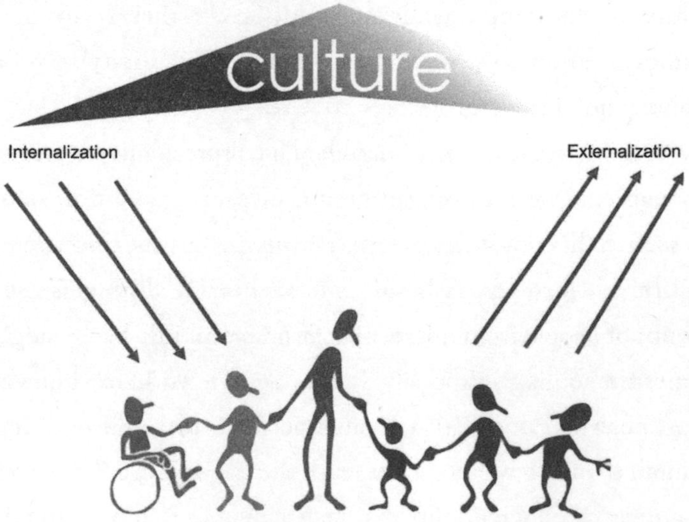

According to sociologist Peter Berger, "Every human society is an enterprise of world-building."[9] That seems obvious enough: we build bridges to connect islands to other islands to the mainland, so that we can build houses and stores and universities and theaters there. We decorate those houses, stock shelves in those stores, hire professors for the universities, and make movies to show in theaters so we can overcharge for popcorn. The big polysyllabic word for this is *externalization*. Humans externalize their values, imaginations, innovations, and ideas on the world around them by what they do. Most of what we do is consistent with our culture, but not always. That's why cultures change: new things are created, and old things are left behind.

When what we do becomes part of our normal way of living together, it's called *objectification*. Cultures are environments, or "worlds," we create for ourselves.[10] For example, automobile ownership is an objectified, or normal, part of the culture in most American communities because we've put things like highways, exit ramps, driver's licenses, stoplights, and well-paying jobs in our communities. In New York City, however, many people forgo owning a car because of the robust public-transportation system, close proximity of stores and employment, and ridiculous traffic. In that sense, and many others, what is normal in New York City isn't normal in Wichita, Kansas, a fact that quickly becomes obvious to the tourist who foolishly rents a car at LaGuardia Airport.

The power of what we experience as normal, though largely unnoticed until we experience a different "normal," cannot be overstated. In fact, cultural norms determine much of our daily lives: our schedules, what we like and don't like, what we buy, what we eat, and how we spend our money. The big polysyllabic word for how culture shapes us is *internalization*. We internalize culture as we settle into its routines, lifestyles, and habits, and as we consume its products, ideas, and assumptions about the world.

So, to summarize, cultures consist of those products of human activity that have collectively taken on a life of their own. The worlds we create powerfully influence our lives by convincing us of what is normal. As we live in a culture, we become committed to its vision of life, unless we're intentional otherwise.[11] In other words, we make our cultures, and then our cultures shape us.

What Culture Is Made Of

When we say that culture shapes us, what do we mean? Primarily, we're talking about how culture catechizes us to its way of life, or forms us into its image.

First, we absorb the *ideas* of our culture. Culture is built on ideas, though these ideas often fly under our radar. What is true? What is good? What is worthy of our love and devotion? In a pluralistic society like ours where so many different ideas about life and the world have a say, it's tempting to embrace the idea that truth, goodness, and beauty are mere matters of opinion rather than objective for all people whether they believe it or not. In cultures dominated by Islam or a Communist ideology, it's different.

"Ideas," as Richard Weaver said, "have *consequences*." These consequences are also part of culture. For example, in parts of the world with bad ideas about work and freedom, many people find themselves trapped in systemic poverty. They may even feel it's hopeless to work harder because there doesn't seem to be any point to doing so. In America, where so many live for the moment and struggle to delay gratification, people tend to think it's normal to live with oppressive personal debt.

Ideas spread in a culture through *champions*. Certainly, this would include philosophers and academics. However, these originators of ideas rarely change culture without significant help from artists, storytellers, entrepreneurs, and educators. For example, the ideas of the sexual revolution—which have dramatically reshaped American culture over the last several decades—owe their origin to folks like Alfred Kinsey, of whom many have never heard. Most people, however, would recognize the name Hugh Hefner, founder of *Playboy* magazine and perhaps the most influential "artist" who championed the sexual revolution

Artists, storytellers, entrepreneurs, and educators communicate their ideas through their *artifacts*—songs, books, classes, tools, and other means. These artifacts become part of our experience and shape our culture. For example, the Protestant Reformation would never have shifted culture in the profound ways it did had the printing press not spiked the literacy rate and made books, especially the Bible, more accessible to everyday people.

When it comes to maintaining and perpetuating culture, *institutions* play the chief role. The primary institutions of a society are the family, church, and government, but other institutions contribute to culture as well. Culture determines how these institutions function and carry with them the power to enforce a certain way of life. For example, educational institutions develop and then enforce certain standards for certification, effectively becoming the gatekeepers of specific professions. In America, the institutions of media decide what counts as news, spending inordinate time on faux controversies while ignoring damning videos about the abortion industry. The effects of institutions ripple throughout the culture. Friends of Brett and mine who have traveled to North Korea, for example, describe a culture-wide distrust resulting from the oppressive regime of Kim Jong Un that divides neighbors, families, and coworkers.

When social institutions change, so does culture. When certain institutions become less influential, others become more influential. In our lifetimes, shifts in the family, such as no-fault divorce, cohabitation, and extended singleness, have significantly reshaped American culture. Now that the legal definition of marriage has changed in the United States, those in other professions (like wedding photographers and county clerks) are being forced to comply. As the church becomes less important in the everyday lives of citizens, other sources of moral authority become more important, for better or worse.

As ideas and their consequences become embedded in a culture, reinforced by the stuff we use (artifacts) and our institutions, our way of life becomes structured. It's now normal to spend our quiet moments looking on our devices for memes, tweets, or texts we may have missed. It's normal to absorb high levels of debt to buy a home or go to grad school. It doesn't seem strange to spend Thanksgiving eating enormous amounts of turkey before trampling security guards and other shoppers in a frenzied quest for 4-D televisions on Black Friday. Many cultures would find it strange that we buy dead trees in parking lots every December only to replant them in our living rooms. But that's what we do!

Culture tends to shape us most deeply by what it presents as normal. We are creatures of cultural habit. Our loves, our longings, our loyalties, and our labors can become products of the liturgies our culture imposes. We live according to them but rarely think through them. Unintentionally, we become culture shaped rather than intentional about shaping culture.

But the Lord Jesus calls Christians not to be "conformed to this world, but … transformed by the renewal of [our minds]" (Rom. 12:2). Thankfully, He's given us a Story bigger than the cultural moment to make this possible.

Discussion Questions

1. What are some of the mistaken ways you've heard people talk about the culture?

2. What are the often unnoticed norms of the local culture where you live? How are they different from what you've seen or experienced in other cultures?

3. Which ideas are most influential in American culture today? Who are the champions of these ideas? What artifacts communicate them?

Chapter Two

Keeping the Moment and the Story Straight

No, the Bible isn't a book of rules, or a book of heroes. The Bible is most of all a Story ... [and] the best thing about this Story is—it's true.

Sally Lloyd-Jones, *The Jesus Storybook Bible*

My (John's) first real exposure to rock music took place in church. Gyrating, big-hair bands and Madonna lyrics rightly concerned my youth pastor, so he decided to confront them head-on with a video about the evils of rock and roll. Unfortunately, it backfired.

Secular musicians were demon possessed, we were told. The proof for that claim was backmasking. Popular rock records, when played backwards, supposedly revealed hidden, nefarious messages. For example, played backward, a popular Cheap Trick song said, "Satan holds the key to the lock," and Queen's "Another One Bites the Dust" commanded its listeners, "It's fun to smoke marijuana."

We were skeptical. I remember thinking at the time, *I can't understand what Ozzie Osbourne says forward*, and that was when he was just talking. Not only that, but cassette tapes had replaced vinyl records by the time we watched the video. They were impossible to backmask. Had new technology really foiled Satan's plot to brainwash us?

Plus, we *liked* the music. *AC/DC is awesome*, we thought and proceeded to the music store. That's not to say we should have liked the chaotic, hypersexualized, darkly violent, and rebellious music dominating the airwaves in the early to mideighties, but we did. Telling us "That's bad, so stay away" didn't work.

In one sense, this anecdote illustrates the age-old struggle between older and younger generations. "Things are getting worse and worse," older generations say. "Music is raunchier, films are more sexually explicit, fashion is immodest, and young people stare at screens all day!"

"This stuff is so cool," respond the young. And this struggle repeats itself over and over and over.

On a deeper level, however, this anecdote illustrates a well-intended but ultimately misguided approach to culture. In the previous chapter, we offered a framework for understanding what culture is and what it does to us. In this chapter, we'll discuss how to approach culture.

The Story and the Moment

Christians say the Scriptures are true. What we mean (or ought to mean) by that is not that they are true *for us* or true to those who believe it or just one truth among many truths. Rather, the Scriptures claim to be *objectively* true, or as Francis Schaeffer used to say, "[True] with a capital T."[1] In other words, the Scriptures describe reality as it actually is.

One might refuse to believe in gravity, but stubbornness doesn't change truthfulness. The Scriptures are like gravity in that they're true whether we believe them or not. But they differ from gravity in that they don't describe just one particular aspect of reality. Rather, they describe the Big Story of reality. Granted, the Scriptures don't give specific details about everything, but they do provide the overarching Story of the world, humanity, and history. They tell us where everything came from, including us, and where everything is going, including us.

We must understand that crucial point to rightly understand and approach culture. No matter how chaotic, grave, disturbing, broken, or troubling our cultural moment may be, its full meaning is revealed only in light of the larger Story of which it is a part. In other words, we must learn to approach our cultural moment from the Big Story. Otherwise, we'll miss the meaning of both the moment and the Story.

Imagine someone abandoning The Lord of the Rings trilogy because he was deeply miffed that Gandalf fell off the bridge and died as he was fighting that demon-like creature near the end of the first book. "What kind of author kills off such a cool character as Gandalf?" he complains. "I quit! I want nothing to do with that kind of story!"

Any Tolkien groupie worth his salt would interject, "Wait! That's not the whole story. (Spoiler alert!) Gandalf doesn't die. He comes back. And he's no longer Gandalf the Grey; he's Gandalf the White. And in the end, he's part of the good that defeats evil."

Like our fictional Lord of the Rings reader, we're also at risk of losing the Story in the heat of the cultural moment, particularly when the world seems to be spinning out of control. Reeling from a tragedy or an election, trying to navigate a world where wrong is right and raunchy is popular, we often become reactionary and approach culture by asking the wrong question first. The anecdote that opened this chapter is a good example.

"Where Should I Draw the Line?"

Many Christians divide the world into sacred and secular, or spiritual and worldly. Everything on the spiritual side is good, and everything on the worldly side is bad. So when they approach culture, their primary concern is to keep from crossing the line from good to bad.

When Brett and I were teenagers, Christian music was good, and rock music was bad (and no one seemed to know what to do with "Christian rock" music). The theater was a bad place for Christians to go, but then some Christians decided to make movies. What now? Believers often champion Christian-themed movies, but what about good films that aren't explicitly Christian? What about historically based films that, though violent, remind us of courageous heroes and defining moments that changed the world? Does Kirk Cameron have to be in a movie for it to be good? If Tom Cruise is in a movie, is it automatically a promo for Scientology?

Asking "Where do I draw the line?"—called the *line approach* to culture—is too simplistic to be helpful. First, not everything labeled Christian is good, and not everything labeled secular is bad. Much that is labeled Christian—movies, songs, leaders, schools, churches, ministries, and organizations—fails to reach basic levels of excellence and honesty. And much that is labeled secular accurately portrays fallen humanity, displays artistic genius, and brings good to the world. As Gregory Thornbury, the president of The King's College, is fond of saying, "'Christian' is the greatest of all possible nouns and lamest of all possible adjectives." It's meant to describe a person, not a thing.

Additionally, an honest look at Christian history reveals we don't always draw lines in the right places. Not that long ago, some Christians drew lines between races by segregating seminaries, condemning interracial marriages, and promoting other ways of keeping apart equally valuable image bearers who looked different than they did. Out-of-context Bible verses and stories were used to prop up this sinful behavior. Mistakes like these reveal just how susceptible we are to cultural pressure. On a lighter note, card playing, dancing, trendy fashions, political careers, and other cultural "stuff" have fallen victim to arbitrary line drawing, and when those lines move, it's not lost on younger generations. Line drawing is a reaction to the cultural moment, not a firm grounding in the Christian Story.

Of course, Christians must have standards. Scripture is clear that we ought not associate with "works of darkness" (Eph. 5:11). At some point, we'll have to ask ourselves, "Does this cross the line?" But that isn't the right question to ask *first*.

Have We Lost the Culture?

Recently, dramatic cultural shifts in areas of sexuality and public policy have many Christians wondering if all is lost culturally. Brett and I understand these sentiments. We don't like the way our culture is currently heading any more than you do. In fact, the rest of this book will examine issues that give the clear impression that our world is spiraling out of control.

The question "Have we lost the culture?" implies that there was a time when we *had* the culture. However, because of the sin that infects all people and all cultures, there has never been a thoroughly Christian culture. Certainly, some cultures are morally better than others, but we risk whitewashing the past when we long for "the good old days."

And if we despair for our cultural moment, we'll lose sight of our responsibility *for* the culture. Throughout history, Christians have found themselves in the midst of cultural breakdowns, many far worse than the one we're in today. In those moments, Christians have been forces of restoration, hope, and redemption in ways that saved lives, both physically and spiritually.

For example, in the Roman Empire, early Christians faced a cultural moment in which children, unborn and born, were considered disposable. Abortion was common, as was infanticide, often through a practice called *exposure*. Roman families who didn't wish to feed additional mouths would abandon newborns in the wild to die from the elements. Though exposure was legally and culturally acceptable at the time, our Christian forebears quickly embraced a different practice: rescuing these children, adopting them into their families, and raising them in the church.

Their actions were redemptive and praiseworthy, but there's more to the story. Because newborn girls were most commonly victims of exposure, a gender imbalance developed in many Roman towns within a few decades. When Roman men wanted to find wives, Christian families had a far greater number of eligible young women than pagan ones did. Math was on the side of the Christians, and many Roman men converted in their quest to marry. According to sociologist Rodney Stark, this is among the factors that explain the explosive growth of Christianity in the second century.[2]

Most important, we must not forget that God is always at work through—and at times *in spite of*—His people. He is at work today as well. Everywhere, for those with eyes to see, is evidence of that work. God is using His people today, as He's always done, to lead nations out of poverty, create brilliant art, tell life-changing stories, parent children, adopt orphans, heal the sick, and restore broken lives and cultures.[3]

Brett and I aren't suggesting that all is well in our cultural moment. In so many ways, it's not. Nor do we wish to imply that things are getting better. In so many areas, they're not. Nor are we suggesting that Christians shouldn't mourn the state of the world around us. But at the same time, we aren't suggesting we should wash our hands and dust off our feet as if we have no responsibility to steward the good things being lost. To be clear, we don't subscribe to the "caring about culture is like rearranging the deck chairs on the *Titanic*"[4] sort of thinking some champion, which has distracted many from their full callings as Christians. In fact, we'll confront that way of thinking head-on in the next chapter.

For the Christian, winning and losing isn't determined in this cultural moment. We belong to a larger Story. When we allow ourselves to be shaped by this Story, we'll approach culture with a better first question.

Starting with the Story

The apostle Peter addressed his first epistle to Christians during a difficult cultural moment. Peter was writing from Rome, where persecution was on the rise, so much so that he called the city "Babylon." And he referred to his audience—Christians dispersed by persecution—as "exiles." The persecution of Christ followers would only get worse, and Peter himself was eventually martyred. The ridicule, unjust treatment, and temptations to compromise morally weren't going away. The cultural pressure would only escalate.[5]

To bolster the church in those trying times, the apostle, who thrice denied Jesus, opened his letter with a reminder not of the ridicule, the persecution, the pervasive immorality of pagan society, or the growing pressures of the cultural moment, but of the gospel Story:

> Blessed be the God and Father of our Lord Jesus Christ! According to his great mercy, he has caused us to be born again to a living hope through the resurrection of Jesus Christ from the dead, to an inheritance that is imperishable,

> undefiled, and unfading, kept in heaven for you, who by God's power are being guarded through faith for a salvation ready to be revealed in the last time. (1 Pet. 1:3–5)

This reality, Peter wrote, would enable Christ followers to endure trials, resist temptation, love their enemies, do good, and live well in the cultural moment. Throughout the letter, as he sought to encourage his troubled audience, he returned again and again to the truth that defined their moment. It defines our moment as well, as it does every moment of human history. Christ has risen from the dead. Our hope is secure.

The Bible in Totals

"The basic problem of Christians," Francis Schaeffer said, "is that they have seen [the world] in bits and pieces instead of totals."[6] At the time he was speaking of how Christians viewed culture, but we could also say it's how many of us view the Scriptures: in bits and pieces, a disconnected collection of verses and stories designed to instruct us, depending on our predilections, in the way of morality, happiness, or financial prosperity.

Missiologist Lesslie Newbigin often wrote of an encounter with a Hindu scholar, who challenged him with these words:

> I can't understand why you missionaries present the Bible to us in India as a book of religion. It

> is not a book of religion—and anyway we have plenty of books of religion in India. We don't need any more! I find in your Bible a unique interpretation of universal history, the history of the whole of creation and the history of the human race.… That is unique. There is nothing else in the whole religious literature of the world to put alongside it.[7]

What the scholar realized, and we often miss, is that the Bible is more than a book of morality and religion. Fundamentally, it's a narrative. It tells the Story of the world, from the creation to the new creation.

Like all good stories, the biblical story line includes an introduction, a protagonist, antagonists, conflict, and resolution. Yet this Story is different from all other stories because it's God's Story. As such, it accurately describes reality, including what has gone wrong and how God will bring history to its conclusion according to His purposes.

"What does this have to do with culture?" you may be asking. *Everything.* If the Scriptures tell the true Story of the world, then our current cultural moment is part of its story line. Thus, the only way to make sense of our moment is by placing it in its true context.

In my (John's) book *Restoring All Things*, Warren Cole Smith and I describe the importance of getting the Story straight in order to understand what's happening in the world:

> Is the world we live in a creation, an accident, or an illusion? Do we live in God's world, or was God an invention we brought into our world? Is the world we live in the one described by Jesus, Richard Dawkins, or Oprah? Are we nothing more than the biological by-products of time plus chance plus matter? Is the world nothing more than a fabrication of our minds?
>
> Different religions and philosophical schemes offer different visions of reality, and it matters greatly which, if any, is right. What we think is real will determine how we live. We need to know which world this is before we can know the answers to other important questions, such as: Is the world fine the way it is? Is something wrong with the world? Is it society? Is it us? Is it "them"? Can it be improved? Can it be fixed? If so, how?
>
> "But I am no atheist!" you say. "I know God created the world and Jesus rose from the dead!" It's possible to get those very important details right and miss others essential to a truly Christian worldview.[8]

The Story in Four Chapters

The Bible is a big book made up of sixty-six smaller books that dozens of people authored over thousands of years. And yet its Story, despite taking many twists and turns, is coherent. In fact, it can be summarized in four chapters: creation, fall, redemption, and restoration.[9]

Creation

"In the beginning, God created the heavens and the earth" (Gen. 1:1). And thus the Story began. God is the author of the Story. The world we inhabit belongs to Him, not us. He is in charge. We are not. Immediately the Story established its *theology* (there is one God who is sovereign, not many gods) and its *cosmology* (the world is not accidental or eternal; it is an ordered creation). God, from the very beginning, was interested and engaged in the world He made. His plan was for it to flourish and be filled with life. It is, God announced, a *good* world (v. 18).

The pinnacle of the Story's first chapter was the creation of man and woman. God's plan for the world would be carried out by His image bearers. They were to "be fruitful and multiply and fill the earth and subdue it." And they were to "have dominion over the fish of the sea and over the birds of the heavens and over every living thing that moves on the earth" (v. 28). It wasn't their world, mind you; it was God's world. But they were to care for it and cultivate it so that it would become the place God intended it to be. This is the Story's *anthropology.* It is, God announced, a *very good* world (v. 31).

I (John) once drove by one of those infamous church billboards in the South that read "Jesus is the only good thing left in a bad world." This is patently untrue. The world God made, *and the capacity humans have to make something of the world*, were good from the beginning.

Of course, the next chapter affirms that there is bad in the world, but the Story began in Genesis 1, not Genesis 3. Only by beginning where the Story began can we grasp the gravity of all that followed. The problem isn't that humans make culture. The problem is the type of culture humans make.

Fall

In all good stories, something has gone wrong. The big bad wolf gobbles up Grandma. The White Witch turns Narnia into a place where it is always winter but never Christmas. Sauron amasses an army of Orcs, goblins, trolls, bad wizards, and other nefarious creatures to conquer Middle-earth.

The biblical Story is no different. In fact, we expect evil to invade any good story because evil has invaded the Story of the world, initially through the sin of our first parents and then through our own sin. Through sin, death entered the Story. God's intent for life and flourishing was threatened. Order was disordered. Our good, God-given capacities have been marred by evil acts, broken relationships, and selfish intentions.

In a talk delivered at the 2016 Q conference in Denver, Colorado, rap artist Lecrae accurately described an important aspect of the biblical Story that separates it from other stories: *We* are the antagonists.[10] The problem to be fixed isn't "out there," as if we were mere bystanders to the brokenness in God's world.

The problem is "in here" too. In the biblical Story, we are both the antagonists causing the problem and the victims in need of rescue.

Therefore, we should always be wary of those who claim, by human ingenuity or effort, that they will fix the world. Utopian visions, like the ones tried throughout the twentieth century (including Communism, eugenics, and sexual autonomy), will always fail. They leave individuals, nations, and entire civilizations riddled with bloodshed and chaos.

To hold together the first two chapters of the Story, we must distinguish between "structure and direction."[11] Just because something has been misused—such as art, authority, politics, or education—doesn't make that thing bad in and of itself. We ought not write off things wholesale, such as movies, politics, dancing, or technology, because fallen people take them in an evil direction. God created the world good, as well as our abilities to make something of it. As the apostle Paul told Timothy, God even "richly provides us with everything to *enjoy*" (1 Tim. 6:17). Good things used in wrong ways can be confronted, restored, and redirected for God's glory.

Even after sin and death entered the world, God never removed the expectation He had of His image bearers to be image bearers. His created intent that humans "be fruitful and multiply and fill the earth and subdue it" remains (Gen. 1:28). To be sure, the fruitful filling part is now accomplished only through the pains of childbirth, and thorns frustrate the subduing part. But the command to fill and subdue the earth still stands.

Redemption

Thankfully, the biblical Story didn't end after Genesis 2. The majority of the Story, in fact, is dedicated to the third chapter. God covered Adam and Eve's nakedness. He saved a family from the flood so the human project might continue even as He wiped wickedness from the face of the earth. He created a nation, Israel, to be His people, among the many nations created and dispersed from Babel. He preserved Israel despite their sin and rebellion, so that through them, all the nations of the earth would be blessed.

Redemption ultimately culminates in the person and work of Jesus Christ, the Word made flesh. He is light, and He is life (John 1:4). Jesus is, as Paul said, "the last Adam" (1 Cor. 15:45), righteous and obedient, though we are not. He took on the sin of the world, suffered God's wrath in our place, and ultimately defeated death by rising from the grave. All who embrace Christ are forgiven and become the children of God. If that was all Christ accomplished, it would be enough to demand our worship and allegiance. But there's more.

In *The Lion, the Witch and the Wardrobe*, Aslan (C. S. Lewis's Christ figure in The Chronicles of Narnia) sacrificed himself to the White Witch to redeem the traitor Edmund. Susan and Lucy, Edmund's sisters, who witnessed the entire horrible event and thought all was lost for Narnia the moment Aslan died, were stunned to see him alive. They wondered what it all meant.

> "It means," said Aslan, "that though the Witch knew the Deep Magic, there is a magic deeper still which she did not know. Her knowledge goes back only to the dawn of Time. But if she could have looked a little further back, into the stillness and the darkness before Time dawned, she would have read there a different incantation. She would have known that when a willing victim who had committed no treachery was killed in a traitor's stead, the Table would crack and Death itself would start working backwards."[12]

In Christ, death is defeated—not only for us as individuals but also on a cosmic level. The Story did not end at Christ's resurrection, or at our redemption. There is a fourth chapter.

Restoration

Christians have long debated the details of how the biblical Story ends. Joining this debate is far beyond the time and space allowed here. However, the final chapter of the Story is summarized in the words of Christ Himself with a present-tense verb: "Behold, I am making all things new" (Rev. 21:5).

The Story that began with the creation of the heavens and the earth ends with a new beginning. The garden is restored in the midst of God's city. As the Old Testament prophet Ezekiel promised (Ezek. 37:27), the God who once walked with Adam and Eve in Eden will make His home with His people. "He will dwell with them, and they will be his people, and God himself will be with them as their God" (Rev. 21:3). When He makes His home with us, all wrongs will be made right, and all lies will be exposed as untrue.

A Better First Question

We live in this cultural moment, but it hovers between redemption and restoration. Thankfully, before His ascension, Jesus offered instructions on how to live in this moment: "A new commandment I give to you," He said, "that you love one another: just as I have loved you, you also are to love one another" (John 13:34). We're to be disciples who make other disciples (Matt. 28:18–20). Paul tells children to obey their parents and husbands to love their wives. We should be good citizens, Peter instructs us (1 Pet. 2:13–15). And we're to wait expectantly for the culmination of the Story, which occurs when Christ returns (Rom. 8:22–24).

There are many more instructions than we have space to walk through, but two deserve attention here. First, as Peter wrote to the exiles facing their tough cultural moment, we are to be defined by hope (1 Pet. 3:15). And he didn't mean a squishy, wishful thinking, things-aren't-that-bad sort of optimism. The believer's hope, secured through the resurrection of Jesus Christ, isn't subject to fickle feelings shaped by the cultural moment.

Second, the New Testament employs all kinds of "re" words to describe life between redemption and restoration: renew, repent, restore, regeneration, reconciliation. Paul offered a mission statement to those who have been made new in Christ: "All this is from God, who through Christ reconciled us to himself and gave us the ministry of reconciliation" (2 Cor. 5:18). Reconciled ones are to be reconcilers.

The Story is the context of our cultural moment. We must live from it and allow it to shape us. That's why there's a better first question with which to approach culture than "Where do we draw the line?" or "Have we lost?"

The better question is "What is our salvation for?"[13]

Discussion Questions

1. If you were raised in a Christian home, how were you taught to think about culture? If you weren't raised in a Christian home, how have your thoughts about culture changed since coming to Christ?

2. Summarize the biblical Story using the four chapters explained earlier.

3. Choose something in culture (e.g., education, movies, law, technology, marriage) and walk it through each chapter of the Story. What biblical insights are gained when you think about this topic from that perspective?

4. Think about an area of brokenness you've noticed in the world around you or experienced. Which biblical "re" word is needed to bring restoration?

Chapter Three

A Vision of Success

Should one go off and build a little house with flowers outside the windows and a garden outside the door and extol and thank God and turn one's back on the world and its filth? Isn't seclusion a form of treachery—of desertion? … I'm weak and puny, but I want to do what is right.

Hans Scholl, Letter to Rose Naegele

"Somebody, after all, had to make a start."[1]

Sophie Scholl was just twenty-one years old when she spoke these words to the chief justice of the People's Court of the Greater German Reich shortly before he ordered her execution. On February 22, 1943, Sophie, her brother Hans, and their friend Christoph Probst were convicted of treason in a kangaroo court and sent to the guillotine.

Hans Scholl led the underground resistance movement known as the White Rose. From June 1942 until their arrest, Hans, Sophie, and several other University of Munich students covertly authored anti-Nazi pamphlets and distributed them on campus and to nearby communities. Retribution for their crimes was swift. Within four days, they were detained, accused, tried, convicted, and executed. Within weeks other members of the White Rose were rooted out and faced similar fates.

Raised in a nominally religious German home, the Scholl siblings came to real, personal faith in Christ while at their university. In *The Fabric of Faithfulness*, Steven Garber describes how their conversions motivated their actions:

> Brother and sister began to find a place to stand. Reading the Scriptures in the light of the challenges presented by their culture, having conversations with friends about the world and their place in it, meeting older, wiser people who offered them their time and their books—together they molded a vision about what was real and true and right.[2]

Many Germans, including Christians, chose to remain silent and do nothing to resist Hitler and the Nazi regime. Others embraced the evil Nazi ideology. But the Scholl siblings' faith drove them from the sidelines into what Dietrich Bonhoeffer called "the tempest of the living." Hans was supposed to meet Bonhoeffer, perhaps the most famous figure of the German resistance, but never did. Instead, Hans was executed the very day the meeting was scheduled to take place.

Hans and Sophie shared more with Bonhoeffer than antipathy toward the führer. Whether they knew it or not, they also shared Bonhoeffer's theological vision for culture, which might be summarized this way: "We are Christians, and we are Germans; therefore we are responsible for Germany."[3]

What Is Our Salvation For?

Christians love to talk about how Christ has saved us *from* sin and judgment *to* righteousness and eternal life with God. The Scholl siblings, however, grasped a vision that they were saved *for* something. Specifically, they believed that God had called them *to* that particular moment in German history.

Perhaps they were wrong and got caught up in all the political chaos of their day, using their newly deepened faith to justify their actions. Or maybe they were right. Perhaps it wasn't incidental that they were both Christian *and* German, and the intersection between the two implied responsibility. Either way, the question needs to be asked. Before we decide how we will deal with culture, we need to know our responsibility. In other words, what is our salvation *for*?

Called for the World, Not from It

This world is clearly a broken place. But it's not a bad place. It's easy to confuse one for the other, especially for those who have only experienced evil, suffering, neglect, or abuse. The Christian, however, must avoid this persistent heretical temptation.

Gnosticism, which has taken various forms throughout the history of the church, divides reality into two parts: the physical, which is evil, and the spiritual, which is good. In this formulation, we should strive for sacred things and avoid as much as necessary that which is secular. A current gnostic tendency is to elevate some jobs as "ministry," while other jobs are not. For example, evangelism, foreign missions, and pastoral duties are considered full-time Christian service, while everyone else does secular work, which is, at best, a way to make money to support those "in the ministry" or, at worst, a necessary evil.

However, as we discussed in the previous chapter, the Bible describes the world differently. Because the world is both physical and spiritual, made "good" by God's hand before it was corrupted by human hands, reality is divided not between physical and spiritual but between the Creator and the creation. Though fallen, God's creation still proclaims His grandeur, kindness, and goodness. And human activity, such as building, growing, selling, inventing, cleaning, or any other work we do, should be seen as God's work.

Living in this good-yet-fallen place means living in tension. Sin and evil have thoroughly infected this beautiful world. People have profound capacities not only for justice, kindness, and love but also for injustice, cruelty, and hate. The Nazi officials who sent Jewish children to the gas chambers of Auschwitz during the day hugged their own children at night.

Two reactions tempt the church in every generation. The first is to flee from culture. Shouldn't we withdraw into the safety of the church, take care of our own, and avoid the darkness?

The other reaction is simply to avoid controversial issues. This way, we're told, we can keep the focus on God's love for all people. Both of these reactions offer ways to escape the tension.

But Christianity, unlike other religions, is not escapist. Buddhism calls its adherents to escape from the world through meditation and mental focus. Hindus consider the physical world an illusion to be escaped through the births and rebirths of reincarnation. America's most popular religion, a syncretistic, New Agey sort of spiritual self-helpism, teaches that we can escape stress and self-doubt by following our hearts (or something like that).

At the center of Christianity, however, is Jesus Christ, the God who put on skin and "moved into the neighborhood" (John 1:14 THE MESSAGE). The Christian faith is *incarnational.* God didn't send laws, prophets, angels, or a book to fix His broken world. Instead, He Himself came in the person of Jesus Christ.

The incarnation means that Christianity is no "Let's get out of here so we can stay safe from the evil world until God takes us out of here" sort of religion. The night before Jesus' crucifixion, He prayed for His disciples and those who would believe because of them: "I do not ask that you take them out of the world, but that you keep them from the evil one" (17:15). In fact, the larger context of the prayer makes clear that Jesus' greatest desire for His disciples—"that they know you, the only true God, and Jesus Christ whom you have sent"—would happen not by escaping the world but as they lived in it (v. 3).

It's important to note that God's people can still make a difference in the world. Proverbs says, "When the righteous increase, the people rejoice, but when the wicked rule, the people groan" (29:2). Even while the Israelites were exiled in a pagan land, God instructed His people through the prophet Jeremiah to live as they had in Israel:

> Build houses and live in them; plant gardens and eat their produce. Take wives and have sons and daughters; take wives for your sons, and give your daughters in marriage, that they may bear sons and daughters; multiply there, and do not decrease. But seek the welfare of the city where I have sent you into exile, and pray to the LORD on its behalf, for in its welfare you will find your welfare. (Jer. 29:5–7)

This perspective will undoubtedly sound strange to some. For example, it won't make sense to those who see the gospel as only a two-chapter Story of how sinners are saved. Christianity isn't less than this, of course, but as we described in chapter 1, it's so much more.

The Christian Story has *four* chapters, not two. God created His image bearers to rule His good world on His behalf. The sin of our first parents and their offspring infects His world, twists it away from God's original intent, and brings death. In Christ, God defeated sin and death on our behalf. We are redeemed. Made right with God. Yet we aren't immediately whisked away to heaven upon conversion. So now what?

Christ didn't save us *from* being human; He saved us so that we would *be* fully human again. Thomas Howard brilliantly describes this in the following passage:

> The Incarnation takes all that properly belongs to our humanity and delivers it back to us, redeemed. All of our inclinations and appetites and capacities and yearnings and proclivities are purified and gathered up and glorified by Christ. He did not come to thin out human life; He came to set it free. All the dancing and feasting and processing and singing and building and sculpting and baking and merrymaking that belong to us, and that were stolen away into the service of false gods, are returned to us in the gospel.[4]

The Story the Scriptures tell clarifies that just as God intended His image bearers to bring life to the world by ruling over it as He would, He intends redeemed humans to join His work in bringing new life to the world. Remember Paul's mission statement that believers had been given "the ministry of reconciliation" (see 2 Cor. 5:17–21)?

Of course, being human looks different since the fall than it did before the fall. Now there's evil to fight and brokenness to restore. Our best efforts and intentions don't always bring the best outcomes. Bad things happen to good people. Still, our salvation employs us in God's redemptive plan for the world.

Writing from Tegel prison on July 21, 1944, Dietrich Bonhoeffer described how he had come to this understanding of Christianity in his own faith journey:

> During the last year or so, I've come to know and understand more and more the profound this-worldliness of Christianity. The Christian is not a *homo religiosus,* but simply a man, as Jesus was a man.... I don't mean the shallow and banal this-worldliness of the enlightened, the busy, the comfortable, or the lascivious, but the profound this-worldliness, characterized by discipline and the constant knowledge of death and resurrection.... I thought I could acquire faith by trying to live a holy life, or something like it.... I discovered later, and I'm still discovering right up to this moment, that it is only by living completely in this world that one learns to have faith.[5]

Called to Our Times, Not Another

Not only are we called to the world; we're also called to a particular time and place. The apostle Paul bluntly stated this in his interaction with Epicurean and Stoic philosophers on Mars Hill in Athens, Greece:

> The God who made the world and everything in it, being Lord of heaven and earth, does not live in temples made by man, nor is he served by human hands, as though he needed anything, since he himself gives to all mankind life and breath and everything. And he made from one man every nation of mankind to live on all the face of the earth, *having determined allotted periods and the boundaries of their dwelling place*, that they should seek God, and perhaps feel their way toward him and find him. Yet he is actually not far from each one of us. (Acts 17:24–27)[6]

As difficult as it can be to admit, particularly as parents longing to keep our children out of harm's way, God determines our cultural moment.

One morning at breakfast, my (John's) wife turned on the worship song "Ten Thousand Reasons." My then-five-year-old daughter asked, "Mommy, is that Justin Bieber?" Though no Justin Bieber song had ever played in our home, and though we had never discussed him, somehow she knew his name.

In short, we cannot escape our cultural moment, even if we try. That's why it was confusing, irritating, and even a little infuriating when the youth pastor of a large, influential church said to Brett, "I'm done talking about same-sex marriage. That ship has sailed." What on earth could that possibly mean? Living in America today ensures we *must* talk about certain things, including topics we'd rather avoid. The kids under that youth pastor's care will grow up, fall in love, and watch their friends, families, and neighbors do the same. Whom will they fall in love with? Are they free to act on all of their romantic feelings, even if they are same-sex attracted? Should they attend a friend's same-sex ceremony? What if they're hired to photograph or cater a same-sex ceremony? What if someone asks about their view on the issue? Not to clarify the cultural issues of our day with the next generation is a dereliction of duty.

Not only is it impossible to escape our cultural situation, but God hasn't asked us to try. Christians should see their culture as the setting for living out their God-given callings to bring life to His world.

Too many Christians, especially in the wake of all of the recent cultural shifts, think it's hopeless to engage culture. "It's all over," they say. Some spiritualize their surrender by suggesting the *culture-changing* business gets in the way of the *people-loving* business. But you can't love people by ignoring the cultural evils that victimize them.

Others retreat, looking for safety. They believe that Christians should get out of the way and wait for God's judgment. "We" tried to warn "them," but "they" didn't listen. So "we" must protect our families, not to mention ourselves.

Protecting our children is a godly endeavor, but sheltering them wholesale is not. Like all Christ followers, they too are called to be reconcilers in whatever cultural moment God has placed them. By all indications, they've got quite a moment ahead of them, so they had better be prepared. Still, safety is never the goal for the Christ follower. Faithfulness is.

Be encouraged, Christian, that we aren't the first Christ followers to face a difficult, or even seemingly hopeless, cultural moment. Nor will we be the last. In fact, it could be worse. Believers throughout history, starting with John the Baptist, lost their lives for speaking truth in a hostile moment. Like depressed and disillusioned Elijah after his great victory against the prophets of Baal (see 1 Kings 18–19), we're tempted to think we're alone. But Elijah wasn't, and neither are we. Those who run the race join the "great cloud of witnesses" who have gone before (see Heb. 11–12).

And remember, there's still much good that can be done. It's tempting to lose hope because we're outraged at what's pouring out of Washington, DC; New York City; Hollywood; and other centers of cultural power. Of course, God has His people in those places, but too often those of us not placed at the so-called top of culture forget to steward the local culture we can influence—like families, churches, community groups, Little League teams, and city councils. These places matter too.

In the World but Not of It

Still, let's not fool ourselves. We've seen so many casualties of culture. Brett and I know students who lost their faith in college, churches that caved to cultural pressures on important doctrines, and entire denominations that have denied Christ. We constantly hear of pastors, fathers, wives, teenagers, and Christian celebrities caught in significant moral failures or suddenly announcing they've changed their minds on historic Christian doctrines so they can keep up with the times.

As I heard Chuck Colson say often, "There's no limit to the human capacity for self-rationalization." Our own frailty, plus the subtle but powerful influences in our culture, makes us susceptible to drifting into compromise. Smaller compromises lead to bigger ones, and like Solomon, we may quickly find our hearts turned toward other gods (1 Kings 11).

We often think of compromise when it comes to beliefs and behaviors, but a particularly subtle temptation is to compromise in our methods. It's tempting to run our businesses, grow our churches, and pursue wealth through an end-justifies-the-means way of thinking. It's tempting to prize stuff over people and political power over righteousness. It's tempting to define success by popularity rather than faithfulness and seek to be relevant to avoid self-sacrifice, conflict, or suffering.

The simple truth is that Christian faithfulness involves not only our doctrine and lifestyle but also our habits, attitudes, and affections. It isn't enough to sprinkle Christian truth on lives shaped more by the cultural moment than the gospel. As Rod Dreher has warned repeatedly over the past few years, we must not underestimate the power of culture to form our deepest allegiances and identities.

In response, Dreher has proposed the Benedict Option, an approach to culture that many people understandably misinterpret as a call to retreat.[7] After all, he did name his option after the founder of a monastic order. Aren't monks the poster children for withdrawing from culture into Christian fortresses to avoid the evils of the world?

Dreher, however, has clearly said that he isn't advocating cultural withdrawal, and as should be obvious by now, neither are Brett and I. Without debating the overall strengths and weaknesses of the Benedict Option, we can note that Dreher offers critical insights for those concerned about whether the next generation will survive this cultural moment with their faith intact.

Dreher insists that, currently, culture is shaping the next generation's understanding of faith far more than their faith is shaping their understanding of culture. Sociologist Christian Smith, who has conducted extensive research on American teenagers, coined the phrase "moralistic therapeutic deism" to describe how they understand religion and spirituality.[8] For these teens, faith is about being nice and happy and believing that God is always there to help them when they need it.

Moralistic therapeutic deists believe that God visits their world, not that they live in God's world. They believe that God serves their agenda, helping them feel good about themselves along the way. God, in their view, demands nothing of them. Rather, He exists to help them in whatever way they wish. Moralistic therapeutic deism is not Christianity at all.

In light of Smith's findings, Christian families and churches must see what they do as more than offering wholesome youth programs and teaching moralistic therapeutic Sunday school lessons. Our agenda for the next generation must be whole-life formation, intentionally countering the dominant cultural vision of what life is about. We must make sure our kids understand Christian faith as more than a set of beliefs and behaviors. Instead, they need to know that a competing vision of life demands their deepest allegiance and grounds their identity.

After all, the question is how they'll respond when the cultural pressure is *really* on. Will they do what is right even when all of the incentives promote doing wrong? Will they recognize the lies and still embrace what is true? And will they not only survive the culture but also be able to engage it with courage, clarity, and resolve, standing for Christ wherever He has placed them and in whatever work He has called them to?

Years ago, a twentysomething dragged her friend up to talk to me at a conference where I was speaking.

"Thank you for saying that we need more Christian fashion designers," she said.

"You're welcome," I responded and inwardly panicked because I didn't even remember saying that, nor had I ever really thought much about a Christian view of fashion.

Thankfully she had more to say about it than I did: "My friend here is moving up the ladder as a fashion designer, and I tell her all the time how important her work is. Fashion designers teach culture what is beautiful."

That's exactly right. When mature Christians engage the culture fully, deeply, and wisely, the culture won't corrupt us. Just the opposite. We'll be teachers of the culture. We'll teach it what is good, true, and beautiful. For two thousand years, among the highest and best artifacts of culture have come from Christians—whether

Dante's *The Divine Comedy*, Gutenberg's printing press, Bach's music, T. S. Eliot's poetry, Arthur Guinness's innovative business culture, Truett Cathy's chicken sandwich, Makoto Fujimura's paintings, or the Human Genome Project. This can still be so.

What is cultural success? It's a life lived like Hans and Sophie Scholl, deeply engaging the moment in which God has placed us and courageously navigating the threatening currents, knowing that we serve a cause, and a God, far greater than ourselves.

Discussion Questions

1. Using the quote from Dietrich Bonhoeffer in this chapter, fill in the blanks: "[I am] Christian, and [I am] _________; therefore, [I am] responsible for ________." (Hint: think beyond geography to any area of your life that God has clearly gifted to you for His purposes.)

2. The secular-sacred split is very common. Give some examples you've seen in your own life or the lives of other Christians. How might this split be corrected from a Christian worldview?

3. Are you more tempted to withdraw from culture or capitulate to it? In what ways?

4. What examples can you think of in which Christians have positively impacted culture, even during a very dark time?

Part Two

A Read of the Cultural Waters

Chapter Four

The Information Age

The endless cycle of idea and action, Endless invention, endless experiment, brings knowledge of motion, but not of stillness; knowledge of speech, but not of silence; knowledge of words, and ignorance of the Word. All our knowledge brings us nearer to death, But nearness to death no nearer to God. Where is the Life we have lost in living? Where is the wisdom we have lost in knowledge? Where is the knowledge we have lost in information?

T. S. Eliot, *The Rock*

Historians not only study past eras; they name them. We know the Roaring Twenties, the Middle Ages, and the Industrial Revolution by name even if we can't recall their dates. Our current era has already been identified for posterity. We live in the "information age."

According to Wikipedia (where else would we get a definition for this?), the information age is "characterized by the shift from traditional industry ... to an economy based on information computerization."[1] This is a complicated way of saying that our world is no longer dominated by farms or factories but by glowing screens. It's hard to think of a single area of human life that information technology hasn't deeply shaped.

Older generations may remember life before 24/7 access to the Internet, but kids today don't. They've never known a quiet world. Every day of their lives, they encounter more information than people who lived in the fifteenth century would have learned over the course of their entire lives. Each time kids go online—which is multiple times a day for this generation—they have access to more information than most of us can even imagine. Each *day*, 500 million tweets are sent, 4 million hours of content are uploaded to YouTube, 4.3 billion Facebook messages are posted, 6 billion Google searches are conducted, and 205 billion emails are sent.[2] A staggering amount of information is at our fingertips, and that's only counting what's online.

Wherever we go, billboards, bumper stickers, web pages, pop-ups, tweets, Facebook feeds, Snapchat posts, banner ads, commercials, songs, movies, television shows, and digital ads compete for our attention. In just about every restaurant, every store, and for some of us, every room in our homes, the music is blaring and the televisions are on. Life in the information age is noisy, and it only becomes noisier as the competition heats up for our ears, eyes, attention, and pocketbooks.

Some of us have been around long enough to realize how dramatically the digital revolution changed life, but kids struggle to imagine a world when phones had cords, libraries had expansive card catalogs, and televisions had only thirteen channels. Since the 1970s—and exponentially since the 1990s—more and more information has saturated the world while people have become more and more addicted to the devices that keep them online and up to speed. Though all of this change is relatively recent, the only world our kids have ever known is, as Thomas Friedman aptly describes it, "flat."[3] By that he meant that everyone now has access to information resources that were, in the past, reserved for a privileged few. For digital natives, glowing rectangles are integral aspects of reality, and information access is essential to everyday human life.

Even digital immigrants—those of us who fondly remember the good old days when the world was quieter and people lived primarily *offline*—often fail to realize just how much the information age shapes us. Communication and information technology make life convenient and more efficient, and we quickly find it hard to imagine life without the new gadgets that deliver information right to our fingertips and earbuds. But as T. S. Eliot said more than eight decades ago, we shouldn't confuse information with knowledge or knowledge with wisdom.[4]

It's Not Just Information

We could also call the information age the age of ideas. Every song, movie, tweet, sermon, news story, podcast, banner ad, and billboard tells us something about what to believe and how to live. Even information we think is inconsequential to our lives still communicates ideas about life and the world.

Ideas are sometimes true and sometimes false. They may be trivial and shallow, or they may communicate deep thoughts about the meaning of our existence. Those peddling the ideas may have the best of intentions, or they may be trying to deceive or harm us. They may be genuinely trying to persuade us, or they could be trying to manipulate our emotions. Ideas take various forms, but they must be taken seriously. Why? Because *ideas have consequences.*[5]

Not all ideas bring equally grave consequences, of course. The more important the idea, the more significant its consequences. That's why it's foolish to think of ideas as innocuous words on a page or as heady concepts that concern only philosophers. If ideas stayed safely in their books, as many people wrongly assume, then batting them around would be as harmless as a friendly tennis match. But they don't stay in books. They grow legs, walk off the page, and head out into the world. They influence the way we think and live. They shape entire societies and drive the course of human history.

That's why we must also say that *bad ideas have victims.* Real people, including innocent bystanders, suffer the consequences of bad ideas. For example, the bad ideas about economics that state power enforced led to tens of millions of deaths in the twentieth century alone. Bad ideas about celebrity, fame, and physical appearance leave teenage girls confused, starving, and purging. Bad ideas about masculinity leave young men in perpetual adolescence, without purpose and addicted to video games. Bad ideas about sex and relationships fuel the hookup culture on college campuses, leaving students broken, used, and lonely.

Ideas are particularly difficult to navigate today not only because there are so many but also because they come at us so fast and from so many directions. For this reason, many of us can't even recognize ideas as ideas, much less think critically or articulate sensibly about them. This is no small problem. If we can't master ideas, ideas will master us. If we passively absorb the information around us, someone else is thinking for us.

It would be helpful, of course, if ideas came with warnings. Movies, television shows, songs, and YouTube videos have disclaimers about foul language, explicit sexuality, and excessive violence, but ideas come with no such warnings. So we must always be alert in the age of ideas and constantly activate our brains—or as author and Christian academic Nancy Pearcey calls them, our "baloney detectors."[6] As a public service, we offer the following disclaimer for life (including, of course, this book):

> The following (song, movie, program, commercial, speech, tweet, post, image, story, book, sermon, etc.) contain ideas in the form of arguments, embodied characters, narrative consequences, satirical exaggerations, and/or emotional outbursts. These ideas will be assumed true, though not necessarily supported by any arguments, and reflect the worldview of the actors, producers, directors, musicians, writers, or speakers. Discretion is advised.

Why Kids Struggle with Ideas

Making sense of ideas in a culture of information overload isn't easy. For starters, *we cannot control which ideas kids will be exposed to, or when they'll be exposed to them*. This is a difficult reality for a generation of parents known for desiring control and safety. Like most parents, Brett and I often find ourselves answering unexpected questions from our kids while thinking, *How do they know about that?* and *Aren't they too young for this conversation?*

So it is in the information age. And it's gotten even worse in just the past decade. If you consider yourself media savvy, but your pop-culture literacy is more than a few months old, you're out of date. Movies rated R a decade ago might not earn even a PG-13 rating today. PG movies and prime-time TV sitcoms contain profanity and sexual references. And as always, G-rated movies and cartoons contain subtle worldview messages.

Access and exposure to new ideas are just a billboard, commercial, song lyric, or mouse click away. A questioning and spiritually vulnerable child who might never have encountered atheistic arguments in another day and age may very well come across a Richard Dawkins video on a Facebook feed. Christian young people who may not even be looking for reasons to question their faith find that non-Christian ideas about God, truth, and morality are looking for them.

That's why it's more critical than ever that parents, church leaders, and mentors create an environment where kids can ask tough questions and wrestle with controversial topics. The ignore-controversial-subjects-and-they'll-go-away approach to raising kids won't do. In the information age, plenty of voices are willing to talk with our kids if we aren't.

The policy in our homes (Brett's and mine) is that any question or topic our kids want to discuss is fair game. Of course, we might say, "I don't think you're quite ready to know about that, but we'll talk about it when the time is right," or we may leave out certain details that would steal their innocence. But we want our kids to know it isn't wrong to be curious. Even more, we desperately want them to come to us with their questions, not to those intent on deceiving or harming them.

Another challenge of the information age is *who to trust.* We'd love for our kids to come to *us* with their questions, of course, but we must realize that this world of competing ideas is also a world of competing authorities. Therefore, kids struggle with who to believe: their pastor or their professor? Who knows more: their parents or their peers? Should they search Google or Galatians for answers? If their course textbook, professor, and the *Huffington Post* all say, "The science is settled" about sexual orientation and gender identity, does that mean the Bible is wrong?

The issue of trust is complicated only if kids think that so-called Christian authorities are *untrustworthy.* For example, children who find their difficult questions aren't welcome, taken seriously, or sufficiently addressed in church will look elsewhere for answers. Brett and I can't even count the number of times teenagers have confessed to hiding doubts from those who could help them most, because they were told it was sinful to question God or that they should "just believe."

We must never give our kids the impression that questioning is doubting or that doubting is sinning. If it is indeed wrong to question God, the book of Psalms needs to be removed from the Bible. How often in Israel's hymnbook did David or another psalmist wonder aloud whether God was truly good—or even there at all?

Of course, sincere questions differ significantly from cynicism. In Proverbs, Solomon distinguished between those who seek God and those who mock Him. Mockers aren't interested in answers, but seekers are. The hearts of mockers are so hard, they wouldn't accept the truth even if they found it.

In our experience (Brett's and mine), seekers become mockers if they're not allowed to wrestle with their doubts and questions. Parents may fear they'll make it worse if they say the wrong thing, but it's far better to answer a question with "I really don't know, but let's work on finding an answer together" than to condemn a child for having sincere questions. Remember, in the information age, if we won't take our kids' questions seriously, others will.

Kids who have seen hypocrisy or immorality in the lives of parents, pastors, or Christian leaders struggle the most with trust.

Years ago after I (John) finished speaking to a group of students, a teenage girl asked me the perennial question that troubles Christians and skeptics alike: Why does God let bad things happen to good people? Ready with my answer, I jumped into explanations about human freedom, resurrection hope, and the failure of other worldviews to explain evil *or* good. I thought I nailed it, but then she said, "Well, that's all well and good, but you weren't able to help me."

She then told me how she had been deeply disappointed by the moral failure of her dad, and how the church he pastored had mistreated their family.

"I'm mad," she told me. "I'm mad at my dad because he let me down. I'm mad at the church because they stabbed us in the back. And I'm mad at God because He let all of this happen." And then she added, "And I'm mad at myself because I know I'm not supposed to be mad at God."

Like so many students Brett and I have worked with, this teen's intellectual doubts were outward expressions of internal hurts. She stopped trusting God because everyone she trusted let her down.

We're not saying that anyone who hopes to maintain trust with the next generation can never fail. After all, perfect people aren't Christians; forgiven people are. And just as the moral failures of parents or pastors can threaten a young person's faith, so can hypocrisy and the constant pressure of unreachable expectations. On the other hand, nothing bolsters faith more than seeing Christ restore a broken life, marriage, or relationship. Hidden failures and pretend perfection are dangerous to us and our kids. Instead, parents and leaders need to be appropriately vulnerable. Kids should know we have questions, struggles, and doubts just like they do. It won't do to proclaim that Christ is the true, revealed, and risen hope for sinful humanity if they never see Him at work up close and personal in the lives of those they know and love.

Kids must also learn how and why to trust the Bible. It's one thing to accept the Scriptures at church or home in an environment where everyone basically agrees that it's the Word of God.

It's another to trust the Bible on a college campus or in some other environment where the Bible is seen as racist, homophobic, or misogynistic, and where its claims are critiqued and reinterpreted under the guise of science and modern scholarship. (See chapter 17 for a quick guide to help kids understand the authority of Scripture.)

Finally, *many students struggle with ideas simply because they don't know how to think.* In the information age, we encounter ideas that are difficult to understand and require intricate and sustained reasoning. Kids have to think their way through this culture, but in our work with students, Brett and I are constantly surprised at how unfamiliar they often are with basic logic and how quickly the silliest ideas and weakest arguments sideline them. Of course, this is often the case with many adult Christians too!

For example, many cannot distinguish an assertion from an argument. The statement "The Genesis account is one of many creation myths in ancient literature, so it cannot be true" is not an argument. It's an assertion that needs to be investigated and clarified if it is to be taken seriously. In what ways is the biblical account similar to myths? In what ways is it different? Which came first? Which stories have the backing of authoritative sources?

Also, many kids confuse feelings for reasons. Too many colleges and universities today are intellectually neutered by speech codes and safe spaces rather than being centers of robust debate and discussion. In this environment, students don't learn to think. Recently, professors at a university in Colorado announced that their course on the environment would not entertain ideas that countered theories of human-caused climate change. When a local news station asked two students what they thought of this course policy, they replied, "Well, I feel that the professors should allow other opinions."[7]

Feeling isn't thinking, but many kids can't tell the difference. They're constantly told that being nice is more important than being right, and that being tolerant is better than knowing truth. However, today's version of tolerance isn't tolerance at all. True tolerance means to treat others with respect even if their views differ from yours. Today tolerance means embracing the views of the majority culture, and those who don't are labeled "intolerant."[8] In a culture like this, people are pressured not to think but to conform.

Also stunting the next generation's ability to think are the ever-present forms of entertainment that perpetually feed what Aldous Huxley called "man's almost infinite appetite for distractions."[9] For entertainment addicts, even the slightest intellectual endeavor seems like too much work in light of the constant supply of on-demand movies, social media, and games courtesy of the glowing rectangles all around us. Way back in 1985, the late social critic Neil Postman wrote a book accusing Americans of "amusing ourselves to death."[10] One wonders what he would think if he were still alive today.

The word *amuse* literally means "not to think" (*muse* is to think, and the *a* at the front negates it). Too much amusement from entertainment stunts our intellectual energy. And this problem belongs not just to younger generations. As I (John) type this, a woman seated across the aisle on my flight is playing a game on her iPad without headphones. She is either unaware or unconcerned that the sound from her game, turned all the way up so she can hear it above the noise of the engine, is bothering other passengers. Captivated by her glowing rectangle, she's not only not thinking; she's not thinking of others. Our addictions to these diversions aren't harmless if by them we create a culture in which we simply stop caring for, or even about, others. (We'll examine entertainment more closely in chapter 14.)

Kids who can't think clearly in the information age are destined to be deceived. They must know enough, and care enough, to make sense of the ideas they encounter. Paul instructed his readers, "See to it that no one takes you captive by philosophy and empty deceit" (Col. 2:8). How can we help our kids think so they can live as God would have them in this noisy culture?

Thinking "Worldviewishly"

In a world of bad ideas, we need good ideas. Knowing what is true is always important, and it's never been more so than in an age drowning in information. But as strange as it sounds, just telling our kids the truth isn't enough.

If true information is merely added to the flood of information, the truth can't be heard. Like a drop of water in the ocean or a single voice in a crowded room, truth can be overwhelmed with lies, half truths, propaganda, or trivialities, rendering it ineffective in capturing our kids' attention, much less their allegiance. Brett and I aren't the only parents who wonder, "Are they even hearing what we are saying?"

As hard as it is to admit, parents and mentors are just one voice among many vying for the hearts and minds of the next generation. We're only one stop on the information bus of their lives, and there are a lot of stops. This means that although we may not be the loudest and certainly not the most entertaining voices they hear, we must be the most intentional.

From us, kids need to not only hear truth, but they also need to learn what it means to think *with* truth. Paul's prayer for the church at Philippi should be ours as well:

> It is my prayer that your love may abound more and more, with knowledge and all discernment, so that you may approve what is excellent, and so be pure and blameless for the day of Christ, filled with the fruit of righteousness that comes through Jesus Christ, to the glory and praise of God. (Phil. 1:9–11)

What Paul offered is a terrific description of discernment, an oft-used but rarely defined word. In Paul's prayer, *discernment* is "the ability to *distinguish* the true and genuine from the false and counterfeit." But in Paul's prayer, there is more to discernment than mental ability. As the eighteenth-century literary genius Samuel Johnson said, discernment is "the power to tell the good from the bad, the genuine from the counterfeit, and to prefer the good and the genuine to the bad and the counterfeit."[11]

If we want to see our kids rise above all the noise and live well in this culture, rote recitation of facts alone won't be enough. Discernment is required. Young people must develop the ability to not only recognize the truth but also to see all of life through the truth—as a lens by which they identify and evaluate every idea they encounter.

All of us have "belief glasses," or a worldview through which we see the world. Like prescription glasses, our worldview will either enable us to see the world as it is or, if it's the wrong prescription, keep us from seeing the world as it is. We don't look *at* our worldview; we look through it. The question isn't whether we have a worldview. The question is which worldview has us.

Our worldview is "the framework of basic beliefs we have, whether we realize it or not, that shapes our view *of* the world and *for* the world."[12] We all have fundamental beliefs about the nature of reality—whether the world is an accident of nature or a creation of God, whether right and wrong are absolute or relative, whether there is or isn't an afterlife, whether humans are animals with a conscience or higher-order beings with some sort of privileged place in the universe. We build our lives and make decisions based on these fundamental assumptions.

Worldviews are caught more than taught. Like a cold, most people "catch" their worldview beliefs from the culture around them. If we never stop and examine our worldview, we'll still have one, but it may not be the right one.

Our worldview, first of all, gives us a view *of* the world. Which world do we live in? Is life random, or does it have purpose? Is history headed somewhere, or are we, as Ernest Nagel put it, "an episode between two oblivions."[13] Our view *of* the world is our explanation of reality, including our beliefs about the following:

- Origins: Where did everything come from?
- Identity: What is a human being?
- Meaning: What is the meaning of life? What is our purpose?
- Morality: Who determines right and wrong? What's wrong with the world, and how can it be fixed?
- Destiny: What happens when we die? Where is history headed?

Forgive the double negative, but we can't not answer these questions. If we don't take time to answer them critically in our hearts and minds, we'll answer them passively by how we live, how we make decisions, and especially, how we relate to others. As Dr. Bill Brown often says, "You may not live what you profess, but you will live what you really believe."[14]

How we answer any one of these questions will shape how we answer the others. For example, if there is no God who created the world (origin), then humans are just products of natural forces like any other life-forms (identity). Or if Columbine High School shooters Dylan Klebold and Eric Harris were correct in their belief that there is no life after death (destiny), then they faced no eternal consequences for their actions on April 20, 1999 (morality). Even if we never take the time to think about them, our fundamental beliefs about life matter.

Our view *of* the world provides the framework by which we make sense of what happens in the world. If life has no ultimate purpose, then neither does suffering. If humans are biological machines, then our value is reduced to what we look like or what we can do. If there is no designer of the universe, then concepts like marriage, sexuality, and government are whatever humans decide they are.

Second, our worldview determines our view *for* the world. Our worldview shapes our values, and our values shape our behavior. Our actions reflect our core beliefs about life. The best way to live, then, is critically so that we can determine what is true and right, and then to build lives from those deeply held convictions. If, however, we aren't intentional about what we believe, we'll simply adopt a worldview to accommodate the values and behaviors in the culture around us.

Shaping Worldview

Despite all the noise of our culture, parents remain the most important voice in the lives of their children. That's good news. And it's good to know that churches and mentors also have considerable influence. In the context of strong relationships, we can help kids form a robust, informed, and thoughtful Christian worldview. Here's how.

1. Talk about worldview early and often. Yes, it's a strange word, but kids need to know they have a worldview, what it is, what it should be, and how a Christian worldview is different from others. They need to know that every song, movie, television program, article, speech, tweet, post, and commercial reflect values and behavior rooted in a worldview.

2. Explain non-Christian worldviews. When ideas are named, they're far less intimidating or powerful. Kids need the ability to identify worldviews when they encounter them. Years ago I (John) received an email from Chris, a student who attended a Summit worldview conference I led.

In the email, Chris described how going to a movie with his friends was different now that he had learned about worldviews. "I tried to veg out during the movie, but I just couldn't. As I watched it, I kept thinking, *Wait a minute, that's secular humanism, and wait a minute, that's not true. And what do they mean by that, and how do they know that's true!* I learned that I just can't turn this worldview thing off!" After the movie, he was able to discuss with his friends the ideas he had spotted in the film. "They thought it was really cool," he said, "and wanted to know how I was able to see all the things in the movie that I did."[15]

3. Strongly encourage your kids to read good books. The saying is true: "Leaders are readers, and readers are leaders." Kids who read good books not only learn good things; they also learn to think. Books, by design, are linear. The Internet is not. A book takes you from page 1 to page 2, then 3, and so on. There is a built-in form of cause and effect. On the other hand, start on page Google, and you go wherever Google determines.

4. Discuss ideas whenever possible. If a song lyric catches your attention in a store, talk about it. If a commercial promises that a product will bring fulfillment, talk about it. If there is a natural disaster or national tragedy, talk about it. Pause a movie and discuss the difference between the good guys and the bad guys. Share an important news item at the dinner table. Opportunities to talk about ideas are everywhere.

5. Ask good questions. The two best educators in history, Jesus and Socrates, were great question askers. There is no better technique to make students wrestle with ideas than through dialogue. Often, we're quick to preach and instruct. We need to learn to ask good questions.

Here are a few simple questions to keep handy:

What do you mean by that? The battle of ideas begins with the battle for definitions. Often we'll find that even if we're using the same vocabulary as others, we aren't using the same dictionary. So it's always helpful to ask kids to define the words they're using. For example, people often proclaim, "We need marriage equality!" But that's a loaded phrase that makes anyone opposed to same-sex marriage appear opposed to equality, when the terms *marriage* or *equality* haven't been clearly defined. Don't fall for the trap. Instead of replying, "No, we don't need marriage equality!" ask instead, "What do you mean by marriage?" After all, no culture allows anyone and everyone to marry, and for good reason. Who should get married depends on what marriage *is.*[16]

Many other words need to be carefully defined in our cultural moment. For example, our culture promotes license and calls it *freedom*. *Truth* is often defined as "what's true for you" instead of what corresponds to reality. Perhaps most important to define properly and thoroughly today is *love*. In our culture, love is thought of as either a fickle emotion or as sexual attraction. As C. S. Lewis pointed out, there are at least four loves that must be clearly understood and properly ordered if we are to relate rightly to God and others.[17]

How do you know that's true? Assertions require arguments. This question will not only force kids to back up what they say and to know why they believe what they believe, but it will also help them identify unsubstantiated assertions.

Of course, kids quickly learn to toss this question back to us! This can be annoying, but teaching them to ask it—even of us—is worth the irritation. Of course, kids need to learn when to ask this question of authority figures and when to simply listen and obey. But its value is that it helps them discern when people don't really know what they're talking about.

What if you're wrong? This question gets at the consequences of ideas. Blaise Pascal famously proposed a "wager" about God. If Christians are wrong and atheists are right about God, nothing is eternally lost. However, if Christians are right, then atheists will face serious consequences for their unbelief.

In the 1970s, advocates of no-fault divorce often said, "The kids will get over it. In fact, they'll be better off with happy parents even if they aren't married." They were wrong. In fact, the results are in, and millions of children, victims of others' bad ideas, are "haunted by powerful ghosts from their childhoods that tell them that they, like their parents, will not succeed."[18]

The next generation can keep their heads and hearts above the noise. They can learn to master ideas. They can become bold champions of truth. But they need our help.

Discussion Questions

1. Are you a digital immigrant or a digital native? How has that shaped your approach to living in the information age?

2. Define the concept of worldview. Describe a conversation or interaction you've had with someone whose worldview differed from yours.

3. Choose a popular song, video, television program, or news story and analyze it from a worldview perspective, identifying its central ideas.

4. Have a friend role-play a conversation with you in which one of you advocates a different belief or worldview. Using the three questions presented near the end of the chapter, discuss the belief or worldview.

Chapter Five

Identity after Christianity

The idols of the nations are silver and gold, the work of human hands. They have mouths, but do not speak; they have eyes, but do not see; they have ears, but do not hear, nor is there any breath in their mouths. Those who make them become like them, so do all who trust in them.

Psalm 135:15–18

On April 29, 2013, in a headline article in *Sports Illustrated,* Jason Collins announced to the world that he was gay. It became a major news story. At the time, the big-three professional sports leagues (the NBA, NFL, and MLB) were among the last remaining sectors of culture largely untouched by the LGBT (lesbian, gay, bisexual, transgender) revolution, and it wasn't clear how this bastion of manliness would handle such a development.

The response was almost universally positive. President Obama called Collins with his personal congratulations, and the First Lady tweeted, "We've got your back." Basketball legends, celebrities, and media lauded the announcement as historic and groundbreaking. The most common refrain, which we've come to expect when anyone reveals their sexual orientation or gender identity, was this: "Finally, Jason Collins can just be himself" or "He no longer has to hide who he is."

Later that day, on the ESPN show *Outside the Lines*, NBA analyst Chris Broussard faced a litany of questions about the story's implications for professional basketball: Would more players now come out as gay? How would his teammates react? Would teams shy away from signing Collins, who had been a solid role player for teams throughout his career? It was a fascinating conversation.

Then it got personal. Broussard, who is open about his own Christian faith, was asked about something that had nothing to do with basketball. Did he agree with Collins's claim that there was no conflict between his Christian faith and living as a sexually active gay man? Broussard answered,

> Personally I don't believe that you can live an openly homosexual lifestyle or an openly … like premarital sex between heterosexuals [sic].… If you're openly living that type of lifestyle, then the Bible says "you know them by their fruits." It says that, you know, that's a sin.… And if you're openly living in unrepentant sin, whatever it may be, not just homosexuality—adultery, fornication, premarital sex between heterosexuals—whatever it

> may be, I believe that's walking in open rebellion to God and to Jesus Christ. So I would not characterize that person as a Christian because I don't think the Bible would characterize them as a Christian.[1]

You can imagine what happened next. Critics demanded that he resign or be fired. He was an intolerant bigot, they said, and clearly hated homosexuals. Even though, if you look carefully at what he said, he condemned the sexual behavior of most of the NBA. Only his views on homosexuality were unacceptable. Broussard should have known that outdated, hateful, and bigoted views like his are to be kept out of the public square, even if he was directly asked to share them. Being a Christian and holding the views of popes, pastors, theologians, and leaders, not to mention a significant portion of the American population, are no excuse.

That same year, the New Mexico Supreme Court found Elaine Huguenin guilty of discrimination for refusing to photograph a same-sex commitment ceremony seven years earlier. At issue wasn't whether she would photograph gays and lesbians in other settings. She had done that. But to participate in a commitment ceremony was celebrating behavior in conflict with her deeply held convictions about marriage.[2] The court rejected that distinction.

In a concurring opinion, Justice Bosson offered a distinction of his own:

> The Huguenins are free to think, to say, to believe, as they wish; they may pray to the God of their

> choice and follow those commandments in their personal lives wherever they lead. The Constitution protects the Huguenins in that respect and much more. But there is a price, one that we all have to pay somewhere in our civic life.
>
> In the smaller, more focused world of the marketplace, of commerce, of public accommodation, the Huguenins have to channel their conduct, not their beliefs, so as to leave space for other Americans who believe something different.[3]

Bosson wrote that "all" must, at times, "channel their conduct," but in the end, only Elaine Huguenin was forced to do so. Bosson went on to call this a "compromise" that was "the price of citizenship."[4] However, the same-sex couple seeking her services wasn't forced to pay it. In fact, the Huguenins had to separate their beliefs from their behavior, Bosson suggested, *so that the same-sex couple would not have to.*

Like the Collins-Broussard incident, this conflict is a highlight reel of contemporary cultural issues: Christian conviction in the public square, the collision between religious liberty and sexual freedom, and the ever-changing sexual norms of our culture. But beneath each story is something else: a vision of human identity now taken for granted as absolute.[5]

When Jason Collins announced his sexuality, he was assured that was *who he is*, but Chris Broussard heard that his Christian faith amounted to little more than personal opinions he should keep to himself. Elaine Huguenin cited deeply held convictions about participating in a same-sex commitment ceremony, but according to Justice Bosson, she had *a civic duty* to celebrate her clients' sexual behavior.

We used to talk of sex in terms of behavior, but now, we're told, it's *who we are*. The overwhelming message to kids today is that Christian faith isn't nearly as important as sexual inclinations and attractions. Religious belief is mere personal opinion, but sexuality is definitive, absolute, and unquestionable. In today's culture, sexuality is identity.[6]

But this is just the latest chapter of a longer story.

The Cultural Identity Crisis

Sexuality triumphed as identity because of what sociologist Peter Berger once called "the permanent identity crisis of modern man."[7] Simply put, long ago Western culture lost what it means to be human. Take, for example, education.

"We've got no philosophy of what … it is we want by the time somebody graduates," said the Duke University student. "The so-called curriculum is a set of hoops that somebody says students ought to jump through before graduation. Nobody seems to have asked, 'How do people become good people?'"[8] Most of us can relate. We were told to go to college, but why? So we could "do" something, make money, buy nice things, and eventually retire? Missing in the process from beginning to end is why we should do anything at all. Who are we, what is our purpose, and why are we here in the first place?

Imagine a car company that stockpiled engines, steering wheels, bumpers, tires, seat covers, and other parts, intending to launch a new line of automobiles.

"What kind of cars will you build?" you ask the CEO. "Full size or midsize? What will they look like when they're finished?"

"No idea," he replies. "We'll just throw the parts together and see what happens." That's not a company with a promising future.

In the same way, if we don't know *whom* it is we're educating and *whom* they should become, education devolves into a disconnected hodgepodge of classes, skill acquisition, test taking, activities, and degrees. Now think of fashion, business, public policy, health care, biomedical ethics, or even youth groups. We won't know what to *do* in these areas if we aren't first clear on *who* humans are. And it's clear we aren't clear about that.

Welcome to identity after Christianity.

Christianity has contributed many things to the world, but none more important than its vision of the human person. As atheist philosopher Luc Ferry describes it, "Christianity was to introduce the notion that … men were equal in dignity—an unprecedented idea at the time, and one to which our world owes its entire democratic inheritance."[9] More than a century earlier, another atheist philosopher, the notorious Friedrich Nietzsche, called human equality "another Christian concept" that "furnishes the prototype of all theories of equal rights."[10]

Human dignity and equality are concepts taken for granted as givens today, but they grew out of the Judeo-Christian doctrine of the *imago Dei,* the biblical vision that God created humans specially and uniquely, endowing them with eternal value. Of course, no society fully achieved this Christian ideal, but no society without Christian influence even imagined, must less attempted to build, such a world in the first place.[11] Today, many want the *fruit* of human dignity while soundly condemning its *roots.*

As the twentieth century demonstrated, severing human dignity from its Christian roots is a fool's errand. Writing in *Time* magazine, Henry Grunwald observed, "One of the most remarkable things about the twentieth century, more than technological progress and physical violence, has been the deconstruction of man and woman."[12] In a century so oft noted for its remarkable human achievement, humans themselves didn't fare so well. Instead, the relentless pursuit of progress, driven by secular ideologies, brought wars, ethnic cleansing, and human bloodshed on a previously unimaginable scale.

Grunwald explained why in this way:

> Our view of man obviously depends on our view of God.… The ultimate irony, or perhaps tragedy, is that secularism has not led to humanism. We have gradually dissolved—deconstructed—the human being into a bundle of reflexes, impulses, neuroses, nerve endings. The great religious heresy used to be making man the measure of all things; but we

> have come close to making man the measure of nothing.[13]

God made us in His image. We can only know ourselves if we know God. Without God, we no longer know who we are. This is true for individuals as well as entire cultures.

Our twenty-first century, having inherited that twentieth-century baggage, is full of contradiction. We strive to champion and expand human rights without knowing what a human is. We educate students with whats and hows but offer no coherent vision of why. We dramatically protect, heal, and save some babies in the womb while targeting others for extinction, particularly those with disabilities. We fill our lives with entertainment, gadgets, experiences, activities, and other distractions but have no clear *telos,* or ultimate purpose. In short, we want human flourishing without God. But it won't happen.

Of course, those who reject God still worship, only at other altars. We may snicker at those who, in the past, carved an ear on a block of wood and then prayed to it, but we have our false gods too: gods that make us into their images. "Those who make [idols] become like them," wrote the psalmist, "so do all who trust in them" (Ps. 135:18).

The modern pantheon of idols includes the following:

> **Self.** The first of the Ten Commandments is "You shall have no other gods before [Me]" (Exod. 20:3). Today we have no other gods before *me.*

> **State.** The apostle Paul wrote, "My God will supply every need" (Phil. 4:19). Today we increasingly look to the state to supply our needs, and even many of our wants.
>
> **Sex.** This very good gift of God, a means of expressing love and marital oneness, is for many life's highest pursuit, an end in and of itself.
>
> **Science.** The word of science (or, more accurately, of scientists) has replaced the Word of God as the source of absolute truth. Rather than pointing us to the God who made the world, science allows us to remake the world, and even ourselves, as we see fit.
>
> **Stuff.** Blaise Pascal famously wrote of a God-shaped void we all have that only God can fill.[14] Today, the constant barrage of commercials and marketing slogans proclaim that our void is stuff shaped. Yet the more we fill our lives with stuff, the less we're satisfied.

Of course, idols can never replace God, but even more, they dehumanize us. We see ourselves and others in the image of whatever it is we worship. People become sexual objects, valued because of their appearance and used for our pleasure, rather than subjects with inherent dignity and value. Just as we value stuff that is useful and convenient, we devalue those with disabilities, and those who aren't sufficiently useful or convenient are targeted and dismembered in the womb. In the twentieth century, many governments, in godlike fashion, eliminated those who stood in the way of Marxist, fascist, or Nazi agendas. In the twenty-first century, many governments ostracize and silence those who refuse the agendas of sexual ideologies.

The cultural identity crisis creates personal identity crises. Young people especially struggle with who they are and why they're here. Many succumb to false identities, such as "I am what I can do," or "I am what others think I am," or "I am my sexual inclinations," or "I am what I look like."

If kids don't know what it means to be human, how can they know what it means to be Christian? As one student told me (John), "I used to think that being gay was just a struggle, but I've come to realize it's who I am."

How sad but, unfortunately, predictable. As his culture faithfully taught him, his Christianity was incidental to his sexual identity rather than his sexuality being an expression of his identity in Christ. Discipleship is the only antidote for this confusion. Young people must know not only what to believe and how to behave but also who they are as redeemed image bearers of the Creator.

Who Are We, Really?

How can kids form an identity, discerning the truth from the lies about what makes them who they are? Brett and I have found critical insights in three areas that contribute to identity formation: story, questions, and community.

Story

Think of the person you know better than anyone else in the world. Is it because you've memorized that person's weight, height, IQ, blood type, and SAT scores? Of course not! Brett and I would never describe our wives by listing their specifications! First, that would be weird. Second ... well, they would kill us!

We know people by their stories. When they tell us where they're from, what their families are like, and what they enjoy doing, they're revealing who they are by offering bits and pieces of their stories. Story and identity are intimately connected. Postmodernism rejects the existence of a universal Story of history and humanity.[15] Young people don't know who they are largely because they live in a postmodern culture without a coherent story.

Throughout the Old Testament, the psalmists and the prophets called Israel to obedience by reminding the people of who they were. They did this by telling and retelling the Story of how God chose, led, and rescued them as His people. The New Testament, particularly in the letters of Paul and Peter, consistently reminds the church of who they are as God's new people by telling and retelling the Story of how God, in Christ, chose, led, and rescued them as His people.

In a Storyless culture, kids must know Christianity as the true Story of all reality and therefore as *their own* Story, not just as a list of beliefs, rules, and historical facts. Christians often talk about, but rarely define, finding our "identity in Christ." Biblically speaking, however, we can't know our identity in Christ without knowing His Story as revealed in Scripture.

As we described in a previous chapter, the Story of Scripture can be told in four chapters: creation, fall, redemption, and restoration. Each chapter reveals core truths about the identity of image bearers: that we were created to make something of the world, ruling God's place for His glory (creation); that we have rebelled, that human sin brought death into the world (fall); that Christ imaged God as Adam failed to do, obeying and exchanging His righteousness for our unrighteousness and accomplishing salvation on our behalf (redemption); that redeemed image bearers are called back to their full humanity as both messengers and agents of the risen Christ who is "making all things new" (restoration). With this Story, the Bible frames all of reality, including our identity.

Unfortunately, many kids are taught the Bible not as the Story of reality but only as a disconnected set of stories, verses, and lessons to be taken randomly at will, distanced from their context, and applied to our lives as we see fit. This "moral McNugget" approach to reading and teaching Scripture, as Philip Yancey calls it, not only treats the Bible as something less than it is but fails to provide the framework of who we are according to God. As a result, robust, framing biblical truths are reduced to virtual Post-it notes that decorate a generation whose identities, morality, and purposes are being shaped by culture, not Christ. (For more on how we can read and teach the Bible to shape identity, see chapter 16: "How to Read the Bible.")

Questions

In the previous chapter, we said that parents and mentors must create space for the difficult questions kids ask about God, life, and faith. This is critical not only for navigating life in the information age but also for helping kids learn who they are. Canadian behavioral psychologist James Marcia has done extensive research on adolescent identity formation, and his insights, we believe, are critical.[16]

Marcia identified four stages of identity formation people reach—diffusion, foreclosure, moratorium, and achievement—based on two critical questions: (1) Have they wrestled with life's big questions (i.e., origins, identity, meaning, morality, and destiny)? and (2) Have they committed to a particular vision of life based on their exploration of the alternatives?

Those in a state of *diffusion* have neither explored life's meaning nor made any subsequent commitments to a particular vision of life. They have no real sense of who they are. Those in a state of *foreclosure* have committed to a vision of life without ever wrestling with the questions themselves. Instead, they embrace the vision of others—for example, their parents or their community. *Moratorium* describes those who constantly explore alternative visions of life but refuse to commit to any of them. Always questioning, they never settle on any answers. Finally, *achievement* describes those who have sufficiently wrestled with the big questions and have sufficiently committed to a vision of life. They know who they are and how they fit in the world.

Our culture leaves kids in perpetual *moratorium*, constantly barraging them with new ideas and information, tempting them to seek pleasure and self-fulfillment while offering them a dizzying array of choices about what to believe, how to live, what to buy, where to go, and what to love. They are constantly told to question everything, to explore every alternative, and to keep an open mind on everything from politics to religion to gender. Social media, porn, and affluence offer relationships and pleasure without commitment. Kids in moratorium are incredibly unstable, prone to deception, disappointment, and cynicism.

On the other hand, Marcia's description of *foreclosure* reminds us of Christian teenagers who've never wrestled with whether Christianity is, in fact, true. Maybe it's because they're living off their parents' faith, or because their youth groups were entertainment-driven, weekly social gatherings of activities and pizza, with a five-minute "Jesus is your best friend" devotional sprinkled on top. But these kids are one atheist professor, sexual failure, or personal tragedy away from losing their faith and their fragile identities. Simply put, their worldview just isn't big enough for the challenges of the real world.[17]

Parents and mentors won't help kids by being casual observers of their identity struggles. Nor will they help by being protective drill sergeants, sheltering them from anything that would challenge their faith while mandating what they should think and how they should live. Instruction is necessary, of course, but discipleship happens not when we talk *at* our kids but when we walk *with* them through their struggles to a place of commitment.[18]

By walking with them, we take their questions and doubts seriously. The capacity for curiosity and struggle is among God's greatest gifts to us. Yet the ultimate purpose of questioning isn't merely to question, as many will surely tell our kids, nor is it to find answers and win arguments. Identity is found when we commit to a life in the service of God, who is the truth.

At times we may have to confront young people with questions they should be asking but aren't. Too many find themselves off at college or out in culture facing basic challenges to Christianity they never knew existed. They then assume Christianity cannot hold its own in the marketplace of ideas. The first time they confront arguments for same-sex marriage and naturalistic evolution or against the Bible and the resurrection, they should be *with us* in an environment where they can find answers.

In other words, kids must be taught basic apologetics. But they shouldn't be left to wrestle alone. Identity requires believing. It also requires belonging.

Community

The God who made us in His image is Himself an eternal community we call the Trinity. This means that He doesn't merely *do* relationships; He is, in His very nature, a relationship. As His image bearers, we'll never know who we are in isolation from others.

In *The Fabric of Faithfulness*, Steven Garber points to three characteristics of young people who find stable identity in Christ, or in his words, "a coherent life centered in their deepest convictions about what is real and true and right."[19] First, they have a worldview that is big enough for the world. (We've talked about that already.) The other two characteristics are specific relationships: They are deeply influenced by mentors who are committed to walking with them through life, and they belong to a community that embodies Christian life together.

This is why, for the Christian, church isn't optional. It's the community of God to which we belong and with whom we're to live and serve. For the believer, there is no substitute for the church.

Older teens and young adults have an alarmingly high church dropout rate. There are many reasons for this, of course, but one is the tendency of churches to age-segregate their members. Age-specific programming for children and youth can be helpful and is often necessary, but many kids, though technically in the church, grow up outside of it. This means they miss out on mentors and therefore fail to learn what it means to be part of a community they desperately need.

We shouldn't be surprised when, after two decades of fun and games, so many twentysomethings lose interest in church when they age out of the youth group. They need to be part of the church community from the beginning, developing relationships with adults, learning to serve, and participating in the mission. They need the church, especially as they enter that new stage of life when they make so many critical life decisions.

And, we should add, the church needs them too.

Discussion Questions

1. Describe the biblical vision of the image of God *(imago Dei)*. How is it different from the vision of humanity that other worldviews offer?

2. What examples of identity crises have you seen in peers, family members, coworkers, or the culture at large?

3. Review the modern pantheon of idols listed in the chapter. Offer examples of these idols that you've experienced in today's world.

4. Using James Marcia's four categories of identity formation (diffusion, foreclosure, moratorium, achievement), how would you evaluate your sense of identity? Why?

Chapter Six

Being Alone Together

The huge modern heresy is to alter the human soul to fit modern social conditions, instead of altering modern social conditions to fit the human soul.

G. K. Chesterton

"Oh yeah," students tell Brett and me, "that happens all the time."

They're referring to a phenomenon we find, well, creepy. Apparently, some people, while physically separated from their phones, can sense when they receive a text message. For students, this is quite normal. In other words, they're in class, and their phones are in their lockers, and yet in some sort of strange violation of the space-time continuum, they know they have a text. They just *know*.

I (John) first heard of this phenomenon from Sherry Turkle, psychologist and professor of social studies and technology at the Massachusetts Institute of Technology (MIT). Turkle was a guest on my weekly radio program, and we were talking about her book *Alone Together: Why We Expect More from Technology and Less from*

Each Other.[1] Most of us have experienced "phantom ringing," a mental false alarm of receiving a call or a text message, but this is different. This is like a technological ESP. The phrase "That kid is attached to his phone" is no longer hyperbole.

For nearly thirty years, Turkle has studied the impact of computer and online technology on people and their relationships. "Not that long ago," she says, "we were trying to figure out how we would keep our computers busy.... [Now,] they keep us busy. It's kind of as though we are their killer app."[2] Along the way, Turkle's perspective on life in the digital age has evolved with the technology she studies.

Her first book, *The Second Self: Computers and the Human Spirit*, was written in 1984, well before the invention of the World Wide Web.[3] Back then, computers were basically enormous calculators, used for spreadsheets, programming code, and primitive games. Yet Turkle saw that computers were becoming more than machines to use. They would become, she predicted, extensions of ourselves. She was correct.

In 1997, Turkle published *Life on the Screen: Identity in the Age of the Internet.*[4] Though many of us were online by then, websites were informational but not interactive. People got together in chat rooms, but social-media platforms like Facebook, Instagram, and Snapchat were still a decade away. Smartphones weren't very smart (no one had heard of an iPhone), emails were sent with annoying swishing sounds, and people spent most of the day off line.

As in her earlier book, Turkle was prophetic. When people went online, she realized, they were doing more than expressing themselves. They were exploring *alternative selves*. Turkle predicted that online life, unlike real life, would make possible new ways of thinking about identity: decentered, virtual, and not bound by gender, age, or physical, ethnic, and geographic limitations. Online, people could be whoever they wanted to be.

What Turkle's first two books had in common, other than eerily accurate predictions, was optimism. When I first read *Life on the Screen* in seminary, I found her celebration of dissatisfied fifty-seven-year-old men becoming virtual eighteen-year-old girls more than a little strange. We were watching the intersection of human evolution and postmodern identity, she believed, and back then she didn't see a downside. Today she does.

When I asked Turkle why the tone of *Alone Together* was so different from that of her earlier books, she replied, "I wasn't prescient." Then she added, "And I do have a teenage daughter." In the fifteen years between her second and third books, her optimism about online life turned into deep concern about the state of human relationships. "We're designing technologies that will give us the illusion of companionship," Turkle says, "without the demands of friendship."[5] With everyone controlling their own little technogadget worlds, no one is vulnerable. Eye contact is rare. Increasingly, as the title suggests, we are learning to be alone together.

How Our Technology Shapes Us

"We do not ride on the railroad; it rides upon us."[6] Historically, each new technology had naysayers who predicted that terrible things would happen to humanity if they didn't resist it. Most of the time, technofears were overblown. However, we share Turkle's concern about how much life is being lived online these days, and how it's affecting all of us, and especially our kids.

Most of us are unaware of and tend to dramatically underestimate how much time we spend with phones, tablets, televisions, or computer monitors.[7] Yet the average time for Americans in front of our glowing screens continues to skyrocket. From 2004 and 2009, according to a Brookings Institution report, the combined average time *each day* spent watching television, browsing the web, and playing video games for children and teens increased by ninety minutes.[8] Remember, technologically speaking, 2009 was a lifetime ago. More recently, CNN reported that Americans now spend *ten hours a day* with screens of some kind.[9]

One way our current technological challenges differ from those of the past is in technology's omnipresence. There is virtually no place in our lives where a screen isn't front and center. Think about it: at work, at school, in the car, on planes, in our pockets, on the nightstand, at the dinner table, on vacation, in church during the sermon, in line at the store, at playgrounds distracting us from our kids, in museums overshadowing the artifacts, at national landmarks surrounded by beautiful things—the list goes on and on. It's no exaggeration to say that life today is lived more indirectly than directly, with our experiences, conversations, and relationships mediated to us through our various devices.

There are consequences when life is lived this way.[10] First, we lose touch with our world. Especially through social media like Twitter, Facebook, and Instagram, we adopt an odd posture toward everyday life. Rather than enjoying the moment we're in, making the most of an experience, and contemplating important lessons learned and memories made, we find ourselves thinking, *How many likes and shares will my picture of this get?*

Recently, on a trip to Alaska, my (John's) family took a whale-watching excursion. It must have been our lucky day, because a whole pod of humpbacks came within fifty yards or so of the front of the boat. You can guess what everyone on the boat did next (including us). Instead of actually absorbing this incredible moment of seeing one of God's most majestic creatures with our bare eyes, we focused all of our efforts on trying to capture video footage with our phones. How many times have we missed fireworks shows, sunsets, sporting events, or even our children's milestones because instead of actually being there, living in the world God created, we were focused on capturing life for social media?

A second consequence of living life through our devices is that we lose touch with one another. Employers have told Brett and me that many in the emerging generation struggle to make eye contact and can't understand nonverbal communication. We've all been frustrated at a friend, spouse, parent, or child engrossed in a digital conversation instead of the one they should be having with us. We've all experienced constant interruptions from buzzing, beeping, and ringing at dinners and meetings.

According to Sherry Turkle, students tell her that they long for eye contact with their parents. Brett and I find that amazing because this generation, having never known anything different, shouldn't know what they're missing! But they do. Those built-in moments of the day that once guaranteed focused attention, such as the obligatory "How was your day, honey?" at the school pickup, are now moments of divided attention. Parents push the swing with one hand while scrolling through texts and emails with the other. Dinner-table conversation is stolen when Mom is watching television, Dad is checking the headlines on his device, and the kids are texting on their phones. Our kids learn their tech habits from us.

Online life also challenges our willingness and ability to be honest and vulnerable with others. Our social-media profiles are highly edited constructs of our lives for friends and family to browse (and perhaps to envy). We don't struggle online. We posture. This is largely responsible for what has become known as the "mommy wars." Browsing the pages of Pinterest or Instagram celebrities, it's hard to measure up to those moms who always seem put together, with clean houses and creative, decorated breakfast ideas for their always-bathed children.

Social media also fosters a false sense of intimacy and connection with others. Today we can have thousands of "friends" but, in reality, not have deep, meaningful relationships. We might even find ourselves wanting "followers" instead of actual friends. Remember that young people, who have never known what relationships were like before the digital age, won't have any context to distinguish deep relationships from manufactured online ones.

On the other hand, Jimmy Kimmel, in his frequent late-night-television-show segment called "Mean Tweets," demonstrates how technology can make us forget the humanity of others. We're far more likely to say things online that we'd never say to someone's face. And we're more likely to engage in risky behavior we'd never consider in person. Many kids are leaving a digital footprint that will haunt them for the rest of their lives.

Often our kids will claim a so-called right to privacy to escape accountability. According to parenting expert Julie Hiramine, parents should know their kids' passwords for anything they do online. However, many parents are scandalized when she recommends this, feeling that it violates some sort of unspoken absolute of the digital age.[11] In junior high, my (Brett's) daughter asked for privacy on the Internet. But John and I don't even afford ourselves that sort of perk. Our wives have an all-access pass to our emails, social-media accounts, and online activities.

A third consequence of online life is that we lose touch with ourselves. The tendency today is to become curators of our own online museums for our carefully selected and polished moments. In doing so, we may think our personal brand of approved images and sound bites are the real us. Because we can only truly know ourselves in community, we lose touch with ourselves when we lose touch with others.

Online life also sells us the false impression that we can separate who we are into public and private realms. Particularly in the case of pornography addiction, kids cultivate deadly sins online under different identities, as if they aren't at the same time reshaping their own souls. On the other hand, they face pressure online to disconnect from their deeply held convictions.

Expressing Christian views on controversial issues like homosexuality, same-sex marriage, or transgender identity comes at a high cost, but "liking" the post of a friend often feels obligatory, even if he or she is boasting about a view or activity that violates Christian morality.

The Lies Technology Teaches Us

Technology today can also deceive teens, according to Dr. Kathy Koch, a popular speaker and an expert in educational psychology and learning styles. In her very helpful book *Screens and Teens: Connecting with Our Kids in a Wireless World*, Koch describes five lies communicated to teens (and us) in our tech-shaped culture.[12]

Lie #1: I am the center of my own universe.

Adolescence is a somewhat recent innovation, brought to life by messaging, marketing, music, and popular culture aimed directly at teens. Today, unlike ages past, teens can live in a world separate from adults. Technology also allows teens to live in online worlds separate from one another, worlds of their own making.

It's not unusual these days to see a group of teens hanging out together but focused only on their devices. As Dr. Koch points out, kids today have never known a world of limitations. Long gone are the days of buying entire albums with songs we don't like or developing entire rolls of film with pictures that don't turn out as we hoped. We're now the creators of playlists and photo albums and online personalities. Even Google tracks our online behavior and delivers custom search results it thinks we desire.

Of course, reality doesn't always bend to our demands. We're forced to interact with others who have their own ideas and wishes that may conflict with ours. Kids who believe they're the center of their own universe are in for a world of hurt and disappointment. Even worse, they're falling for the very first lie: "You will be like God, knowing good and evil" (Gen. 3:5).

Lie #2: I deserve to be happy all the time.

The great irony of a culture with so many distractions and devices is that our kids can seem perpetually bored. The great tragedy is that so many of them struggle with apathy and depression. According to the Centers for Disease Control and Prevention (CDC), suicide is the second leading cause of death for ten- to twenty-four-year-olds.[13]

Today's technology promises kids immediate gratification. They can get what they want when they want it. Theirs is an on-demand world: movies, music, sexual pleasure, adventure, violence, revenge, gadgets, games.

Unless they learn differently, young people will absorb the three chief virtues of modern society: convenience, efficiency, and choice.[14] In other words, they'll learn by technological osmosis that the best life is one that is faster, easier, and on their own terms. Along the way, they'll miss developing the essential character qualities of patience, prudence, and perseverance.

Lie #3: I must have choices.

I (John) was in a small corner grocery store in Montego Bay, Jamaica. Fresh out of college, I had committed the next year to hosting short-term teams for a missions organization there. A dedicated morning-cereal guy, I was confused to find this store didn't have an aisle, or even a shelf, full of the choices I was accustomed to finding back in the States. Even worse, there were only three brands to choose from, and none of them was Honey Bunches of Oats!

Westerners have long been addicted to choice, and our technologies have only made it worse. There's always something better, newer, upgraded, and cooler. Infinite choices of movies, songs, games, tablets, phones, experiences, and relationships (real or virtual) teach kids that infinite choice is required for happiness and fulfillment.

Choice, in and of itself, isn't bad, of course. However, when kids are trapped in the lie that choices are necessary prerequisites to happiness, two things result. First, rather than seizing the opportunities in front of them, they will always be looking for the next better thing. Second, addiction to choice leads to ungratefulness.

Lie #4: I am my own authority.

One of the illusions of the modern world is that we are in control. Technology enables that illusion by giving us the world on our own terms. Digital reality is infinitely customizable. When so much of life is lived online, it's only a small jump to thinking that's the way all of reality should be as well.

The heart of moralistic therapeutic deism, the dominant worldview of our time that we discussed in an earlier chapter, is the mistaken assumption that this is our world, not God's. Craig Gay calls this "practical atheism," or the idea that even if God exists, we're the ones who run the world.[15] It's not difficult to see how our technologies foster this unspoken, but very real, impression.

Lie #5: Information is all I need, not teachers.

Parents and mentors have a lot of competition these days. So do pastors and teachers. Why seek wise counsel when kids can just google the answers to their questions? Why ask Mom and Dad, when Siri is always available?

In an earlier chapter, we discussed the many challenges of living in the information age. For example, kids are tempted to confuse information with knowledge and completely forgo the pursuit of wisdom. Here's another challenge: having all the answers at their fingertips teaches students that teachers aren't necessary. Gray hair used to indicate wisdom. Now it identifies someone who is out of touch.

Helping Kids Avoid Being Alone Together

So how can parents and mentors counter the tech tsunami engulfing our kids and families? An obvious practical step is to limit access to screen time as long as possible, especially smartphones. Parents face enormous pressure to help our kids keep up with their friends, and it can feel like a losing battle. But stick to your guns and don't let the wrong considerations determine when and how certain technologies are introduced into your child's life. Develop a set of criteria, such as habits, character qualities, and indicators of maturity, to help you decide whether or not your child is ready.

Also, for families, implement technology fasts. Perhaps it's every day after dinner, Sunday afternoons (except for football!), one day a week, or weekends. If your family is already drowning with gadgets, any limits will seem excessive to your kids. So have a plan for how to replace the time.

Both Sherry Turkle and Kathy Koch recommend establishing device-free zones, times and places where everyone unplugs. Here are four:

> **1. The car.** As the parents of young children, Brett and I understand the benefits of movies, audiobooks, and games to pass the time on long road trips. However, most car rides should be tech-free. Obviously, texting while driving is dangerous. More than that, however, rides to and from school, church, and shopping are when parents have a captive audience.
>
> **2. The dinner table.** Research points to mealtimes as critical components of a healthy family and as indicators of a child's long-term success.[16]

Too often today, family meals are disrupted by technology that pulls each member into separate worlds.

3. Bedrooms. It's madness to allow children unfettered, unfiltered access to the Internet in the privacy of their bedrooms. Internet pornography is waiting for them there. Period. Also, glowing screens, midnight texts, and social media are obstacles to good rest. Parents should make their own bedroom a device-free zone as well. How much physical and emotional intimacy do our devices steal from us as couples? Set a nightly curfew when devices are retired until morning.

4. Vacations. Going away as a family is one of the best opportunities for deep relationship building. Don't let your devices get in the way.

Remember to use these device-free times wisely. Develop a list of questions for your kids that will help you dive into their beliefs, hopes, dreams, disappointments, and aspirations. Bring up a hot topic from the news that day or tell a story from your childhood. It doesn't have to be a serious discussion. Laugh together, think together, imagine together. Demand eye contact and dig deeper than "Yes," "No," and "I dunno" discussions. Initially it will be hard for both our kids and us, but it will be worth it.

At times we'll need to make difficult decisions to unplug for good from a device, an online activity, or an app. Involve your kids in these decisions. If you see an addiction develop, confront it early and work with your child to initiate appropriate boundaries and limits. In my family and Brett's, screens are to be used only in public areas. Isolation equals temptation.

There is simply no substitute for deliberately taking the time to know our kids on a personal level and opening up ourselves for them to know us. Only in the context of a true relationship can we demonstrate to them who they are beyond their gadgets, profiles, and online posturing. They need to hear that from us.

This requires us to be appropriately vulnerable with our kids. We need to be willing to share the hard memories as well as the good ones, and our struggles and failures along with our successes and wins. That way, they'll see that our identities are secure outside of our social-media projections, and that we, too, are real people who long to belong and be known.

The glowing rectangles aren't going away. Short of some sort of apocalypse, we'll never again know a dark, quiet world. Our kids inhabit an online world, but we can help them know that they, and everyone they meet, are more than their digital appendages.

Discussion Questions

1. Have you ever lost your phone or handheld device? What was your reaction? Have you ever witnessed someone whose reaction revealed a deep addiction to his or her technology?

2. Have you or anyone you know ever been deeply wounded on social media? What happened?

3. Which of the five technology lies have you experienced or witnessed? What happened?

4. Do you have a device-free zone in your life? If so, what is it and why did you implement it?

Chapter Seven

Castrated Geldings and Perpetual Adolescence

For the first time in human history, the young have become a model of emulation for the older population, rather than the other way around. Culturally speaking, be that in terms of dress codes, mentality, lifestyles and marketing, the world that we live in is astonishingly youthful and in many respects infantile.

Robert Pogue Harrison, *Juvenescence: A Cultural History of Our Age*

"Once, there was a world without teenagers."[1] What Diana West meant by that opening line of her book *The Death of the Grown-up* was not that there was ever a world without teen*aged* humans, but that teen*agers*, as a group distinct from children and adults, are a relatively new human phenomenon.

In virtually every culture throughout the history of the world until quite recently, kids usually became adults by way of some rite of passage. Not anymore. Now they become teenagers or, to use the more scholarly word, adolescents. According to West, it all started with Chubby Checker.[2]

Before the Twist craze of the 1950s, there was no distinct youth culture. Young people went to the dances on Friday nights with the adults, dressed like the adults, dancing to the music of the adults. The Twist changed all that. This was a dance just for young people, and the adults lined up around the outside of the dance floor wondering what sort of debauchery they were witnessing.

Then there was the automobile. Before the existence of the family car, young people were trapped at home on Friday nights. Transportation made possible a new way of life for youth. Now they could borrow the car, hang out with friends, drive the strip, find a part-time job, head to the drive-in movies, and most important, create a world without adults. Then there was Elvis and the Beatles, and suddenly there were teenagers.

And these teenagers had money. Once marketing executives and advertising professionals discovered this new audience segment, targeted products, messages, films, and music followed. And suddenly there was youth culture.

Neurologically speaking, there are reasons to see the teen years as a distinct stage of life. Teen brains, though more developed than those of children, still lack the full "wiring" connections of adults. Thus, they tend to be more prone to risky behavior and not always able to connect actions with consequences. In the past, most cultures assisted the maturation process by treating teens like adults, with commensurate responsibilities and expectations.

Not anymore. Today we fully expect kids to lose their minds during their teen years. The perils of adolescence, despite its recent emergence, goes largely unquestioned as a fixed stage of human development. "Kids will be kids," we say. But we aren't talking about kids. We're talking about what most cultures called young adults, at least until the fifties. Not that long ago, these "kids" would have been expected to manage farms, take over the family business, marry, have children, and fight in wars.

Strictly speaking, adolescence isn't limited to teenagers anymore. Typical indicators of adulthood, such as moving out of the family home, settling on a career path, marrying, or having children are happening, on average, later in life than ever before. Eighteen once marked the end of adolescence; today it barely marks the middle. And not only are people leaving adolescence later than ever; they're entering it earlier than ever. "Preteens" have their own television networks, music, cell phones, fashion lines, and subculture too.

But that's not all. In many ways, adolescence is now—and this must not be missed—the *goal* of our culture. Somewhere along the way, we ceased to be a culture where kids aspire to be adults, and we became a culture where adults aspire to be kids, or at least adolescents, forever. Just consider the cinematic history of the "knucklehead."

When Brett and I were growing up in the golden age of movies (you know, the 1980s), teenagers were responsible for the shenanigans. Remember, Ferris Bueller, Marty McFly, and the Goonies? But when we went to college in the nineties, the knuckleheads got older. It was college students and young adults, usually played by Adam

Sandler or Chris Farley, who acted like idiots and refused to grow up. Today, from *The Hangover* movies to anything starring Amy Schumer or Jason Sudeikis, the idiots are adults trying to escape from grown-up jobs or responsibilities, like marriage or kids.

Some call it the Peter Pan syndrome. Others call it "failure to launch." Diana West calls it "perpetual adolescence."[3] Whatever we call it, it's a problem for kids and those who love them.

The Perfect Storm

Three additional factors have greater consequences than usual for perpetual adolescence. First, kids are exposed at earlier and earlier ages to things like romance, graphic sexuality, and gratuitous violence. In other words, as a culture, we steal away our kids' innocence at a very young age, but then we fail to give them the tools they need to grow up. That's a recipe for disaster.

Second, young people are delaying marriage. When Brett and I started working with teenagers nearly two decades ago, Brett as a youth pastor and I with Summit Ministries, we wondered what we could do to help our students stay sexually pure for another four or five, or maybe seven years. Today because young people aren't considering marriage until their late twenties, the question for parents and mentors is how they can help teenagers stay sexually pure for ten to fifteen years in a hypersexualized culture where they're bombarded with porn.

Delayed marriage is particularly hard on young women. Dr. Mark Regnerus explains why with a model called "the Economics of Sex."[4] Economics is about supply and demand. Men tend to have a demand for sex, but women, who control the supply, are able to decide how much they have to pay for it. When the supply of sex isn't kept low through social expectations of chastity and marriage, men can have it without having to grow up, get married, or be employed. In other words, sex becomes a cheap commodity. Women are pressured to give in sexually to obtain what they demand, such as relational security.[5]

Third, and most important, perpetual adolescents live in a culture where robust moral concepts like sin, moral responsibility, and virtue have been abandoned. They're taught that a successful life is not a good life but a happy one. In this "dictatorship of relativism," as Pope Benedict calls it,[6] "safe spaces" and "trigger warnings" protect fragile and perpetual victims from anything that disturbs them. They're rarely told they are wrong or that their feelings aren't reliable. The cultural mantra, as Del Tackett once described it, seems to be, "You don't judge me, and I won't judge you."[7]

In other words, perpetual adolescents are moral infants. In his book *The Road to Character, New York Times* columnist David Brooks writes,

> Sin is a necessary piece of our mental furniture because it reminds us that life is a moral affair.... When modern culture tries to replace sin with ideas like error or insensitivity, or tries to banish words like "virtue," "character," "evil," and "vice" altogether, that doesn't make life any less moral; it just means we have obscured the inescapable

> moral core of life with shallow language. It just means we think and talk about these choices less clearly, and thus become increasingly blind to the moral stakes of everyday life.[8]

If we love our kids and care about their futures, we can't allow them to settle into perpetual adolescence. Rather, we must directly confront it and call them instead to maturity and moral responsibility. Otherwise, we'll become living embodiments of what C. S. Lewis described in one of his most memorable passages: "men [and women] without chests." According to Lewis,

> Such is the tragi-comedy of our situation—we continue to clamour for those very qualities we are rendering impossible. You can hardly open a periodical without coming across the statement that what our civilization needs is more "drive", or dynamism, or self-sacrifice, or "creativity". In a sort of ghastly simplicity we remove the organ and demand the function. We make men without chests and expect of them virtue and enterprise. We laugh at honour and are shocked to find traitors in our midst. We castrate and bid the geldings be fruitful.[9]

Kids who wallow in adolescence won't be men and women who stand against evil and injustice. They won't shape the culture toward the true, the good, and the beautiful. Instead, it will shape them.

Virtue as an Antidote for Perpetual Adolescence

Virtuous people understand and take moral responsibility. Even if the right thing isn't the easy thing, and even if the right thing isn't clear, they possess both the desire and the skill to figure it out. Edmund Burke called this "the moral imagination." Dallas Willard used the phrase "a well-kept heart." We might also call it maturity.

As we said earlier, God created human beings to care for the world. Moral responsibility is, in reality, a form of stewardship and reflects the sort of people we are. "Those with a well-kept heart," Willard wrote, "are persons who are prepared for and capable of responding to the situations of life in ways that are good and right."[10] In other words, the best way to encourage maturity in the next generation is by the cultivation of virtue.

Because, as a culture, we rarely use moral language, champion virtue, or think in terms of being the right sort of people, we rely on insufficient means to keep people in line. Christian parents and mentors are also tempted to resort to these methods to get the behavior we want from our kids. For young people at certain ages or in specific situations, these methods may be helpful and necessary. However, in the long run, if we never get beyond them to the cultivation of virtue, we'll only perpetuate adolescence.

The most common substitute for virtue is *more rules and regulations*. Whenever something goes wrong, like a mortgage crisis or terror attack or hurt feelings, our culture punts to more oversight, typically from the federal government, to "protect" us.

Some Christian communities turn to rules and regulations as well. "If the girls have long skirts and the boys have short hair," the thinking goes, "all will be well."

Rules can provide wise and appropriate boundaries, but following rules shouldn't be confused with Christian maturity. Rules can't show us the heart of a person. While rules may help limit the bad influences and temptations "out there," they leave unaddressed the problems "in here," in the human heart. Often, kids raised in a rule-based environment become strategically compliant, highly trained at not getting caught. The virtue questions are, How do we become the sort of people who know the right thing even if there's not a rule to follow? Will we do the right thing even if we won't get caught?

Of course, as parents and mentors, we're tempted to go the rule route because our culture seems so committed to the idea that there should be *no rules*. Under the guise of freedom, kids are told to follow their hearts and do whatever makes them happy. "Just look inside," they're told, "and be yourself."

Telling those who aren't virtuous to look inside is like telling them to find their way out of a wilderness using a compass that always points at them. A compass works because it points to something fixed and unchanging by which we can orient ourselves and find our way. In the same way, unless there is a fixed moral reference point outside of ourselves by which we can make moral decisions, we'll always be lost. Following your heart won't work unless your heart knows where it's going. Or as Michael Miller, research fellow at the Acton Institute, says, "We've told a whole generation to go find themselves. What if they find themselves, but when they do, they're jerks?"[11]

Freedom cannot be sustained without virtue. We cannot trust ourselves unless we're trustworthy. We must *be* the right people if we are to *do* the right things. As Edmund Burke said,

> Men are qualified for civil liberty in exact proportion to their disposition to put moral chains on their own appetites.... It is ordained in the eternal constitution of things, that men of intemperate minds cannot be free. Their passions forge their fetters.[12]

Another common substitute for virtue is *motivation*. An amazing story or compelling speech can certainly inspire us to action, but what gets us started rarely keeps us going. Many Christian kids can tell you all about the camp "high," making a spiritual decision in an emotionally charged moment at a conference, and how they struggle to follow through when the feeling is gone. Living off emotion is a very adolescent thing to do, but a trait of virtue is doing the right thing *even when we don't feel like it*.

We can also be tempted to elicit good behavior through *incentives*. Of course, bribery often works. Both Brett and I, for example, had great success with bribery when potty training our toddlers. However, what if, ten years from now, we were still giving our kids candy to get them to use the "big-kid potty"? At that point (and far before), there would be a serious problem.

Kids who do the right thing only if there is something in it for them aren't virtuous. They're junkies. Plus, if they're conditioned to behave for the rewards, they're destined to do the wrong thing in this culture, which incentivizes instant gratification, not virtuous lives.

Each of these methods aim at outward behavior instead of the heart. There's a better way.

Cultivating Virtue: Wise Counsel from Ancient Sources

We'll never be able to prepare kids for each specific ethical challenge they'll face. Instead, we should cultivate them to be people of virtue. Two ancient voices can help us.

Aristotle and Habits

Aristotle contributed one of the first works in Western civilization on ethics.[13] Most contemporary textbooks and college classes on the topic do little more than compare ethical theories. Aristotle, however, was concerned with producing ethical people who would be good citizens.

Aristotle emphasized the role of *habits*. Most of us don't have to think about how to tie our shoes, when to brush our teeth, or whether to stop at Starbucks on the way to work. We do these things out of habit. Ethical habits, however, aren't passively formed or maintained, Aristotle argued. Because culture so powerfully shapes our habits, we must be intentional in fostering and cultivating the right sort.

At first glance, the following five areas may not seem like habits, but they are, and they require active, intentional attention. Even more, they are areas of our lives most susceptible to culture's influence, and they have incredible influence over our lives, especially our relationships.

What Are My Loves? The greatest commandment, Jesus said, was to love—first God and then our neighbors. We're love-shaped people. Therefore, as Saint Augustine taught, we must love the right things, and we must love the right things in the right order. The essence of idolatry is to love something more than God. A proper love of God shapes all of our other loves, including our love of other people.

Love must be carefully defined, however. Though often considered a strong, romantic *feeling* that happens to us, we learn to love whatever it is we're habitually intimate with. Love is active, not passive. We can say that we love our spouses, but if our most intimate moments are spent playing video games, working, or seeing other women rather than our spouses, we're lying. Too many kids today exhaust their intimacies on virtual images brought to life on glowing screens rather than the people around them whom they are called to love.

What Are My Longings? Just as our loves refer to intimacies, our longings refer to our imaginations. We coddle those visions of life we most desire, and these longings set the trajectory for our love and decisions. Because longings are among the most powerful assets humans have, we must vigilantly guard them. What we long for, we pursue.

Humans long for all kinds of things: relationships, success, revenge, acceptance, attention, affection, and things. We must constantly evaluate what we long for and what is creating those longings in us. For example, entertainment powerfully shapes our longings. Commercials sell more than a product. Often, they sell fulfillment, a way of life to meet our deepest needs. Christians, on the other hand, are told to long for the kingdom of God and pray for it to be realized "on earth as it is in heaven" (Matt. 6:10).

What Are My Loyalties? The most common excuse we make when we don't want to do something is, "I don't have the time." But we always find the time and the resources for whatever we really want to do. Because there are so many demands on our time and attention, we might, if we aren't careful, find our hearts drawn to things that are unworthy of our loyalty.

Loyalties are rarely tested in dramatic ways. It's unlikely we'll ever face a life-and-death decision about whether to deny Christ, but our loyalties are tested each day by things that attempt to pull our hearts away from Him, and that's demonstrated by where we spend our time. Every parent would say they love their children more than their iPhones, but the true test of their loyalties happens when they have to choose whether to devote their attention to their children or their social-media accounts.

"Where your treasure is," Jesus said, "there your heart will be also" (Matt. 6:21).

What Are My Labors? What gets our dedicated and focused effort? A lot of teenagers these days are far better at video games than relationships. A lot of young men are far better at wasting time than using it. Apathy is a chronic disease of this generation. Many kids just don't care. Some seem to work harder at making excuses than it would take to live in such a way that no excuses would be required!

According to the Genesis account, God created humans with the capacity to make something of the world. We work because it's how we were made. Work matters because it's an expression of worship. Are our kids committed to making something of the world? Are they takers or makers?

What Are My Liturgies? In the context of church worship, *liturgy* refers to the "order of worship," such as the ordered services found in Lutheran, Anglican, or Catholic churches. The fixed arrangements were designed to create rhythms, or habits, of the various elements of worship.

Our culture has its own liturgies, including rhythms of work, play, sports, shopping, entertainment, and eating. We may say "Jesus is the reason for the season," but in American culture, we're cultivated to treat Christmas as shopping season. As we noted earlier, after spending the day giving thanks as a nation, we trample security guards for the latest toys and electronics. It has become a well-established rhythm of our culture.

Families should adopt intentional and alternative rhythms of life to counteract bad habits that waste time in front of television and computer screens. For example, make dinnertime sacred: no phones or any other screens. Make extended face-to-face conversation a normal and expected part of every day. Don't allow texting to replace talking. Make church a priority rather than subject to sports schedules and other activities. Make Sundays a day of family rest and conversation. Schedule dates with spouses and children.

Many families don't know that the church has provided Christians with an alternative calendar that includes different holidays and significant dates for preparation, remembrance, and celebration. We often don't realize how much our culture's calendar of sporting events, television schedules, and shopping seasons shapes our values. Brett and I have found that by using the church calendar, especially to honor the seasons of Lent and Advent, our families have established countercultural rhythms that prioritize better things.[14]

These five questions get at the heart of our deepest habits. To use them effectively, start with the first question and carefully work through each one with the following guidelines in mind:

- Devote time alone to answering these questions. Ask the Holy Spirit to reveal the truth about your heart and mind. Write down your honest reflections in a private journal.
- Ask a trusted mentor, parent, or friend to answer these questions about you. Before you begin, ask the Holy Spirit for humility. As much as possible, ask for specific examples of any observations and write down the person's reflections.
- Review those areas where change is needed, and humbly repent before God of bad habits

that have taken root. Make a plan for change that includes accountability to others.

- *For families*: During a dedicated time (a date night, a weekend away, etc.), parents can ask these questions regarding their families. Consider things like how you spend leisure time, how you celebrate holidays, the role of entertainment and technology in the home, and so on.
- *For churches and youth groups*: As leaders, evaluate congregational habits. What loves, longings, loyalties, labors, and liturgies are sermons, programming, and classes cultivating?

C. S. Lewis, Eustace, and Reepicheep

C. S. Lewis is the second ancient voice who can help us cultivate virtue in our children. Every parent, youth pastor, mentor, and leader should read (and reread) the opening essay from *The Abolition of Man*, "Men without Chests."[15] In it, Lewis critiqued education that fills the head with knowledge and the belly with passion but fails to cultivate the chest. Aristotle, in his work on ethics, taught that the head was the seat of reason, and the belly was the seat of passion or desire. Virtuous people rule the belly with the head, and Aristotle thought that could be done solely through habit.

Habit helps, but we've all experienced the war that can take place between what we *know* and what we *want.* Often the belly wins. That's why Lewis thought that the head needed help. To master our passions, we need the moral will. Lewis called this "the chest." He went on to say,

> It still remains true that no justification of virtue will enable a man to be virtuous. Without the aid of trained emotions the intellect is powerless against the animal organism.... The head rules the belly through the chest.[16]

To borrow an illustration from Michael Miller, imagine that the belly is an eight-hundred-pound gorilla that constantly demands, "Feed me! Feed me! I want!" The head, on the other hand, is like an eighty-pound professor with a bowtie trying to articulate reasons for self-control. The gorilla will usually win. That's why we need a chest.

What's great about Lewis is that whenever his nonfiction is difficult to understand, you can always turn to Narnia. For example, *The Lion, the Witch and the Wardrobe* beautifully contains much of what he taught in *Mere Christianity.* In the same way, in *The Voyage of the Dawn Treader*, we meet the boy without a chest.

"There was a boy called Eustace Clarence Scrubb, and he almost deserved it," the book begins.[17] Eustace was the product of the sort of education Lewis complained about in "Men without Chests." He knew facts about things, but he didn't know how to live. A self-entitled jerk, Eustace thought he was better than he actually was. By the end of the story, and for the rest of his time in Narnia,

Eustace developed a chest. We can't retell the entire story here (plus we want you to read the book), but following is a summary of what we can learn about cultivating virtue from the life of Eustace.

First, knowing right from wrong is not enough. The Christian vision is more than just how to avoid evil. In the story, Eustace knew a lot about ships, but he didn't know how to be part of a ship crew on a voyage on a mission toward a destination. Along the way, especially through the mentorship of the mouse Reepicheep, Eustace learned of the glories of old Narnia, of battles won and lives lived well for causes greater than self.

Proverbs says, "Where there is no prophetic vision the people cast off restraint" (29:18). We rightly wonder how kids who know all the right answers to the Sunday school questions rebel and make choices that go against everything they know to be right. Proverbs explains it. Kids need to have a vision for that which is ultimately worthy of their allegiance. They need to know that Christianity isn't just about how they're to behave; it's about who they are. They need to know not just what to stay away from but what to live for.

For example, telling kids "Don't have sex" is important. But it's more important for them to know the very good purpose of sex and how God gifted us with sex as a means to fulfill our purpose. They should never hear that sex is bad. They should know that sex is good and must be protected because of how valuable it is.

Second, the chest is a muscle. To be a weight lifter, one must lift weights. To be a virtuous person, one must do virtuous things. We can't put on virtue like a helmet; it must be strengthened like a muscle.

"Life is a long obedience in the same direction," writes Eugene Peterson.[18] Parents and mentors often ask students what they're going to do when they grow up. However, far more important than what they're going to do *one day* is what they're going to do *next*. If they can't handle the next situation, the next problem, the next failure, the next temptation, the next success, or the next relationship, they won't reach a life of virtue.

Third, because we won't always do the right next thing, we must practice repentance. In Lewis's story, Eustace became a dragon because of a series of poor decisions. Then he met Aslan, the Christ figure of Narnia, who invited Eustace to cool off in a lake.

But first, Aslan said, he had to undress. Eustace tried, but he was unable to scratch off his itchy scales. The more he tried, in fact, the itchier they became.

"You will have to let me undress you," Aslan said, and in one of the greatest redemption scenes in all of the Narnia stories, he ripped away the dragon flesh with his sharp claws and threw Eustace into the water. When he emerged, Eustace was once again a boy, but a different boy than before.[19]

We cannot fix ourselves. We cannot do better on our own. Repentance is the gift of God to sinful people that allows us to walk away from our sin and bad choices as new creations.

Too many kids, and too many adults, see God's demand for repentance as proof that He is mad at us. Yes, He despises our sin, but repentance is, Scripture says, proof that God is kind (Rom. 2:4). As Frederica Mathewes-Green writes, "Confident expectation of mercy draws repentance out of hiding by taking away our fear.... God wants us to repent of our sins, not suffer because of them."[20]

Repentance makes us right with God. Even more, repentance is a moral workout. We're far more likely to repeat sins we've hidden than those we've confronted and taken to God for forgiveness.

Finally, *we can never be virtuous by ourselves.* One of the unsung heroes in Eustace's transformation was Reepicheep, who, after a rocky first encounter with the boy, became a mentor, friend, and trusted guide on Eustace's journey toward developing a chest.

"There is no limit to the human capacity for self-rationalization," Chuck Colson often said. He knew this all too well. A hard-working former marine, Colson became President Nixon's special counsel and determined to remain uncorrupted by power. Yet he found himself convicted and sentenced to prison for a Watergate-related offense. Even so, in the midst of Watergate, he found Christ and became a tremendous Christian leader, living the rest of his life in accountability.

We need accountability, quite simply, because *sin makes us dumb.* Without wise voices and accountability, we fool ourselves. We need other people.

"Iron sharpens iron," Proverbs 27:17 says. That's why parents and mentors should always be concerned with the friends who surround their kids. In addition to strong peers, young people need *old people.* They need adults who are older and wiser to help them navigate life's challenges.

Our culture tempts kids with isolation. As we said in the previous chapter, technology gives the illusion of connection, but it allows our kids to hide in front of a plethora of glowing screens. If they aren't relating to and communicating with others, that's a sign of trouble.

Discussion Questions

1. Describe adolescence as the media portrays it in today's culture. In what ways has this stage of life changed over the years?

2. Which of the bad substitutes for virtue have you employed? What happened?

3. Discuss the five questions about habits. What cultural forces have shaped your loves, longings, loyalties, labors, and liturgies?

4. Do you know another story of virtue like *The Voyage of the Dawn Treader*? How does it portray the formation of virtue?

Part Three

Pounding Cultural Waves

A Guide to Part Three

It's time to get really practical. In part 3, we tackle eight contemporary cultural challenges that are pounding away at our young people, and they need our help to navigate each powerful wave. Every chapter has been organized into four distinct sections.

The first section is "Don't Buy the Cultural Lies." In this section, we attempt to expose the false narratives of the culture and show how they're mistaken. Cultural lies undermine God's truth, and therefore, Jesus followers have an obligation to "destroy arguments and every lofty opinion raised against the knowledge of God" (2 Cor. 10:5). That's what we'll do in each chapter.

The second section, "Recapture the Wonder of God's Story," reminds us of the deep truths found in God's Story. Christians must return to Scripture as their primary source for the knowledge of reality. In this section, we illuminate each individual topic with relevant ideas and passages from God's Word. As we return to the biblical worldview, we'll rediscover God's beautiful and glorious design for His creatures.

"Action Steps," the third section, is designed to help you make biblical truth really practical. Don't be overwhelmed by the long list of suggestions, thinking you have to take on every step immediately. Start with one or two suggestions and move on from there. Progress is your goal, not perfection.

Wading through the culture can be messy, a bit frightening, and ultimately disheartening. However, followers of Jesus must never despair. As our Lord has said, "In the world you will have tribulation. But take heart; I have overcome the world" (John 16:33).

In the fourth section, "Hopecasting," we'll forecast hope, reminding ourselves that God's Story continues to play out all around us.

Chapter Eight

Pornography

There is no dignity when the human dimension is eliminated from the person. In short, the problem with pornography is not that it shows too much of the person, but that it shows far too little.

Pope John Paul II, *The Theology of the Body*

"The question," Christian apologist Josh McDowell says, "is not 'Will my kids see porn?' but 'How will they handle it when they do?'" He's right. The vast majority of kids have had some exposure to pornography before they leave home. Many seek it out, but even if they're not looking for porn, porn is looking for them.

The Covenant Eyes website offers the following statistics:

- 90 percent of boys and 60 percent of girls said they were exposed to pornography before the age of eighteen.
- 64 percent of Christian men and 15 percent of Christian women admit to watching porn at least once a month.

- One out of every eight online searches and one out of every five mobile searches is for porn.
- Pornography takes up one-third of the Internet's bandwidth.[1]

The news gets worse. Moral views about pornography have shifted, especially in the emerging generation. Only one in twenty young adults and one in ten teenagers report that their friends think watching porn is bad. In fact, teens and young adults think it's *more immoral* to refrain from recycling than to view porn.[2] Not only are kids watching it; they just don't think it's that bad.

Porn isn't confined to a particular gender, ethnicity, or socioeconomic status. It has no demographic barriers. It isn't relegated to the backroom of a video store or the seedy part of town. It has no geographical barriers. It's just one click away. Friends, we don't have a porn problem. We have a porn *epidemic*.

We know, this is heavy stuff. For those who are fighting their own porn battle, maybe it feels a little hopeless. But it's not. As we wade into this difficult topic, remember, hope is always found in the gospel of Jesus Christ. Always.

Don't Buy the Cultural Lies

Lie #1: Porn is a harmless expression of human sexuality.

A morally desensitized culture simply shrugs at the latest porn stats. Pornography, we hear, is just another legitimate avenue of sexual expression, an unobjectionable personal preference. Combine our culture's moral indifference with its insatiable desire for instant gratification, and you have a recipe for disaster.

First, porn is addictive. In their groundbreaking book *Hooked: New Science on How Casual Sex Is Affecting Our Children*, Drs. Joe McIlhaney Jr. and Freda McKissic Bush demonstrate how chemicals released in our brains during sexual activity can lead to addiction.[3] In fact, those addicted to pornography show changes to the structure of their brains that are similar to individuals addicted to drugs and alcohol. Porn actually changes the physical makeup of our brains. For the undeveloped brain of a young person, the addictive consequences can be lifelong.[4]

Second, porn has serious personal ramifications. It distorts attitudes about sexuality and leads to increased sexual permissiveness and risky sexual behaviors. It also decreases marital satisfaction and breaks down trust between spouses. In the end, it leaves people with perpetual feelings of shame and guilt.[5]

Lie #2: Porn is a personal matter, and it's really no one's business what people do in their private lives.

The consequences of porn aren't limited to the individual. Porn is dehumanizing. It treats people as objects to be used for the gratification of our own desires, resulting in a number of social costs. Porn fuels sex trafficking and leads to increased violence and sexual aggression, as well as the exploitation of women and children. Porn also produces broken marriages and families.

But do we really need statistics? Common sense tells us that porn is poisonous. Pornography kills productivity. It kills sexual intimacy. It kills our marriages. And it kills our spiritual lives. Porn brings destruction.

Recapture the Wonder of God's Story

God's Story—the true Story about all of reality—began with Genesis 1:1 when "God created the heavens and the earth." Humanity isn't the end product of a purposeless collision of atoms. No, we were fashioned by the Grand Designer. We were crafted in the furnace of His will. Each body and soul was constructed carefully and purposefully. Human beings are "fearfully and wonderfully made" (Ps. 139:14).

Thus, human identity can only be properly understood in light of human origins. Where did we come from? Psalm 100:3 declares, "It is [God] who made us, and we are his." If we want to know what humanity is designed *for*, we must know the One who designed it. If we have questions about the way we ought to live, we must consult the Designer. In particular, we need to refer to His design manual: Scripture.

God's Story begins with the triune God creating us and fashioning us in His image. A massive implication of those facts is that we were made for relationship. Just as Father, Son, and Holy Spirit experience loving relationship with one another, we were designed for relationship.

First and foremost, we are to be properly related to God. The garden of Eden story indicates that Adam and Eve were in intimate relationship with God.

Second, we are to be properly related to one another. Human sexuality is an important aspect of human connection and thus is intrinsically relational. Sexuality was intended to be experienced not in isolation but in a one-flesh union between husband and wife: "Therefore a man shall leave his father and his mother and hold fast to his wife, and they shall become one flesh. And the man and his wife were both naked and were not ashamed" (Gen. 2:24–25). There is no shame in God's design for sexuality—only beauty and delight.

Scripture never endorses sexuality in isolation. Never. But porn severs sexuality from its relational context. As we noted earlier, it harms relationships by dehumanizing people, treating them as mere objects for sexual gratification. It disconnects sex from a relationship between two people who love each other and converts it into a means for personal indulgence. Watching porn is a thoroughly selfish pursuit.

In addition, God is clear in His prohibition against all forms of lust: "You have heard that it was said, 'You shall not commit adultery.' But I say to you that everyone who looks at a woman with lustful intent has already committed adultery with her in his heart" (Matt. 5:27–28). To look at a woman lustfully—pornography's fundamental objective—violates God's design and carries severe consequences.

Adultery of body or heart sets us on a trajectory of disgrace and destruction. Listen carefully to the solemn warning in Proverbs 6:

My son, keep your father's commandment,
    and forsake not your mother's teaching.
Bind them on your heart always;
    tie them around your neck.
When you walk, they will lead you;
    when you lie down, they will watch over you;
    and when you awake, they will talk with you.
For the commandment is a lamp and the
        teaching a light,
    and the reproofs of discipline are the way
        of life,
to preserve you from the evil woman,
    from the smooth tongue of the adulteress.
Do not desire her beauty in your heart,
    and do not let her capture you with her
        eyelashes;
for the price of a prostitute is only a loaf of bread,
    but a married woman hunts down a
        precious life.
Can a man carry fire next to his chest
    and his clothes not be burned?
Or can one walk on hot coals
    and his feet not be scorched?
So is he who goes in to his neighbor's wife;
    none who touches her will go unpunished.
People do not despise a thief if he steals
    to satisfy his appetite when he is hungry,

but if he is caught, he will pay sevenfold;
    he will give all the goods of his house.
He who commits adultery lacks sense;
    he who does it destroys himself.
He will get wounds and dishonor,
    and his disgrace will not be wiped away.
        (vv. 20–33)

Is God against sex? No! Look no further than the Song of Solomon. This divinely inspired book reveals that in God's Story, He has wonderful intentions for human sexuality in the context of relationship. In contrast to the culture's lustful passions and untethered sexual desire, God's Story paints a breathtaking picture of the beauty of marital bliss.

Action Steps

1. Wake up! Open your eyes to the breadth and depth of the consequences of porn. Read *The Porn Phenomenon*, an in-depth study and assessment of the current porn crisis conducted by leading researchers from the Barna Group in partnership with the Josh McDowell Ministry.[6] Visit the National Center on Sexual Exploitation's website (www.endsexualexploitation.org), and download the free ebook *Pornography: A Public Health Crisis*. Educate yourself regarding the destructive effects of porn. Knowing the truth should motivate you to take immediate action.

2. Confront *your* porn problem first. As we've said, porn has no demographic boundaries. It's not just a problem for our kids; it's a problem for us all. Maybe you have your own battle with porn. To be the kind of leader your kids need, you must engage in this battle right alongside them. Men, confess your porn habits to God and to one another—such as a close and trustworthy friend, pastor, or counselor. Women, do the same. Husbands, confess to your wives. Wives, confess to your husbands. Pastors, confess to one another and to trusted leaders in your church. You may need to seek the help of a professional Christian counselor to begin repairing the damage of porn in your life. Let the grace of the gospel wash over you as you experience God's forgiveness and let the Holy Spirit sanctify you by His power as He begins the process of removing this sin from your life. And then inject some major accountability into your life.

3. Take preemptive action. Do *not* wait until you discover porn in your kids' lives. The average age of exposure to porn is eleven, but our kids don't have to be a statistic. Do something now. As Josh McDowell once said, "I would rather put a fence at the top of the cliff than an ambulance at the bottom." Prevention is better than recovery. Porn is coming for them, so prepare your defenses now. Here are your first preemptive steps:

- *Filtering.* Internet filters restrict access to explicit material and block pornographic content. Therefore, access can and should be filtered on every Internet device in your home. This includes desktop computers, laptops, tablets, smartphones, and gaming consoles.

- *Monitoring.* Internet monitors allow you to keep track of online activity, creating an avenue for accountability. In addition, monitoring creates a second line of defense for parents of tech-savvy teenagers who know how to get around filtering software. Again, monitoring software should be installed on every Internet device in your home.
- *Restrictions.* If you are using an iOS device (e.g., iPhone, iPad), under the "General Settings" you can "Enable Restrictions." This will allow you to set up password-protected controls on that particular device. For instance, you can prevent kids from downloading apps without your permission, turn off internet browsers, or set content ratings.

There are myriad choices for Internet filtering and monitoring, but here are five trusted resources John and I recommend:

- OpenDNS Family Shield—www.opendns.com/home-internet-security/
- Net Nanny—www.netnanny.com
- Mobicip—www.mobicip.com
- Covenant Eyes—www.covenanteyes.com
- Circle with Disney—https://meetcircle.com

Preemptive action is a vital step in protecting your family from pornography, but there is no foolproof method of protection, and even a tech-savvy student can find ways around filtering and monitoring. Thus preemption is just one tool in this battle and can never be a substitute for close relationships and honest conversations with your kids.

4. Expose the darkness of the porn industry. The apostle Paul warns us to "take no part in the unfruitful works of darkness, but instead expose them" (Eph. 5:11). One strategy to strip porn of its allure is to pull back the curtain and expose the truth about the porn business. It's an industry filled with sexually transmitted diseases (STDs), prostitution, drug abuse, emotional abuse, violence, and even the exploitation of women and children for sex trafficking. Knowing what really goes on behind the scenes can help weaken rationalizations for viewing porn.[7]

5. Initiate conversations about pornography. First, adults must be proactive and initiate conversations about porn. Most kids will never bring up the topic of sexuality voluntarily with an adult. Second, it must be a conversation, not merely a one-way teaching time. Ask your kids the following questions:

- Do you know what porn is?
- Have you viewed it before?
- Do your friends ever talk about it or watch it?

- What are your thoughts about porn?
- Do you think it's harmful or harmless, and why?

Ask open-ended questions initially and sustain the dialogue. Of course, don't turn it into an interrogation, but a conversation. Allow kids space to share freely, but also take opportunities to provide wisdom and clear instruction.

6. Paint a vivid picture of the consequences of viewing porn. Warn your kids about the clear and present dangers of porn. Simply do a Google search on the "negative effects of pornography." You'll find research demonstrating its ability to rewire the brain and create addicts, especially at young ages. You'll discover data that links porn with social anxiety, depression, low motivation, lack of productivity, and feelings of guilt and shame. You can also read about porn's harmful effects on marriages: how it decreases interest in sex with one's spouse and increases divorce among the addicted. And the list goes on.

7. Always be ready to respond with forgiveness and grace. In a world where porn is the norm, most of our kids will view it. They'll battle feelings of guilt and shame that could potentially short-circuit their relationship with Christ. With all of the protection and warnings and conversation, never stop proclaiming the gospel. Declare the good news of the forgiveness of sins only available through the cross of Christ. Remind your kids—and yourself—that "there is therefore now no condemnation for those who are in Christ Jesus. For the law of the Spirit of life has set you free in Christ Jesus from the law of sin and death" (Rom. 8:1–2). Only Christ can offer freedom from addiction and hope amid the guilt and shame. Only Christ can restore the willpower to resist sin and temptation. The culture may recognize the porn problem and its corrosive effects, but it can't provide the true path to freedom. Only the New Testament church, equipped with the power of the gospel, can show an addicted culture the way to hope and healing.

8. Love your spouse and your children. No Internet filter or monitoring system can replace loving relationships between husband and wife or parent and child. The best defense against pornography is a close family. Let us suggest two vital components for a close-knit family. First, spend time together. There is no replacement for quality time among family members. Start with something simple like weekly family dinners or a monthly outing. Second, worship together. Work hard to find a solid local church, commit to it, and then plug in. The body of Christ is essential to our spiritual growth and thus our growth as loving families.

Further Resources

- Covenant Eyes—www.covenanteyes.com
- National Center on Sexual Exploitation—www.endexploitationmovement.com
- Protect Young Eyes: Defending Kids from Online Danger—https://protectyoungeyes.com

Hopecasting

We started this chapter on a somber note, but could the tide of pornography be turning? There are signs of hope. In 2015, the worldwide Hilton hotel chain—with 540 properties in more than eighty countries across six different continents—announced that it would remove porn channels from all of its hotels.[8] The decision came in response to a three-year public campaign spearheaded by the National Center on Sexual Exploitation.

Hollywood celebrities are also joining the chorus of voices speaking out against pornography. English comedian and actor Russell Brand posted a YouTube video warning about the damaging effects of porn on relationships.[9] Former NFL player-turned-actor Terry Crews posted a series of Facebook videos titled *Dirty Little Secret*, in which he confessed his own porn addiction and acknowledged his need for professional help.[10] Now he campaigns against the dangers of porn.

Even former *Playboy* model Pamela Anderson is weighing in. She and a Jewish rabbi coauthored an op-ed article titled "Take the Pledge: No More Indulging Porn" that appeared in the *Wall Street Journal*. The article warns of pornography's "corrosive effect on a man's soul and on his ability to function as husband and, by extension, as father. This is a public hazard of unprecedented seriousness given how freely available, anonymously accessible and easily disseminated pornography is nowadays."[11] If a former *Playboy* centerfold can issue such a dire warning, then there's hope for change!

The porn culture can seem unstoppable, and we'll certainly need a seismic societal shift on this issue to conquer it. However, we can view this epidemic as an opportunity for Christians to lead a stumbling culture out of the darkness of sexual sin and brokenness into the light of Christ. It starts with hope and healing in our own homes.

Discussion Questions

1. When was your first exposure to pornography, and how did you respond? When was your most recent exposure to pornography, and how did you respond?

2. How have you seen pornography damage lives and families?

3. Do you have adequate filtering and monitoring measures in place for your online activities? What is missing?

Chapter Nine

The Hookup Culture

Christians should keep talking about sex so that they can learn to speak about it more adequately, that is, more theologically.

Mark Jordan, *The Ethics of Sex*

It may be difficult to find love in the twenty-first century, but it's pretty easy to have sex. That's the promise of the hookup culture.

What exactly does it mean to hook up? The answer depends on whom you ask. Many young people prefer an ambiguous definition because they face conflicting social pressure. By disguising details, they can still walk the socially acceptable line of being sexually active while avoiding all-out promiscuity.

"Hooking up" is a catchall phrase that can mean anything from simply making out to touching sexual body parts to engaging in oral sex or intercourse. However, all of this sexual activity takes place *outside* the context of a committed relationship. Hookups are typically brief, casual, and commitment-free. It's sex, no strings attached. Kids can sidestep messy relational entanglements when they have friends with benefits.

A multiyear survey of more than twenty-four thousand college students from twenty-two different US colleges and universities found that just as many students are hooking up as are dating. Sixty-two percent reported having hooked up since the beginning of their college experience, while 61 percent reported going out on a date.[1] Clearly, hooking up is widespread. And so are the repercussions.

Don't Buy the Cultural Lies

Lie #1: Everyone is hooking up.

Not everyone is doing it. In fact, despite the alarming statistics, the hookup trend seems to be heading downward. A recent study in the *Archives of Sexual Behavior* demonstrated that millennials are twice as likely to be sexually *inactive* than previous generations.[2] In the study, millennials reported fewer sex partners than any group since the 1960s. That means kids today report fewer partners than their parents did. The number of high school students who reported having sex fell to 30 percent in 2015 from 34 percent in 2013 and 37.5 percent in 1991.[3]

Make no mistake, young people are still experimenting with sex. Indeed, most Americans will have sex at some point before they marry.[4] However, the data tells us that promiscuous sexual activity isn't the inescapable and unavoidable result of our hookup culture. Could the decrease in sexual activity among millennials signal the moral exhaustion of the culture?

Lie #2: Dating is dead.

Dating isn't dead, but it is on life support. Young people are hooking up at times *and* dating at other times. Hooking up hasn't replaced dating as much as it has changed the way young people think about it. Nowadays, there are just no norms for dating. Have sex first and then date? Sure, no problem. Dinner and a movie? If you want, but a late-night text message and hookup are just as acceptable. Ask a girl's father for permission? Open doors and pay for dinner? Not so much. That's a little too old fashioned. You see, the hookup culture has remade dating, but the makeover is a mess.

Lie #3: Hooking up is consequence-free.

A one-night stand. Sexual favors with no strings. Pleasure without problems. All the sex without any of the stigma. Right? Wrong.

First, hookups increase the risk of sexually transmitted diseases. According to the Centers for Disease Control and Prevention, the infection rate for sexually transmitted diseases like chlamydia, gonorrhea, and syphilis are on the rise, especially for young people. The "CDC estimates that nearly 20 million new sexually transmitted infections occur every year in this country, half among young people aged 15–24," even though they represent only 25 percent of the sexually active population.[5] The rates of gonorrhea and chlamydia are highest among young people ages fifteen through twenty-four.[6] The consequences are severe. Chlamydia can cause permanent damage to a woman's reproductive system, even leading to infertility. Some types of the human papillomavirus (HPV), the most common sexually transmitted infection, can cause head and neck cancer, cervical cancer, and genital warts. Worse yet, there is no treatment for HPV.[7]

Second, hookup behavior during college is correlated with depression and poor mental health.[8] Ohio State University surveyed approximately ten thousand young people about their romantic relationships and found that teens who experienced depression were more likely to have casual sex as young adults.[9] A 2014 study concluded, "For emerging-adult college students, engaging in casual sex may elevate risk for negative psychological outcomes."[10]

Third, hooking up is associated with other risky behaviors. According to the *Journal of Sex Research*, 53 percent of women drank during hookups—and 38 percent drank heavily. The less they knew their hookup partner, the more likely they were to drink, and drink heavily, before sex. An astounding 89 percent of hookups involved drinking when the partner was a random stranger.[11]

Lie #4: What you do when you're young won't impact your future.

Hooking up now undermines marriage later. Eighty percent of young people see marriage as an important part of their life plans.[12] However, permissive sexual behavior sabotages marital stability.

Individuals with more sex partners before marriage report less marital satisfaction. Conversely, having fewer sexual partners results in higher marital quality.[13] A third of marriages today began as a hookup. Those couples report lower quality of marital satisfaction.[14]

Cohabitation greatly increases marital dissatisfaction. The social-science data on this is clear. First, cohabitation leads to higher divorce rates after marriage. "People with cohabiting experience who marry have a 50 to 80 percent higher likelihood of divorcing than married couples who never cohabited."[15] Second, it leads to a lower-quality marital relationship. Researchers at UCLA "found that cohabitors experienced significantly more difficulty in their marriages with adultery, alcohol, drugs and independence than couples who did not cohabit."[16] Living together is no replacement for marriage, nor is it a trial run.

Today's sexual orthodoxy proclaims so-called sexual freedom and insists that all consensual sex acts are good. Anything that interferes with or restricts sexual expression is therefore inherently bad. But clearly, sexual liberation doesn't deliver what it promised. Instead, it's a burden that's breaking our young people.

Recapture the Wonder of God's Story

Can we Christians stop *not* talking about sex, please? For too long, we've let other voices direct and dominate the cultural conversation on sex. Much of the church's contribution has been to shout "Don't do it!" from the margins of society. We've given the impression that Christianity has a negative view of sex. But God's Story offers so much more than a simple no to unsanctioned sex. For every prohibition, there is a beautiful, life-giving yes!

As we've already highlighted, God's Story begins with God as creator and designer. Human design and identity are grounded in His nature. Questions like "Who am I?" "What am I?" and "How do I function properly?" find their proper starting point in God's existence and creative activity.

Every discussion of human identity begins with the image of God: "God created man in his own image, in the image of God he created him" (Gen. 1:27). Shortly after that passage, we discover God's intention for men and women: "A man shall leave his father and his mother and hold fast to his wife, and they shall become one flesh" (2:24).

Embedded in God's design of humanity is a holistic union of men and women within the husband-wife context: they are intended to become "one flesh." This one-flesh union entails sexuality. The sexual desire men and women have for each other is a good thing. If God designed sex, it only makes sense that we look to Him for vision, guidance, and wisdom in this area.

First and foremost, God's *primary* purpose for sex isn't personal pleasure but procreation. That's right, sex is for making babies. God's first command to Adam and Eve was to "be fruitful and multiply and fill the earth" (1:28). Therefore, sex must not be completely severed from reproduction. Why? Because our creator fashioned family in such a way that the permanent commitment between husband and wife is the proper and ideal environment for childbearing and child rearing and, thus, filling the earth. While a husband and wife can certainly enjoy sexual pleasure with each other, they should also have in view God's other purposes for human sexuality.

Second, sexual desire and pleasure aren't the problem. Disordered sexual desire and pleasure are. God says yes to sexuality between husband and wife but no to lust. Young people must know that sex is good, and that's why it must be protected and cultivated. Consider Proverbs 5:15–19:

> Drink water from your own cistern,
> flowing water from your own well.
> Should your springs be scattered abroad,
> streams of water in the streets?
> Let them be for yourself alone,
> and not for strangers with you.
> Let your fountain be blessed,
> and rejoice in the wife of your youth,
> a lovely deer, a graceful doe.
> Let her breasts fill you at all times with delight;
> be intoxicated always in her love.

Yes, those verses are in the inspired Word of God.

Think about it. Only an amazing God could think up something so beautiful and wonderful and thrilling as sex, which *also* serves His purpose of populating the world. God's design unites pleasure *and* purpose. Sexuality is God's gift, and His gifts are good: "For everything created by God is good" (1 Tim. 4:4).

In contrast, our culture says that sex is merely a means to our personal satisfaction, divorcing the pleasure God intended from His procreational purposes. But God's Story is the full story about sex.

The gift of sexuality belongs only within the context of a husband-wife marriage (1 Cor. 7:2). Why? First, the exclusivity and commitment of marriage are the best context within which to care for the product of sex: children. Second, marriage is the best environment in which to cultivate the love, safety, security, and trust needed for sexual intimacy to flourish.

Incredibly, Christ Himself is offered as the model for marital love: "Husbands, love your wives, as Christ loved the church and gave himself up for her" (Eph. 5:25). The love of Christ for His bride, the church, is exemplified in the sacrifice of His own life. This kind of life-sacrificing love and commitment is a picture of marriage. In such a context, all of the aspects of marital love, including sexuality, can be experienced as God intended.

The hookup culture is powerless to deliver such love and intimacy. The reason we must exhort young people to stay sexually pure and say no to the hookup culture is so they can say yes to God's big, bold, beautiful plan for sex.

Although Christians must do a much better job telling the yes of God's design for sexuality, we must continue to communicate the nos as well. God's Story sheds light on another important aspect of human nature. Yes, we're made in God's image, but we're also fallen, sinful creatures. We are beautiful *and* broken. Dignified yet depraved. The ugly consequences of fallen human nature are undeniably laid bare in the realm of human sexuality. For this reason, Scripture offers strong warnings against illicit sexual activity:

- **Say no to sexual immorality:** "For this is the will of God, your sanctification: that you abstain from sexual immorality; that each one of you know how to control his own body in holiness and honor" (1 Thess. 4:3–4).
- **Say no to lust:** "Everyone who looks at a woman with lustful intent has already committed adultery with her in his heart" (Matt. 5:28).
- **Say no to adultery:** "Let marriage be held in honor among all, and let the marriage bed be undefiled, for God will judge the sexually immoral and adulterous" (Heb. 13:4).

God's nos—His moral rules—are meant to protect and provide for us. The culture conditions young people to cast aside biblical morality and instead pursue all sexual avenues available to them. They're told to delay marital love as long as possible. The result? They're losing out on both. In the hookup culture, young people settle for a cheap imitation of real love. The result is pain, suffering, regret, and shame. It's time to recapture the wonder of God-ordained and God-glorifying sexuality for our young people.

Action Steps

1. Become your kids' authority on sex. If kids don't look to parents and Christian leaders as the authority on this topic, they'll turn to someone or something else. We cannot wait for them to initiate conversations about sex, especially in a culture that bombards them with bad messages about it all the time. We must start the conversations. We don't mean just having the comprehensive, one-time "sex talk" that both kids and parents dread. It must be an ongoing, open-ended dialogue.

I (Brett) remember initiating a conversation about sex with my son, who was ten at the time. I wanted to let him know it was okay to broach the topic. I simply asked him, "Do you know what sex is?"

Without hesitating, he answered confidently, "Yes, Dad. It's on your driver's license and Mom's. Your license says *M* and Mom's says *F*."

I smiled at his innocence, but his answer helped me gauge what he knew. Throughout his teenage years, I've continued to initiate each conversation, assuring him that sex is a safe topic, and I have some knowledge and wisdom to offer. By doing so, I've become his authority on the matter and can ultimately point him to God's plan for sex.

2. Never ever shut down your kids' questions about sex. If you shut down your kids on this subject, they won't stop asking questions. They'll just ask someone else. Or they'll google it. That's something you can't afford to risk. Peers, teachers, professors, and even pornographers are willing and ready to educate your kids on sex.

3. Emphasize the yes as well as the no. Often parents begin sex talks with moral rules and prohibitions and unwittingly communicate a negative view of sex. Beginning with the nos prompts the wrong questions. Too many kids just want to know "How far is too far?" But sexual purity isn't merely a line they shouldn't cross; it's a direction of life that moves them toward marriage. Remind your kids of the long-term vision of marriage. Paint marriage as a beautiful yes to God's design for men and women, and sex as the beautiful gift God gives to His image bearers to fulfill His purpose for their lives together.

4. Don't let your kids navigate dating alone. The pain of rejection can be lonely. The guilt and shame of sexual sin can crush your kids. Instead, walk by their side. Tell them you want to be involved and help them navigate potential minefields. Get to know their dates and the families. Help your kids make rational dating decisions when emotions are running high. Be there to extend God's love and forgiveness when they stumble.

5. Encourage healthy dating. As the father of daughters, it's difficult for me (Brett) to even think about them dating. However, we must help our kids learn to how to develop healthy and proper relationships, especially with those of the opposite sex. First, talk to your kids about the purpose of dating when they're young. Instilling wisdom starts early. It will be too late when their emotions and hormones are running wild. Explain the connection of dating to marriage, and help them understand the wisdom of waiting to date. In doing so, you'll help your kids think through not just the what but also the why of dating.

Second, walk with them through the dating experience. Take your kids on dates before their peers do. Mom, date your boys, and Dad, date your daughters. It's a great opportunity for some one-on-one time with each kid, but it also allows you to model for them how they should treat others and how they should be treated on a date. When that first date comes along, celebrate with them. Help them think up creative ways to date. Find ways to join them sometimes. It's tempting to dread this unique period in your kids' lives, but enjoy it instead. Most of all, stay involved.

Third, help establish boundaries for healthy dating. Here are some boundaries John and I use with our kids:

- *Never be alone with a date.* Isolation often encourages sexual temptation.
- *Stay in public places.* Staying in public creates accountability. And kids can still have private conversations in public.
- *Stick to a reasonable curfew.* Not much good happens when guys and girls stay out late together.
- *Encourage group dating.* Every date doesn't have to be a group date, but having other couples around helps take some of the pressure off.

- *Don't date exclusively during high school.* Avoiding exclusivity helps keep young people from getting serious too quickly. It helps girls guard their hearts from premature emotional attachments and prevents boys from feeling entitled to a girl's affections.
- *Listen to Mom and Dad.* As parents, we reserve the right to say no to unhealthy relationships and unwise plans.

6. Teach your young men how to be gentlemen. Call us old-fashioned, but John and I think men should be initiators. They should ask girls out, have manners, go to the front door, meet the parents, plan the date, pay for the meal, and more. Let's raise the bar for our young men once again. Boys have to be taught to be gentlemen. It doesn't happen by accident, and today's coarsening culture actually opposes such efforts. Thus, Christian men play an invaluable role in raising young gentlemen. Dads, in particular, need to be intentional about training up their sons.

7. Share your own stories about love, dating, and sex. Kids typically love to hear personal stories about our lives. Tell your kids funny stories about past crushes. Explain what, why, and how you did dating back in the day. Admit your own sexual failures and mistakes, and how you experienced God's grace. Authenticity at age-appropriate levels will help kids relate to you and open up about the topic of sex.

8. Make your marriage a beautiful model. Don't let your marriage be the reason your kids want something other than marriage. Work hard to cultivate a loving relationship with your spouse. Be intentional about growing a healthy marriage. Date regularly. Read books about marriage. Attend marriage-enrichment conferences. If need be, go to counseling and work out your problems. Let your kids see that unlike the hookup culture, marriage is about self-giving, not self-interest. By building a strong marriage, you embody sexual wholeness and give them a living picture of the beauty of marital love.

9. Pray and trust God. For many of us, this is a scary topic to navigate. Maybe you carry scars from your own sexual sin and desperately want your kids to avoid the same experience. Or maybe your own parents never modeled healthy dialogue and direction on this topic when you were growing up. Whatever the reason for your fears, you need to continually lay them at God's feet and put your trust in Him. Remember, the power of God is greater than the power of our sexualized culture.

Further Resources

- *Before "I Do": What Do Premarital Experiences Have to Do with Marital Quality among Today's Young Adults?* by Galena K. Rhoades and Scott M. Stanley (Charlottesville, VA: National Marriage Project, 2014)—free downloadable ebooklet available at www.nationalmarriageproject.org

- *The Ring Makes All the Difference: The Hidden Consequences of Cohabitation and the Strong Benefits of Marriage* by Glenn T. Stanton (Chicago: Moody, 2011)

Hopecasting

What hope is there for kids growing up in a sexually promiscuous culture? Know this: violating God's moral reality will catch up with the culture and leave it gasping for the true, good, and beautiful. His truth about sexuality is indeed true and good and beautiful. We may proclaim it confidently and courageously in a sexually broken culture.

Recently during a Q-and-A session at a high school summer camp in California, a girl approached the microphone and asked, "I have a question from my friend. If you're in a sexually active Christian relationship that is healthy and not dependent or defined by sex, can an individual in this situation be 100 percent committed to Christ, given that they have prayed about their situation and they did their actions out of love and not lust?"

I (Brett) gently but firmly pointed out that the only healthy sexually active relationship is between a husband and wife. This is the clear teaching of Scripture. Thus, two unmarried high schoolers having sex is unhealthy by definition.

After I finished answering her question, another female student approached the microphone. She admitted, "This is my question. This is my relationship. I've been in it for over a year now. I have run this by psychologists, nurses, and church leaders. We prayed about it for about ten months and came to this decision. So am I not 100 percent committed to Christ?" Suddenly it was no longer just a question to be answered but a real life at stake. I softened my posture but pressed forward with the truth.

"This is actually a decision you didn't need to pray about. God has already spoken, and sex between a boyfriend and girlfriend is sin. If you thought you heard God say this is okay, that was not God."

Tears began to stream down her flushed cheeks, and she returned to her seat.

My heart broke for her, so I added, "I don't say this out of anger or disgust but out of love. I love you students like my younger brothers and sisters, so that's why I am compelled to speak the truth to you. This will harm you, it will harm your relationship with your boyfriend, and it will harm your relationship with God."

That was a difficult conversation to have in front of other students and camp leaders. I did my best to exude grace without compromising God's truth. I walked away not knowing whether she would open herself to the Holy Spirit's conviction. Thankfully, through a youth-pastor friend who was also at the camp, I heard the rest of the story. Later that week, this high schooler called up her boyfriend and broke it off. She had been lovingly confronted with God's truth, the Lord opened her eyes, she repented of her sin, and she responded in obedience. Praise God she took the path of redemption and restoration. Such stories should ward off the Christian's temptation to become discouraged and despair. Instead, we're reminded there is always hope in Christ.

John and I are not only seeing students redeemed; we're seeing them make efforts to redeem the culture. Sade Patterson, a student at the University of New Mexico, watched two years in a row as her school hosted its annual Sex Week, a student-led event designed to "educate" students on all things sexual. After hearing about workshops like "How to Be a Gentlemen and Still Get Laid" and "How to Have Threesomes," seeing "educators" like Dirty Lola (an advocate of sadomasochism and other deviant sexual practices) invited to teach, and listening to presentations containing all kinds of falsehoods,[17] she decided to do something.

Through her Students for Life pro-life campus club, Patterson put together an alternative event at the university called the Real Sex Week. Instead of crude content and a focus on sexual gratification, the event provided students with beneficial sex education. Workshops dealt with topics like the male and female body, the impact of sex on students' minds and relationships, support for pregnant and parenting students, the negative effects of abortion, the biology behind intercourse, and the promotion of abstinence. She reported that attendance for the event was "strong."[18]

Without question, we must broadcast Jesus' offer of grace, forgiveness, and redemption to a sexually bankrupt culture. However, we must also offer God's vision for human sexuality *before* kids wade into the waters of sexual activity. It's far easier to build sexual health and virtue in our kids than to try putting back together sexually broken men and women. That task begins with us—in our homes, Christian schools, youth groups, and churches.

Discussion Questions

1. What characterizes our culture's attitudes and habits regarding sexual behavior and relationships?

2. What relational habits are needed to see members of the opposite sex in an honoring, respectful, and life-giving way?

3. What conversations about sex and relationships have you had with the kids under your care and influence? What conversations are still needed?

Chapter Ten

Sexual Orientation

How do we make an identity out of temptation? By collapsing what you desire with who you are. By collapsing what tempts you or what trips you up with who you will become.... God's revealed purpose for my identity always nails me to his cross.

Rosaria Butterfield, *Openness Unhindered*

Christians are obsessed with homosexuality. Many in our culture think we just can't stop talking about it. Worse, when we identify ourselves as Christians, many assume we must hate gay people. "You might as well have it tattooed on your arm: antihomosexual, gay-hater, homophobic."[1] But do these perceptions match reality?

While Christians have held a consistent view throughout two millennia of church history, homosexuality was never a prominent issue in the church. Nor is there a massive emphasis on this topic in Scripture. The Bible addresses issues like salvation, the poor, money, the kingdom of God, heaven, hell, and a host of other issues much more than it does homosexuality.

Prior to the last thirty years, where was all the Christian activism and outrage on the subject? many wonder. The answer is that no one really talked about it prior to thirty years ago. Historically, Christians haven't been obsessed with this topic because the culture hasn't been. LGBT rights have become the issue of our times, and some are looking for Christians to fully and unconditionally surrender.

We may not like how we got here, but here we are. We need to know what to do. The cultural momentum is ready to bury the church on the "wrong side of history" and carry our kids directly into treacherous waters. Around the country, Christians have been punished for their views on gay and lesbian relationships, from losing their jobs and being forced to close businesses to being fined large sums of money by state commissions. Surveys reveal a significant gap between the views of younger and older generations on LGBT issues. This issue may cost us dearly. So how should we move forward?

Jesus was "full of grace and truth" (John 1:14), and He is the model for our engagement on *all* issues. We must bring truth to bear by thinking carefully about the intellectual issues surrounding sexual orientation. We must bring grace to bear by engaging individuals with love, kindness, and hospitality.

Don't Buy the Cultural Lies

Lie #1: Christians are characterized by their terrible treatment of gays and lesbians.

Christians simply hide their bigotry and hatred under the guise of religion, right? I (Brett) recall a conversation on homosexuality with a Christian teenager who sincerely wanted to love his gay friends but was bothered by his perception of the church's response to gays and lesbians. He declared, "Christians have treated gay people terribly." I was curious where this impression of Christians came from, so I asked a few questions.

"You've grown up and have been active in the church, right?" He nodded. "So that means you've observed Christians carefully almost every week for the last sixteen years of your life." He nodded again. "In those sixteen years, how many times did you personally witness a Christian treating a gay person terribly?"

He sat back and thought for a moment. "Actually, I've never seen it myself," he finally answered.

Think about that. Here was a young person who had grown up in the church and had a very negative perception of Christians' actions toward the homosexual community but had never personally observed such mistreatment. I've begun regularly asking this question of Christians and have discovered that the vast majority have never seen another Christian treat gay people with anything but kindness.

Now, I'm *not* saying that mistreatment doesn't happen at the hands of Christians. Surely it has and still does, and both John and I unequivocally condemn such actions. All people, gay or straight, are God's image bearers and should be treated with dignity and respect. However, the cultural perception among non-Christians *and* Christians is that this bad behavior is widespread in the church. Where does this impression come from if it's not clearly evidenced in the lives of actual Christians? It comes from a media-saturated culture that constantly posts images of picketing "Christian" groups like Westboro Baptist Church and their "God hates fags" signs in an effort to characterize all of Christendom. Of course, neither John nor I know a single reputable Christian leader, or any Christian for that matter, who thinks such actions are anything other than utterly deplorable. But here's the key point we're trying to make: the perception that the vast majority of Christians mistreat gay people isn't rooted in reality.

Why is this important? This false cultural narrative builds immense barriers between the gay community and the Christian community. If the gay community perceives the church to be full of vitriol and hatred, they will shun us. However, Christians have what the world, including the gay community, so desperately needs: the redemption and restoration that only Jesus can offer. We must not allow cultural lies to sever our relationships with gay people. We must overcome the false narrative of Christian hatred and oppression with generous, loving action.

Lie #2: Gay people are born that way.

From Lady Gaga's album *Born This Way* to the lyrics of Macklemore's hit song "Same Love"—"And I can't change, even if I tried, even if I wanted to"—to television sitcoms and movies, pop culture repeats this mantra over and over: Gay people are born that way, same-sex attraction is innate, and sexual orientation cannot be changed. Therefore, we're told, same-sex behavior is a legitimate form of sexual expression. So how can one be against homosexuality?

First, an action or disposition isn't morally justified simply because it has genetic origins. For example, if researchers discovered genes that contribute to alcoholism or violent behavior, would that justify the morality of drunkenness or murder? Even if a gay gene is discovered, the moral question of homosexual activity would still be unsettled.

Second, there is no compelling scientific study proving homosexuality is biologically determined,[2] but there is evidence against this claim. For example, twin studies undermine the claim that there is a gay gene. Since identical twins share identical genetics, if homosexuality was biologically determined, whenever we find one gay twin, it would follow that the other should be gay as well. However, researchers found that in cases where one twin is gay, the other twin is also gay less than 15 percent of the time.[3]

The American Psychological Association (APA), which is gay affirming, recognizes the lack of scientific evidence for the claim that homosexuality is genetic: "Although much research has examined the possible genetic, hormonal, developmental, social and cultural influences on sexual orientation, no findings have emerged that permit scientists to conclude that sexual orientation is determined by any particular factor or factors."[4] Even gay-rights activist Martin Duberman, founder of the Center for Lesbian and Gay Studies (CLAGS) at the City University of New York, agrees: "No good scientific work establishes that people are born gay or straight."[5]

Third, the fact there is an ex-gay community clearly undermines the born-this-way theory. Men and women whose same-sex attractions have changed don't fit the gay-gene narrative. Their stories are rarely told, but they are plentiful.[6]

If people aren't born gay, what other explanations might be considered? Many suggest gay people simply choose their same-sex attractions. Here it's helpful to distinguish between action and attraction. Gay men and women certainly choose the actions or behavior they engage in and, as such, are accountable for them. However, the evidence doesn't suggest they choose their attractions or orientation. Just as heterosexuals don't claim to choose their attractions but simply discover them, homosexuals find themselves with attractions and often report them as unwanted. Instead of thinking of sexual orientation as either innate or chosen, we suggest a third explanation. There is strong evidence that both developmental and environmental factors play a prominent role in forming a same-sex attraction between birth and young adulthood.[7]

Lie #3: The gay lifestyle is just as normal and healthy as heterosexuality.

When you pull back the curtain on the gay lifestyle, this claim is clearly false. First, monogamy is almost nonexistent in homosexual relationships. Only 4.5 percent of homosexual men in current relationships report being faithful to their partners. In contrast, 75 percent of heterosexual men and 85 percent of women reported they were faithful to their spouses.[8] A study of the sexual profiles of 2,583 older homosexuals found that only 2.7 percent of these men reported having sex with only one partner.[9] Promiscuity among lesbians is higher as well. Between 75 and 90 percent of women who have sex with women (WSW) report sexual activity with men as well,[10] and lesbian women were 4.5 times more likely than heterosexual women to have had fifty or more lifetime male sexual partners.[11]

Second, homosexual behavior greatly increases the risk of sexually transmitted diseases like HIV, chlamydia, gonorrhea, and syphilis. For example, men who have sex with men (MSM) have by far the highest rate of syphilis infections (83 percent) among men.[12] Gay and bisexual men are at greater risk for HIV infection than any other group in the United States. They make up approximately 2 percent of the population but account for 55 percent of the HIV infections. Among males thirteen and older, "gay and bisexual men accounted for 83% of estimated new HIV diagnoses."[13]

For many gay men, the lack of sexual fidelity also involves risky sexual behavior. Between 2005 and 2011, there was an increase in MSM who reported having unprotected sex.[14] Risky sexual activity with an abundance of partners results in greater rates of sexually transmitted diseases.

Third, gay men and women are more likely to experience emotional, psychological, and physical harm. According to gay activists David Island and Patrick Letellier, "The incidence of domestic violence among gay men is nearly double that in the heterosexual population."[15] The CDC found the following to be more prevalent among gay, lesbian, and bisexual students than heterosexual students:

- Physical dating violence (17.5 percent compared to 8.3 percent)
- Sexual dating violence (22.7 percent compared to 9.1 percent)
- Feelings of sadness or hopelessness (60.4 percent compared to 26.4 percent)
- Serious contemplation of suicide (42.8 percent compared to 14.8 percent)
- Suicide attempts (29.4 percent compared to 6.4 percent)[16]

Many in our culture dismiss the prevalence of psychological disorders and substance abuse or claim these problems are the result of discrimination and poor treatment of the gay community. However, even in gay-friendly countries like the Netherlands, where same-sex marriage has been legal since 2001, or in countries like England or New Zealand that are recognized for the liberty afforded LGBT citizens,[17] rates of anxiety, depression, drug dependence, and suicide are still much higher among gay men and women.[18]

John and I didn't walk through all of this data to denigrate our gay family members and friends or to make them look bad. Our culture often dispenses with truth in order to endorse any sexual identity and all forms of expression. Because the lives and well-being of people are at stake, we need to take an honest and sobering look at the cold, hard facts before we promote a lifestyle that causes great harm. We should also be moved to love and compassion for our hurting gay family and friends.

Recapture the Wonder of God's Story

As we said earlier, because Western civilization has abandoned God, it has lost what it means to be human. At the heart of every issue in sex and sexuality is the question of identity. The issue of sexual orientation is a prime example. We must return again to the garden.

After all, that's what Jesus did. When asked about marriage and divorce, Jesus took his questioners to the creation account:

> Have you not read that he who created them from the beginning made them male and female, and said, "Therefore a man shall leave his father and his mother and hold fast to his wife, and the two shall become one flesh"? So they are no longer two but one flesh. What therefore God has joined together, let not man separate. (Matt. 19:4–6)

God's Story doesn't start with "Thou shalt not" but with "God saw that it was good" (Gen. 1:10). The primary emphasis of His Story is not homosexuality and its sinfulness but the way

He designed males and females to become husband and wife. This one-flesh union is God's true, good, and beautiful plan for humanity. Men and women were designed for each other, and this union alone achieves God's purpose of filling the earth with more image bearers who will follow His command to "be fruitful and multiply and fill the earth" (v. 28).

In light of God's design, we can examine homosexuality and draw implications. First, homosexuality violates God's creational norms. Men and women weren't designed to engage sexually with a partner of the same sex. That's why the apostle Paul described gay and lesbian behavior as exchanging "the natural function for that which is unnatural" (Rom. 1:26 NASB). Homosexual behavior is unnatural because it disregards God's natural order of creation. And any departure from God's creational norms will be deficient by definition.

Second, homosexual behavior is sin. Romans 1:24–28 makes the clearest pronouncement in all of Scripture on the subject:

> Therefore God gave [people] over in the lusts of their hearts to impurity, so that their bodies would be dishonored among them. For they exchanged the truth of God for a lie, and worshiped and served the creature rather than the Creator, who is blessed forever. Amen.
>
> For this reason God gave them over to degrading passions; for their women exchanged the natural function for that which is unnatural,

> and in the same way also the men abandoned the natural function of the woman and burned in their desire toward one another, men with men committing indecent acts and receiving in their own persons the due penalty of their error.
>
> And just as they did not see fit to acknowledge God any longer, God gave them over to a depraved mind, to do those things which are not proper. (NASB)

Homosexuality is addressed elsewhere in Scripture as well (e.g., Lev. 18:22; 20:13; 1 Cor. 6:9–10; 1 Tim. 1:8–11). Sin is the violation of God's moral law. Just like all other sinners, gay men and women aren't victims of their biology; they are free moral agents responsible for their choices.

Third, homosexuality attempts to replace God-given identity with self-identity. The culture replaces God's governance with self-governance. We don't answer to God; we answer only to ourselves. We're autonomous, declaring, "I'm in charge," and the culture shouts back approvingly, "Do whatever is right for *you*!" Every desire is legitimized. Everyone sanctions their own sexual decisions.

Even our identity becomes what we make it. Think about the statements "I'm gay" or "I'm lesbian." For the first time in human history, we define ourselves in terms of our sexual proclivities. Being gay or lesbian isn't merely what you do; it's who you are. As we said in an earlier chapter, this is identity after Christianity.

No matter how much we resist it, we'll never escape God's reality. Attempts to redefine reality serve only to run us head-on into it. Broken and shattered people are the aftermath.

The apostle Paul strongly warned,

> Do not be deceived: God is not mocked, for whatever one sows, that will he also reap. For the one who sows to his own flesh will from the flesh reap corruption, but the one who sows to the Spirit will from the Spirit reap eternal life. (Gal. 6:7–8)

> Do not be deceived: neither the sexually immoral, nor idolaters, nor adulterers, nor men who practice homosexuality, nor thieves, nor the greedy, nor drunkards, nor revilers, nor swindlers will inherit the kingdom of God. (1 Cor. 6:9–10)

That's bad news for all of us, not just our gay friends. Thank God for the good news of the gospel. Immediately following these verses, Paul declared, "And such were some of you. But you were washed, you were sanctified, you were justified in the name of the Lord Jesus Christ and by the Spirit of our God" (v. 11). God's forgiveness and healing are available to all, gay or straight. Not only does God's Story describe our fall into sin; it also proclaims our redemption by His grace.

Action Steps

1. Acknowledge that sexual brokenness isn't confined to homosexual behavior. Don't give the topic excessive attention to the exclusion of other kinds of sexual sin. There's an abundance to go around. In fact, premarital sex, adultery, and pornography are much more common and therefore need to be addressed more often with our kids.

2. Maintain an open dialogue on this subject with your kids. Young people are talking about this issue all the time. On the screen, on social media, and at school, kids will be disproportionately exposed to questions of homosexuality and sexual orientation. Don't make this a taboo subject. Talk about it even if you're not ready when they bring it up. Ask them questions and attempt to answer theirs. Also get some help, like Tom Gilson's book *Critical Conversations: A Christian Parents' Guide to Discussing Homosexuality with Teens.*

3. Resist the culture's false view of love. The culture tries to tell us that love equals full acceptance. If you truly love your gay friends and family members, you'll embrace them on *their* terms. Not even true tolerance—disagreeing yet dignifying the other person—is enough. Only full acceptance will do. But Jesus always loved without compromising the truth. We must show kids where He modeled this in the Gospels. (For example, see Jesus' interaction with the woman at the well in John 4:1–30.) Loving people often requires telling them the truth—even if they don't respond well to it.

4. Watch video presentations from Living Hope Ministries. The following resources are so important and helpful that John and I took them out of the list of resources at the end of this chapter and put them here. Please stop reading and order these DVDs online right now:

- *Why? Understanding Homosexuality and Gender Development in Males*—https://livehope.org/resource/why-dvd/
- *Why? Understanding Homosexuality and Gender Development in Females*—https://livehope.org/resource/femaledvd/

Once you receive these DVDs, watch them *with* your teenagers.

5. Spend time with gay family members and friends. If they're unbelievers, don't avoid or shun them. The apostle Paul made it clear that we aren't to dissociate ourselves from "the sexually immoral of this world … since then you would need to go out of the world" (1 Cor. 5:9–10). Of course, it's a different story regarding sexually immoral believers (vv. 11–13). So invite non-Christian gay neighbors over for dinner and model God's loving-kindness and Christian hospitality. However, realize this may not be as easy as it sounds. Be prepared for potential complications, such as a gay couple showing affection, and help your kids understand how to navigate them. Or consider how you would handle a difficult conversation with your guests. Loving people in a broken world can get messy, so never neglect prayer for your gay friends.

6. Counter the culture's narrative regarding sexual orientation. The culture's worldview commentary on this topic is ever present. Look for it and address it. For example, if a movie or television show has a gay character, ask your kids whether the character is negatively or positively portrayed and what messages are being communicated about family and sexuality. Look for news reports related to this topic, listen to them with your kids, and then discuss them. John's daily *BreakPoint* commentaries are a great source for worldview commentary.

7. **Make Jesus, not homosexuality, the main issue.** When your kids ask questions about homosexuality, answer them. But just because it's the most prominent topic in the culture doesn't mean it's the most prominent topic period. Always point your kids back to Christ. For example, if your teenager asks you what he should say to his gay friend, remind him that what someone does with Jesus is your top concern. The priority isn't converting your non-Christian gay friends to heterosexuality but pointing them to Christ for salvation. Frame this issue, and all issues, in light of God's Story of creation, fall, redemption, and restoration. The most important thing about us isn't what we believe about homosexuality but what we do with the claims of Christ. Likewise, our identity is found in the image of God, not in our sexual orientation.

8. Prepare your family for the social costs of affirming biblical views. The days of socially acceptable Christianity are over. Christians are now mocked, ostracized, and punished for merely holding biblical views on homosexuality. There's even a word to describe our so-called discrimination[19] against any nonheterosexual form of behavior or identity: *heterosexism*. Ignorant people used to be racist; now they're heterosexist. Prepare your kids to pay the price for holding firmly to biblical truth. Remind them of Jesus' words in John 15:18–20:

> If the world hates you, know that it has hated me before it hated you. If you were of the world, the world would love you as its own; but because you are not of the world, but I chose you out of the world, therefore the world hates you. Remember the word that I said to you: "A servant is not greater than his master." If they persecuted me, they will also persecute you.

Further Resources

- *The Ambassador's Guide to Understanding Homosexuality* by Alan Shlemon (Signal Hill, CA: Stand to Reason, 2013)
- *A Parent's Guide to Preventing Homosexuality* by Joseph Nicolosi and Linda Ames Nicolosi (Downers Grove, IL: InterVarsity, 2002)

- *Same-Sex Marriage: A Thoughtful Approach to God's Design for Marriage* by Sean McDowell and John Stonestreet (Grand Rapids: Baker, 2014)
- *What Does the Bible Really Teach about Homosexuality?* by Kevin DeYoung (Wheaton, IL: Crossway, 2015)

Hopecasting

No matter how far the culture strays from the truth on this issue, there is always the hope of redemption in Jesus Christ. Beautiful, real-life stories remind us of this.

Rosaria Butterfield was a lesbian college professor of English and women's studies at Syracuse University. She was living happily with her partner when Presbyterian pastor Ken Smith befriended her. In two years of friendship with Smith and his wife, Rosaria was confronted with the truth of Christ in His Word. Now she's the wife of a pastor, a mother of four children, and a homemaker.[20]

Christopher Yuan, the son of Chinese immigrants, never fit in with his American classmates when he was growing up. Early exposure to pornography awakened his same-sex attractions, and while attending dental school, he started down a path to homosexuality. After Yuan came out to his family, he slowly descended into a fast-paced gay lifestyle, as well as doing and dealing drugs. He was eventually arrested and sentenced to prison. During his incarceration, he discovered he was HIV positive. Through the prayers of his parents, who had become Christians, and exposure to God's Word by means of a Gideon Bible he pulled from a prison garbage can, Christopher Yuan gave his life to Christ. He now teaches at Moody Bible Institute and has a worldwide speaking ministry.[21]

Read Rosaria's and Christopher's biographies. Their stories, and thousands like them that will never be published in books, remind us that hope and healing are always possible in God's Story. Jesus is reconciling gay *and* straight sinners to the Father and restoring them to new life through the power of His resurrection.

Discussion Questions

1. What are the most prevalent lies about sexual orientation in today's culture?

2. How would you respond to someone who says, "Homosexual behavior isn't sinful because love is love"?

3. In what ways has sexual orientation been confused with identity? What is identity from a Christian worldview?

Chapter Eleven

Gender Identity

At the heart of the problem is confusion over the nature of the transgendered. "Sex change" is biologically impossible. People who undergo sex-reassignment surgery do not change from men to women or vice versa. Rather, they become feminized men or masculinized women.

Dr. Paul McHugh, "Transgender Surgery Isn't the Solution"

The newest word John and I have learned is *cisgender*.

Even if you haven't heard it before, your teenagers likely have. According to Wikipedia, *cisgender* refers to individuals "who have a gender identity that matches the sex that they were assigned at birth."[1] Assigned by whom? Parents, medical professionals, and society. Of course, in one sense, almost everyone who has ever lived fits this definition. But in order not to alienate those who don't, a new word was created.[2] Two assumptions are embedded in Wikipedia's definition of *cisgender*. First, that sex is "assigned" and not a biological reality. And second, that gender is chosen, not innate.

These same two assumptions are deeply embedded in our culture. Within the span of a few months in 2016, the cosmetic company CoverGirl announced that seventeen-year-old James Charles would be its first Cover boy,[3] and *Time* magazine ran a cover article on the new phenomenon of "chest-feeding" titled "My Brother's Pregnancy and the Making of a New American Family." Author Jessi Hempel wrote, "My brother Evan was born female. He came out as transgender 16 years ago but never stopped wanting to have a baby. This spring he gave birth to his first child."[4]

In this brave new world, gender is so fluid that men give birth. We have to help our kids navigate this issue of gender identity.

Don't Buy the Cultural Lies

Lie #1: Gender is merely a social construction.

When it comes to gender and sexuality, our culture says there are no objective truths, only subjective preferences. If you feel it, declare it, and it is so. Gender, we're told, is not a fixed trait rooted in biology; instead, it's a social construct that culture creates. Some identify with the gender they were "assigned" at birth, while others are transgender.[5] High-profile celebrities like Miley Cyrus reinforce public-school sex-education lessons that teach children as young as kindergarten age that there are "many ways to express gender" and tell kids as young as third grade that they can choose whether they are male, female, both, or neither.[6]

Jill Soloway, director of Amazon's award-winning online television series *Transparent* (a show about an older father coming out trans to his adult children), claims, "In a few years, we're going to look back and say, 'When we were little, we used to think that all women had vaginas and all men had penises, but now, of course, we know that's not true.'"[7] You may wonder how a biological fact can stop being true. According to Soloway and the culture, we'll make it so. We will no longer construct the terms *male* and *female* the traditional way. Instead, we'll give them new meanings. Or get rid of them altogether.

One way to undermine the claim that gender is merely a social construction is to test-drive the idea and see where it leads. In logic, this form of reasoning is known as *reductio ad absurdum* (literally "reduction to absurdity").

A video that went viral on YouTube[8] illustrates the absurdities of this claim about gender identity. Joseph Backholm, president of the Family Policy Institute of Washington, asked students on the University of Washington campus about their views on gender identity and public-restroom policy. At first the students affirmed the right of every individual to choose the bathroom that corresponds to their perceived gender. Backholm followed up with a series of questions designed to show the resulting absurdities:

- "If I told you that I was a woman, what would your response be?"
- "If I told you that I was Chinese, what would your response be?"

- "If I told you that I was seven years old, what would your response be?"
- "If I told you I'm six feet five inches, what would you say?"

Amazingly, the vast majority of student interviewees were unwilling to say that Backholm wasn't anything he claimed to be. One particular student's answer sums up the responses: "If you thoroughly debated me or explained why you felt that you were six foot five, I feel like I would be very open to saying that you were six foot five or Chinese or a woman." Here's the rub: Joseph Backholm is a five-foot-nine-inch white guy. So we have to stop and ask ourselves, Why were seemingly bright, young college students unwilling to counter obvious absurdities? Intellectual consistency.

The culture's dominant vision of gender identity offers no nonarbitrary stopping point for social construction. Indeed, we're beginning to see where the absurdity leads. There are people who wear pet collars, eat from a bowl, and identify as dogs.[9] There are people who perform major body modifications to look dragon-like and identify as reptiles.[10] There are grown men who identify as little girls.[11] There are individuals who marry themselves (it's called *sologamy*).[12] Social construction is free to go anywhere our minds will take us. The absurdities are endless.

But this logical slippery slope can't hold up under the weight of its own consequences. If we self-identify as sixty-five-year-old men, should the federal government start sending us Social Security checks? If we self-identify as six-year-old girls, should we be able to enroll in a first-grade class at the local public elementary school? If we self-identify as a particular minority, should we be able to receive college scholarships earmarked for that minority group? If the answer is no to any of these questions, then why is a biological male who identifies as a female allowed to impact the laws of the land so that he can use the restroom or locker room of his choice or make sure fines are imposed on those who don't use transgender pronouns?[13] Social construction cannot maintain logical consistency; therefore, the idea should be rejected.[14]

Lie #2: We should validate people's thoughts and desires so they'll flourish.

The culture says, "Be who you are" and "Do what you want." Whatever reality you select for yourself is just fine. Moreover, the choice to defy reality is often hailed as an act of courage (as in the case of Bruce Jenner). Absolute autonomy, we're told, is the path to one's authentic self. In fact, this is our culture's new vision of human dignity. Unrestrained by any external limitations, one can never be defined by anyone except oneself. Human dignity is grounded in the autonomous will of an individual. This path of unfettered choice is how humans flourish, our culture declares.[15]

Anyone who denies people their ultimate right to choose reality is labeled a bigot. Since dignity is derived from self-determination, standing in someone's way or merely disagreeing with his or her choices strips a person of dignity. Tolerance is no longer sufficient these days. We must be affirming. If a man thinks he is a woman in his own mind, he must be a woman in your mind also. Dissent indicates bigotry. Bigotry is animated by hatred. Therefore, all bigots must be silenced.

Wow. Those are heavy-duty accusations. How can we respond? First, it's not about bigotry; it's about biology. We must distinguish between physical reality and psychological perception. How do we know biologically that someone is a male or female? Objective facts about physiology, anatomy, chromosomes, and DNA exist. Maleness and femaleness are undeniable physical realities.

On the other hand, there are no objective medical or scientific tests to determine transgenderism. It exists only in the mind of the individual. It's purely subjective. Essentially, a doctor cannot diagnose an individual as transgender. The individual diagnoses him- or herself. Worse yet, the individual prescribes his or her own treatment.

Instead of treating someone's psychological confusion, the gender-identity movement says that biology must conform via sex-reassignment surgery. However, reshaping the physical doesn't change the deeper biological realities of chromosomes.

In addition, the mental makeup of sex-reassignment patients isn't entirely transformed either. How do we know? If sex reassignment was indeed a biological fix for gender-identity confusion, transgender people wouldn't regret their sex-change surgeries. But a significant number do.[16] In addition, a University of Birmingham (England) review of more than one hundred international medical studies of postoperative transsexuals "found no robust scientific evidence that gender reassignment surgery is clinically effective."[17]

You can alter someone's physical appearance, but reality remains. The empirical data demonstrates that sex-reassignment surgery isn't helping the transgender community. Many don't flourish after surgery; they flounder.

As difficult as it may be for transgender people to hear, we must examine possible psychological causes for gender confusion. If gender is rooted in one's biological sex, then help with gender confusion may be found in mental health treatment. Even the *Diagnostic and Statistical Manual of Mental Disorders* (DSM)—the psychiatrist's bible—refers to this condition as *gender dysphoria*, "a marked incongruence between one's experienced/expressed gender and assigned gender."[18]

Of course, an incongruence between one's psychological and physical reality isn't unfamiliar to most of us. For example, a ninety-pound teenage girl who struggles with anorexia may believe she is grossly overweight, but doctors won't tell her to accept her feelings and change her body. They don't doubt her feelings, but they consider her self-perception incorrect. Because the anorexic holds a distorted view of herself, her mental and emotional health must be treated.

People with body integrity identity disorder (BIID) also believe their physical form doesn't match how they feel they should look, so they want to amputate otherwise healthy limbs. Doctors don't cooperate with their feelings by hacking off undesired body parts.[19] Instead, they recognize an underlying psychological condition that must be treated.

Only in the case of transgenderism are physical solutions offered for a psychological incongruence. As a result, the proposed cure harms the patient. Two-thirds of transgender people suffer from multiple psychological disorders, such as depression and phobias.[20] Transgender rates of depression and anxiety "far surpass the rates of those for the general population."[21]

There are serious consequences when we buy into cultural lies. For instance, Seattle Children's Hospital has opened a gender clinic, offering pubertal blockers to stop "the body from making the hormones that start puberty" and cross-sex hormones to "help make a person's physical body match their inner gender."[22] Certain segments of society are now taking serious steps to transition young children. However, the American College of Pediatricians warns against these treatments for kids, outlining the dangers in an official statement on its website.[23] In defiance of the data, the majority listen to political and pop-culture voices. We would do better, for our children and for our transgender friends and family, to listen to the testimony of an ex-transgender man:

> The shame of being so narcissistic and self-absorbed as a transgender female and knowing I had hurt the ones I loved resulted in deep depression and regret. I started to consider suicide. That's what I mean when I say my once successful transition turned on me. I discovered much too late that gender change surgery was not a medical necessity at all. I can admit that transition was the biggest mistake of my life.[24]

Recapture the Wonder of God's Story

You won't find the word *transgender* in Scripture, but that doesn't mean the issue isn't addressed. God speaks directly and explicitly about gender in the creation account: "Male and female [God] created them" (Gen. 1:27). God didn't make gender-neutral humans. Gender isn't a social construct, nor is it assigned. It's part of God's design, deeply grounded in His created order and woven into the fabric of reality. Thus, gender is a gift from God.

The distinction between male and female does nothing to undermine the value and dignity of either. Both are made in the image of God, and our equality is secured by that fact alone. No distinction—ethnicity, gender, age, sex—threatens the equality of human beings. All are image bearers. All have equal and inestimable worth in the sight of God. Within this framework, there is also room to affirm distinct gender roles while preserving gender equality.

Transgender people understand that something is amiss. They feel as if they're broken and need to be fixed. They say they feel like a woman trapped in a man's body or vice versa. And we would agree: something is amiss. However, in light of God's Story of reality, their diagnosis is incorrect. Gender isn't something to overcome, ignore, suppress, or remove. Human wholeness comes not by denying reality but by conforming to it. When transgender people pursue a physical fix, they're pursuing a solution that won't put them back together.

For the person struggling with gender identity, God's Story offers not only an accurate diagnosis but also the singular cure.

Rather than baptizing any and all desires as good, Scripture offers a contrasting picture: "Let no one say when he is tempted, 'I am being tempted by God,' for God cannot be tempted with evil, and he himself tempts no one. But each person is tempted when he is lured and enticed by his own desire" (James 1:13–14). Not every human desire is proper. Many lead us straight into sin, bringing brokenness into our lives: "Then desire when it has conceived gives birth to sin, and sin when it is fully grown brings forth death" (v. 15). Recall the distinction between structure and direction in chapter 2. God created the world structurally good, but as a result of the fall, we take that structure, and the corresponding desires, in the wrong direction. Our transgender friends have a good desire for wholeness, but they've taken it in the wrong direction. The result is sin and brokenness.

Let's be brutally honest. Every issue related to sex and sexuality that we've discussed—whether pornography, the hookup culture, homosexuality, or transgenderism—is open defiance of our creator. We're not just broken; we're rebellious. Romans 1:21–32 graphically captures humanity's revolt and its results:

> For although [people] knew God, they did not honor him as God or give thanks to him, but they became futile in their thinking, and their foolish hearts were darkened. Claiming to be wise, they became fools, and exchanged the glory of the immortal God for images resembling mortal man and birds and animals and creeping things.

Therefore God gave them up in the lusts of their hearts to impurity, to the dishonoring of their bodies among themselves, because they exchanged the truth about God for a lie and worshiped and served the creature rather than the Creator, who is blessed forever! Amen.

For this reason God gave them up to dishonorable passions. For their women exchanged natural relations for those that are contrary to nature; and the men likewise gave up natural relations with women and were consumed with passion for one another, men committing shameless acts with men and receiving in themselves the due penalty for their error.

And since they did not see fit to acknowledge God, God gave them up to a debased mind to do what ought not to be done. They were filled with all manner of unrighteousness, evil, covetousness, malice. They are full of envy, murder, strife, deceit, maliciousness. They are gossips, slanderers, haters of God, insolent, haughty, boastful, inventors of evil, disobedient to parents, foolish, faithless, heartless, ruthless. Though they know God's righteous decree that those who practice such things deserve to die, they not only do them but give approval to those who practice them.

Taking steps to change one's God-given gender is rebellion against God's created order, and the aftermath is the shattered lives of transgender men and women, their families, and increasingly, children.

But that's not the end of God's Story! The only thing that will put a fractured human being back together is the One who fashioned him or her. First, God redeems us from our sin through the work of Christ on the cross. Second, His Story shows us how we were made and how He intended us to function properly.

Human beings fail to flourish when we remove God-given gender distinctives. Gender is a gift, and "every good gift and every perfect gift is from above, coming down from the Father of lights, with whom there is no variation or shadow due to change. Of his own will he brought us forth by the word of truth, that we should be a kind of firstfruits of his creatures" (James 1:17–18). God made us male and female, and the unique design and functioning of the sexes isn't something to eradicate; rather, it's a good gift to celebrate.

We aren't bound to the confusion of the cultural moment. We must tether ourselves instead to God's Story. This is good news for our friends and family members who struggle with gender identity.

Action Steps

1. Let God move you to compassion for men and women who struggle with gender-identity issues. They are hurting and broken people. Forty-one percent of transgender men and women attempt suicide. That's a staggering statistic in light of the rate among the general population, which is only 1.6 percent.[25] In your relationships with transgender friends or family members, lead with grace and then with truth. Ask questions and show genuine interest in their answers. Pray for them regularly.

2. Talk to your kids about gender. Teach them about God's created order and point to Him as the source of gender distinctiveness. Give them a theology of the body. Discuss what it means to be male and female, even when your kids are young. Teach them to make appropriate biblical gender distinctions, but don't overemphasize cultural expressions of maleness and femaleness (e.g., that boys never like to dance, and girls never like rough-and-tumble activity). Help them identify with the appropriate gender.

3. Fathers, from the beginning cultivate warm, loving relationships with your sons and daughters. Be a strong yet gentle father. Give your kids the three As—attention, affection, and affirmation—and evaluate yourself regularly. Affirm your son's masculinity and mentor him into the world of men. For a more sensitive boy, connect with him and affirm his unique personality. With daughters, be affectionate from the beginning. Show respect and appreciation for their feminine distinctives. By cultivating loving relationships with your kids, you and your wife will lay a lifelong foundation for physical, psychological, and spiritual health.

4. Mothers, from the beginning cultivate caring, nurturing relationships with your sons and daughters. Build a strong emotional connection with your daughter. Help her embrace a feminine identity and build a positive body image. Don't treat her as an extension of you, but help her develop a stable sense of herself. With your son, be warm and affectionate, but don't be overbearing. Don't coddle him; instead, give him healthy space and try to tolerate some of the typical rough-and-tumble activity (without letting him get away with destruction!).

5. Work hard to cultivate a strong, healthy marriage. Marriage takes work, but the payoff is tremendous. A loving marriage is a powerful model of gender identification and healthy sexuality. Let your kids absorb proper views of gender as they watch your relationship. Husbands and wives, show each other attention and affection. Admit your faults and forgive one another. Date regularly. Pray together regularly. By building a strong marriage, you will also be contributing to the health of your kids' future marriages.

6. Watch two DVD presentations from Living Hope Ministries. Remember this action step from the previous chapter? You may be tempted to think that John and I are getting a kickback from these presentations, but we're not. We simply think they're so important and helpful that we're recommending them again:

- *Why? Understanding Homosexuality and Gender Development in Males*—https://livehope.org/resource/why-dvd/
- *Why? Understanding Homosexuality and Gender Development in Females*—https://livehope.org/resource/femaledvd/

Once you receive them, watch them *with* your teenagers.

7. Speak the truth carefully, with an extra dose of compassion. The culture affirms and celebrates transgender confusion. Few people are willing to tell the truth. Speak the truth on this issue, but know what you're talking about. Study the source notes for this chapter and equip yourself with the facts. Affirm the goodness of what transgender people are seeking: wholeness. However, help them to see that the solution isn't mutilating their bodies but transforming their hearts, minds, and souls. In every conversation, be extravagant with showing grace and kindness. Remind people that your motivation is love, not hatred. If the bridge ahead is out, the most loving thing to do is to tell people and try to protect them from harm.

8. Take the long view on this issue and be prepared for things to get worse. The ideas that have brought Western culture to this point have been baking for a long time. There is incredible cultural momentum behind transgender ideas right now, and change won't happen overnight. In fact, many in our culture seem committed to punishing all dissent. Count the cost now and prepare for the consequences.[26] Through it all, fix your hope on Jesus Christ and trust in the power of the gospel.

Hopecasting

There are brave men and women who are committed to speaking truth on this issue and refuse to be bullied by the culture. Walt Heyer, a former husband and father of two children, previously identified as a transgender woman but has transitioned back. He publicly shares his heartbreaking yet hopeful story and regularly addresses contemporary transgender issues.[27] Even though transgender proponents vilify him, he still speaks out. Why? Heyer says, "Changing genders is short-term gain with long-term pain.… Instead of encouraging them to undergo unnecessary and destructive surgery, let's affirm and love our young people just the way they are."[28]

Dr. Paul McHugh has spent more than forty years as the Distinguished Service Professor of Psychiatry at Johns Hopkins University School of Medicine, with twenty-six of those years as the psychiatrist in chief at Johns Hopkins Hospital. He has authored six books and at least 125 peer-reviewed medical articles. For the past forty years, he has studied transgenderism and sex-reassignment surgery, working closely with many transgender individuals. He's an expert on the subject, and he's speaking out, even though he's taking plenty of heat.

What motivates this doctor to speak the truth and risk the reputation of his highly distinguished career? In Dr. McHugh's words,

"I do so not only because truth matters, but also because overlooked amid the hoopla … stand many victims.… [Transgenderism] is doing much damage to families, adolescents, and children and should be confronted as an opinion without biological foundation wherever it emerges."[29]

Neither of these men is motivated by hatred. Rather, they're compelled by their care and concern for people who are hurting. With the same truth-in-love approach, we can help our own kids successfully navigate gender identity.

Discussion Questions

1. In what ways does our culture shape our understanding of gender? Are the dominant views on gender in our culture healthy or harmful? Why or why not?

2. How did you come to understand your identity as male or female? What were the most important influences? What were the most harmful?

3. How would you respond to a young person who shared his or her gender-identity struggles with you?

Chapter Twelve

Affluence and Consumerism

Indeed if we consider the unblushing promises of reward and the staggering nature of the rewards promised in the Gospels, it would seem that Our Lord finds our desires not too strong, but too weak. We are half-hearted creatures, fooling about with drink and sex and ambition when infinite joy is offered us, like an ignorant child who wants to go on making mud pies in a slum because he cannot imagine what is meant by the offer of a holiday at the sea. We are far too easily pleased.

C. S. Lewis, *The Weight of Glory and Other Addresses*

Americans love stuff. The sheer amount we buy and own exposes our love of stuff. Consider these statistics:

- The average American home contains three hundred thousand items.
- The average American house has almost tripled in size over the past fifty years.
- Of the world's children, 3.1 percent live in America, but Americans purchase 40 percent of the toys sold worldwide.
- On average, American women have thirty outfits (that figure was nine in 1930).
- On average, American families spend $1,700 a year on clothes and dispose of sixty-five pounds of clothing.
- There are more television sets than people in the average American home.
- America has more shopping malls than high schools, and for 93 percent of teenage girls, shopping is their favorite activity.[1]

Not only do we love our stuff; we love unnecessary stuff. Americans spend $1.2 trillion annually on nonessential goods like jewelry, alcohol, candy, recreational vehicles, gambling, and more. (That's 11.2 percent of total consumer spending compared to only 4 percent in 1959.)[2]

We scoff at the bumper sticker that reads "Whoever dies with the most toys wins"—but then we live life according to that mantra. What's underneath all the piles of stuff? Our culture is infected with materialism and consumerism.

Don't Buy the Cultural Lies

Lie #1: Wealth and material possessions bring happiness and ensure the good life.

People in our culture rarely take time to ask, "What is the good life?" Unwittingly carried along by the cultural currents, we've absorbed the idea that material prosperity is at least a, if not *the*, goal of life. We think wealth and possessions will bring human flourishing. And our young people are all in:

> Voices critical of mass consumerism, materialistic values, or the environmental or social costs of a consumer-driven economy were nearly non-existent among emerging adults.... The consensus position of emerging adults was this: As long as people can afford it, they may buy and consume whatever they happen to want without limit. It is completely up to them as individuals. There is nothing at all problematic about America's consumer-driven socioeconomic system. Shopping and buying as a way of life is just fine, and owning some of the nicer things in life is a natural part of the purpose or goal of life.[3]

How's this plan working out for Americans? Well, we have more money, disposable income, material goods, technology, leisure time, vacations, square footage in our homes, quality health care, computers, cars, and conveniences than past Americans. We have more wealth and more possessions than any civilization in the history of humanity. As a result, we're happier and more fulfilled than previous generations, right? Wrong.

Americans today report more symptoms of depression and anxiety than over the past fifty years. Antidepressant use has increased almost 400 percent among all ages in the past two decades.[4] The suicide rate among Americans thirty-five to sixty-four years of age increased 28.4 percent between 1999 and 2010.[5] Teen depression has increased dramatically (a fivefold increase) over the past five decades and is the most common mental-health disorder among US teens.[6]

Surely middle- and upper-class kids, with their education and affluence, are insulated from the struggles of others. Not at all. In *The Price of Privilege*, Madeline Levine found the opposite to be true:

> America's newly identified at-risk group is preteens and teens from affluent, well-educated families. In spite of their economic and social advantages, they experience among the highest rates of depression, substance abuse, anxiety disorders, somatic complaints, and unhappiness of any group of children in this country. When researchers look at kids across the socioeconomic spectrum, they find that the most troubled adolescents often come from the affluent homes.[7]

That's not exactly a picture of human flourishing, is it? According to our culture, the God-shaped hole in our hearts is a stuff-shaped hole, but all of our possessions fail to provide happiness and fulfillment.

Lie #2: You are what you own.

Certain brands and products communicate value and status to the world, and celebrities often flaunt their possessions as proof of their significance. We're tempted to think we are the sum total of our wealth and possessions. Many attempt to validate their existence by acquiring and consuming material goods, even saddling their futures with copious amounts of debt. The average American household carries more than $132,000 in debt, including over $16,000 in credit-card debt.[8] We live beyond our means even though wealth and consumption don't buy emotional or relational stability.[9]

Beneath consumerism, idolatry lurks. It sells an approach to life that says, "I'm the center of the universe. Everything exists to meet my needs and satisfy my desires." We seek identity in our stuff because it validates our worship of self. Reinforced by media, entertainment and the endless stream of advertising, we devour goods, services, and even people in an attempt to satisfy our souls.

However, when we've exhausted the fleeting pleasures of affluence and consumerism, what remains? Boredom, depression, and meaninglessness. As a wise man once wrote, "I have seen everything that is done under the sun, and behold, all is vanity and a striving after wind" (Eccles. 1:14). The disappointment of pleasure leaves a void, and we slowly uncover the truth that we've created emptiness out of our own affluence. As Ravi Zacharias explains, "I am absolutely convinced that meaninglessness does not come from being weary of pain; meaninglessness comes from being weary of pleasure. And that is why we find ourselves emptied of meaning with our pantries still full."[10]

But there's a silver lining. The emptiness of our affluence and consumption, and the ensuing anxiety and depression, should point us elsewhere. We're tempted to live in order to consume, but we were created instead to contribute. God didn't design us to be only takers; He created us to be makers. When we've exhausted ourselves with the resources of this world, we should look beyond this world. We find inexhaustible meaning and wonder only in God Himself. As Charles Spurgeon said, "Nothing teaches us about the preciousness of the Creator as much as when we learn the emptiness of everything else."[11] In God alone do we find the source of human flourishing.

Recapture the Wonder of God's Story

Happiness hasn't always had the contorted meaning it now has in contemporary culture. The "pursuit of happiness" in the Declaration of Independence wasn't the unbridled pursuit of affluence, pleasure, and personal satisfaction. Happiness was found in a life well lived, characterized by wisdom, virtue, and character. The Old Testament writers had a word for it: *shalom.*

God's prophets continually warned the people of Israel how life could go wrong. In contrast, they used the word *shalom* to indicate how life is supposed to be: a life in which human beings flourish. Cornelius Plantinga Jr. explains the Old Testament meaning of *shalom*:

> The webbing together of God, humans, and all creation in justice, fulfillment, and delight is what the Hebrew prophets call *shalom*. We call it peace, but it means far more than mere peace of mind or a cease-fire between enemies. In the Bible, shalom means *universal flourishing, wholeness, and delight*.... Shalom, in other words, is the way things ought to be.[12]

We get a vivid picture of *shalom* in Psalm 1:

> Blessed is the man
>   who walks not in the counsel of the wicked,
> nor stands in the way of sinners,
>   nor sits in the seat of scoffers;
> but his delight is in the law of the LORD,
>   and on his law he mediates day and night.
>
> He is like a tree
>   planted by streams of water,
> that yields its fruit in its season. (vv. 1–3)

Shalom represents human flourishing and is found in God's plan of creation, redemption, and restoration.

The New Testament continues to paint this picture. The Sermon on the Mount is rich with the language of flourishing as Jesus examined the question of which life is the good life. In the Beatitudes, the Greek term used for "blessed" is *makarios*, which is akin to the Hebrew word *shalom*. According to Jesus, "blessedness," the goal of Christian living, is human flourishing.

In God's Story, human flourishing is grounded in God Himself. As the psalmist said, "For me it is good to be near God" (Ps. 73:28). He is our highest good, our ultimate end. Our souls are thirsty for fulfillment, but affluence is a false god unable to quench that thirst. Only God can truly satisfy our souls, as the writer of Psalm 42 declares, "As a deer pants for flowing streams, so pants my soul for you, O God. My soul thirsts for God, for the living God" (vv. 1–2). God is the one who fills us, not earthly goods.

The early church father Augustine tried to fill his life with the pleasures of the world, but when he found God, he concluded, "You stir man to take pleasure in praising you, because you have made us for yourself, and our heart is restless until it rests in you."[13] For this reason, the greatest commandment is to "love the Lord your God with all your heart and with all your soul and with all your mind" (Matt. 22:37).

We were designed in God's image and made for relationship with him. We were also tasked with caring for His creation (Gen. 1:28–30). Certainly, God created good things for us to consume and enjoy (vv. 29–30), but that isn't our final end. We're also to give back, to steward and embellish God's world by creating good things ourselves.

To be clear, pleasure isn't the problem. All the good cooks John and I know, our wives included, enjoy the food they prepare. But even more, they derive pleasure from seeing others enjoy it. When pleasure is our goal, rather than the by-product of a higher end, it becomes distorted. God created us with the capacity for pleasure because He is kind. However, because He made us creators and not merely consumers, we confuse the ends with the means when we live for stuff. We can love the good things God gives us, but our loves must be in the right order.

Wealth isn't necessarily evil, but loving wealth more than God or others is. God has given some of His servants an amazing capacity to generate profit, and as they do, they lift others out of poverty. There's nothing evil about that at all. We're blessed to be a blessing to others. But when wealth or the accumulation of things becomes life's pursuit, loves are disordered.

Because we're so tempted to confuse the ends and the means when it comes to possessions and wealth, Jesus gave us adequate warning:

- Do not lay up for yourselves treasures on earth, where moth and rust destroy and where thieves break in and steal, but lay up for yourselves treasures in heaven, where neither moth nor rust destroys and where thieves do not break in and steal. For where your treasure is, there your heart will be also. (Matt. 6:19–21)

- No one can serve two masters, for either he will hate the one and love the other, or he will be devoted to the one and despise the other. You cannot serve God and money. Therefore I tell you, do not be anxious about your life, what you will eat or what you will drink, nor about your body, what you will put on. Is not life more than food, and the body more than clothing? (vv. 24–25)
- Take care, and be on your guard against all covetousness, for one's life does not consist in the abundance of his possessions. (Luke 12:15)

Simply put, affluence and consumption are poor substitutes for God. Jesus put it this way: "If anyone would come after me, let him deny himself and take up his cross daily and follow me. For whoever would save his life will lose it, but whoever loses his life for my sake will save it. For what does it profit a man if he gains the whole world and loses or forfeits himself?" (Luke 9:23–25).

Jesus wasn't giving a command; He was describing reality. We can accumulate all the riches of the world and never achieve true life. Jesus was explaining how we were made to flourish in God's Story.

Action Steps

1. To help our kids navigate this consumer-driven culture, the first step is to repent of our own sinful pursuit of affluence. Adults aren't immune to the sway of cultural values. We must first examine our own lives, repent of materialistic pursuits, and resolutely resist affluence as the path to the good life. The example of our lives will shout more loudly than our words.

2. Forgo financial benefits to spend time together as a family. The consumerism of the culture puts financial pressures on us to overwork in order to keep up with the culture's standards of the good life. Sociologists have found that since 1969, "the time American parents spend with their children has declined by 22 hours per week."[14] We work more today, even with good intentions, when in reality, kids need more time with their parents, not less. Protect your family time from work demands.

3. As a family, avoid high amounts of debt. Other than in cases of unexpected medical emergencies or other tragedies, high amounts of debt indicate an inability to delay gratification. Add to this instant-gratification approach to life our own emotional instabilities, and consumerism becomes a quick fix to soothe our souls. However, this wrong approach to life can easily lead to financial ruin. Furthermore, it teaches our kids the terrible idea of living for the moment instead of for the future. Teach your kids to delay immediate gratification by forgoing debt. Instead, model for them living within your means, while at the same time saving money consistently to use for larger purchases.

4. Learn to say no to your kids, and tell them why. Resist the urge to buy things just because your kids ask for them. Of course, blessing your kids with gifts is good, but never if the purpose is to appease them, bribe them, or compensate them for your lack of time or attention. When you do say no, explain why. Involve your kids in setting financial goals for future plans, such as college, a family vacation, or a missions project. This will teach them to think about the future and others when they have their own resources to steward.

5. From the start, teach your kids to work hard and contribute to the family. John and I try to live by a simple family rule: never do for your kids what they can do for themselves. It's a bit of an overstatement, but it represents our general posture. Kids can set the table and clean up after meals, pick up their toys, vacuum the house, prepare breakfast, make lunch, and more. Learning how to work should begin when your kids are young. A two- or three-year-old is more than capable of taking utensils from the dinner table to the sink or picking up toys. Responsibility is learned through practice, and the sooner you start building a work ethic in your kids, the better. Through work you help them learn that the reward for their labor isn't just what they get but whom they become.

6. Give your kids an allowance based on household chores. Allowances should always come with strings attached. Weekly chores help kids connect work with earning money. Use a chore chart to outline daily duties, and help your kids stay on track. Communicate that just as Mom and Dad work hard to contribute to the well-being of the family, your kids can also contribute in ways that benefit everyone.

7. Help your kids create a budget. We want our kids to understand that the purpose of money is not merely to fulfill our own desires. John and I use three budget categories for our kids: giving, saving, and spending. Giving is first because we want our kids to recognize that all we have comes from God, and our first obligation is to give back to His kingdom. Second, we want them to learn how to save wisely, and then they can use their remaining finances for personal needs and desires.

8. Teach your kids to pay for the things they want. It's not wrong for a child to desire a toy or for a teenager to purchase clothing or a tech toy. However, we lose a tremendous opportunity to teach our kids responsibility and a work ethic if we simply pay for everything. Help your children understand that responsibility precedes privilege by giving them the opportunity to work and save for their purchases. It will also help them see the real financial costs of consumption.

9. Create a family giving box. You can establish a box or bank that the entire family contributes to, and use the funds to meet the needs of others as they arise. For instance, when you discover a family in need of groceries or a single mom in need of diapers, the family can decide together to help with those needs out of the funds accumulated in the giving box. It's another way to shift the focus off ourselves and actively look out for the needs of others.

10. Let your kids see you give away money and resources. Many of us give regularly to our churches and to nonprofit organizations.

Often this is done out of the sight of our children. But the next time you write that check to your church or donate online, pull your kids aside and explain to them what you're doing and why you're doing it. Model generosity for them.

11. Have your kids give things away regularly. As a family, regularly weed out toys, clothes, and other possessions. Have your kids choose a quality item to give away to a friend or someone in need. Take the items to a local charity or shelter together and explain how this benefits others.

12. Expose your kids to the reality of poverty. If we live in a comfortable suburb, it's easy for our kids to be insulated from the harsh realities of the world. Be intentional about opening their eyes to the needs of those who live among them and around the world. If your church has programs to help the poor, get involved and bring your kids along. Make sure your teenagers participate in the missions trips available through the church's youth ministry. Volunteer with your kids at a local shelter or food bank. Let them see with their own eyes the world's needy, and protect them from the tendency to think the world revolves around them.

13. Practice gratitude on a daily basis. Use mealtime prayers as an opportunity to pause and recognize God's good gifts. Have family members share specific things they're thankful for and then offer prayers of thanksgiving for these things. When God provides that work bonus or a material blessing, gather the family together, share the good news, and give thanks to God.

Further Resources

- *Financial Peace Junior: Teaching Kids How to Win with Money* by Dave Ramsey (Brentwood, TN: Lampo Group/Ramsey Press, 2015)—curriculum for kids
- *The Price of Privilege: How Parental Pressure and Material Advantage Are Creating a Generation of Disconnected and Unhappy Kids* by Madeline Levine (New York: HarperCollins, 2008)

Hopecasting

There are hopeful signs that our kids have become disillusioned with the consumerism of our culture. For all the complaints about millennials as lazy, self-absorbed, entitled individuals, there is reason for optimism because they may be more generous than we are. They may give differently (for instance, through mobile platforms) and be more inclined to give to causes rather than institutions, but they're still giving. In 2014, researchers discovered the following about millennials:

- 84 percent made a charitable donation.
- 78 percent made individual donations.

- 70 percent spent at least an hour volunteering for a cause they cared about.
- One-third volunteered eleven hours or more.
- 45 percent participated in a company-wide volunteer day.
- 32 percent used paid time off to volunteer.
- 16 percent used unpaid time off to volunteer.[15]

As young people discover the empty promises of affluence and consumerism, we have an opportunity to teach them about true human flourishing. Let's guide them back to their creator as the source of true purpose and meaning. Let's model lives of flourishing, just as we lose our lives for the sake of Jesus' kingdom.

Discussion Questions

1. In what ways are we shaped by the constant commercials and sales pitches we hear on a daily basis?

2. In what ways is consumerism a form of idolatry?

3. What values did you learn growing up about money, debt, savings, and shopping? Were they positive or negative?

Chapter Thirteen

Addiction

I have absolutely no pleasure in the stimulants in which I sometimes so madly indulge. It has not been in the pursuit of pleasure that I have periled life and reputation and reason. It has been the desperate attempt to escape from torturing memories, from a sense of insupportable loneliness, and a dread of some strange, impending doom.

Edgar Allan Poe, *Life and Poems of Edgar Allan Poe*

Empty. That's our culture.

According to many psychologists, we've become a culture of empty selves. Philip Cushman explains:

> [American culture] has shaped a self that experiences a significant absence of community, tradition, and shared meaning. It experiences these social absences … as a lack of personal conviction and worth, and it embodies the absences as a chronic,

> undifferentiated emotional hunger.... [The empty self] seeks the experience of being continually filled up by consuming goods, calories, experiences, politicians, romantic partners, and empathic therapists in an attempt to combat the growing alienation and fragmentation of its era.... One of the wealthiest nation[s] on earth is also one of the emptiest.[1]

As we've seen in previous chapters, we express and cope with our inner emptiness in myriad ways, from sexual immorality to chronic consumerism. And today, more people, especially kids, are turning to drugs and alcohol to soothe their souls.

In a culture of increasing dependence on *and* acceptance of drugs and alcohol, how do we help our young people navigate the cultural currents?

Don't Buy the Cultural Lies

Lie #1: Drug and alcohol abuse aren't that big of a problem in our culture.

While certainly acknowledging that people abuse drugs and alcohol, our culture tends to dismiss it as a fairly small problem. Maybe it's a problem in the inner cities, but not in the relative safety of the typical suburban neighborhood. Recent headlines, however, have highlighted the growing problem of drug and alcohol abuse throughout the United States:

- "Americans Are Drinking More—a Lot More"[2]
- "30 Percent of Americans Have Had an Alcohol-Use Disorder"[3]
- "Alcohol Problems Affect about 33 Million U.S. Adults"[4]
- "Ten Percent of Americans Admit Illegal Drug Use"[5]
- "Daily Marijuana Use among College Students at Highest Rate in 35 years"[6]
- "Heroin: The Poisoning of America"[7]

These problems aren't confined to adults. In a survey of high school students, researchers found the following over a twelve-month stretch:

- 58 percent of twelfth graders used alcohol.
- 35 percent of twelfth graders used marijuana.
- 7 percent of twelfth graders used amphetamines.
- Nearly 24 percent of twelfth graders used illicit drugs.[8]

Among college students,

- 79 percent reported drinking alcohol;
- 35 percent reported binge drinking;
- approximately 6 percent reported daily or near-daily marijuana use—the highest rate since 1980;

- marijuana use over a twelve-month period rose from 30 percent in 2006 to 34 percent in 2014; and
- cocaine use rose sharply from 2.7 percent in 2013 to 4.4 percent in 2014.[9]

An increasing number of young people abuse all kinds of substances, not just alcohol. The list includes legal and illegal substances like marijuana, sedatives, tranquilizers, cocaine, club drugs, bath salts, pain killers, opioids, methamphetamines, heroin, hallucinogens, inhalants, and more. Statistically speaking, chances are that our kids and/or their friends will experiment with alcohol and drugs, if they aren't already.

Lie #2: Legal drugs and alcohol are primarily used for recreational purposes. Even if you abuse them, you're only hurting yourself.

Look carefully at alcohol advertisements. What do you see? Sharply dressed, suave men. Scantily clad, seductive-looking women. Groups of beautiful people, smiling and laughing, having the time of their lives. The culture communicates that alcohol, in all its forms, is a harmless means to fun, pleasure, and enjoyment. Consider the advertising slogans:

- "Enjoy the high life." (Miller beer)
- "The adventure starts here." (Molson Canadian)

- "Find your beach." (Corona Extra)
- "The happiest hour on earth." (Jameson whiskey)
- "Great times are coming." (Budweiser)
- "Always worth it." (Bud Light)
- "A shot of adventure." (Jose Cuervo tequila)
- "Clean, crisp refreshment that never stops." (Coors Light)

Essentially, the culture tells us that consuming alcohol is for the most part harmless and is an indispensable part of the good life.

Increasingly, marijuana is perceived in the same way. In fact, 58 percent of Americans favor legal marijuana use.[10] There are currently twenty-eight states that allow legal medicinal marijuana, and eight states—Alaska, Colorado, Oregon, California, Maine, Massachusetts, Nevada, and Washington—have legalized recreational marijuana. These numbers will grow as more states legalize marijuana use in the coming years.

When we look underneath the slick alcohol advertisements and the growing chorus of approval for marijuana, we discover a great amount of damage when these substances are abused. There's plenty of data to show the harm that accompanies drinking. For example, college-age students have reported assaults (including sexual assaults and rape), unintentional injuries, academic problems, unsafe sex, health problems, property damage, confrontations with the police, suicide attempts and deaths, all related to alcohol abuse.[11]

Marijuana isn't harmless either. Today's marijuana products are much more potent, with higher levels of tetrahydrocannabinol (THC), the psychoactive ingredient in marijuana that is shown to be addictive, mind altering, and harmful to the brain, resulting in detrimental cognitive and psychological effects.[12]

In the state of Colorado, the legalization of recreational marijuana has led to a number of unanticipated problems. Marijuana-related hospitalizations have tripled, emergency-room visits have increased 30 percent, drug-related school suspensions have increased, drug cartels have started operations in the state, drug-related crime has increased, and border states like Oklahoma and Nebraska have filed lawsuits, arguing that Colorado has violated federal drug law and contributed to the illegal drug trade in their states.[13]

The physical harm and destruction that substance abuse cause are just the tip of the iceberg. We haven't discussed issues like the heroin epidemic breaking out in places like Ohio and West Virginia, where in a town like Huntington, West Virginia, "one in four residents ... is hooked on heroin or some other opioid."[14] Drug and alcohol abuse seem to be growing problems in our culture.

As followers of Jesus Christ, we know there's a more fundamental matter than physical harm that must be dealt with. Addiction is the result of an emptiness in the soul, not of what's put into the body. Spiritual harm is much more insidious and is the real reason empty selves turn to drugs and alcohol. In a culture of alienation and fragmentation, people search for something to save them from their pain. For many, drugs and alcohol become substitute saviors. However, these substances are an inadequate replacement for the real thing. Drugs and alcohol can only anesthetize people, dulling life for a few fleeting moments, but they cannot satisfy empty souls. Instead, they compound brokenness and multiply the devastation of sin. Real rescue can be found only in God's Story.

Recapture the Wonder of God's Story

Substance abusers find themselves antagonists and victims in God's Story, desperately seeking salvation. The situation is tailor made for the gospel. Jesus came for wounded, broken sinners, which includes you and me. When the self-righteous Pharisees questioned Jesus about the company He kept, He made His mission clear: "Those who are well have no need of a physician, but those who are sick. I came not to call the righteous, but sinners" (Mark 2:17).

We are desperately sick, looking for a substitute savior. Some seek salvation in sex or consumption, while others turn to substance abuse. However, these false gods cannot give "liberty to the captives" or restore "sight to the blind" (Luke 4:18). As Peter preached in the book of Acts, "There is salvation in no one else, for there is no other name under heaven given among men by which we must be saved" (4:12). In this third chapter of God's Story, Jesus rescues, redeems, and reconciles addicts to their creator. And the good news gets even better.

The addicted and sinners of all stripes can now say, "I have been crucified with Christ. It is no longer I who live, but Christ who lives in me" (Gal. 2:20). Not only are we saved *from* our old lives of sin and corruption; we're saved *to* a new life in Christ. We're new creations (2 Cor. 5:17), and that means there's a new way to be human.

In this new life, we recognize that our lives are no longer our own: "You are not your own, for you were bought with a price. So glorify God in your body" (1 Cor. 6:19–20). By ourselves, we've made a mess of body and soul. However, through the cross of Christ, God has bought us back (redeemed us), and His Spirit now resides in us. As we "present [our] bodies as a living sacrifice, holy and acceptable to God" (Rom. 12:1), the Holy Spirit begins to sanctify us in this new mode of existence.

In the old life, sin controlled us (Rom. 6), but in this new life, we discover the fruit of self-control as we allow the Holy Spirit to control us (Gal. 5:23). Living a self-controlled life in the power of the Spirit is the emphasis of the New Testament. That's why Paul warns us not to "get drunk with wine, for that is debauchery, but be filled with the Spirit" (Eph. 5:18). Drunkenness is one way we give control of ourselves to something other than God. In contrast, "if the Spirit of him who raised Jesus from the dead dwells in [us], he who raised Christ Jesus from the dead will also give life to [our] mortal bodies through his Spirit who dwells in [us]" (Rom. 8:11). A Spirit-filled, self-controlled new life brings wholeness to body and soul and is a beautiful contrast to the destruction wrought by substance abuse.

Interestingly, the Bible never condemns drinking alcohol, but it does condemn drunkenness. When Christians see something abused, we often resort to wholesale condemnation of the thing in question rather than promoting its proper use. If some people get drunk on beer or wine, we make a rule that no one should drink at all. However, Paul directly challenged this approach to sanctification:

> If with Christ you died to the elemental spirits of the world, why, as if you were still alive in the world, do you submit to regulations—"Do not handle, Do not taste, Do not touch" (referring to things that all perish as they are used)—according to human precepts and teachings? These have indeed an appearance of wisdom in promoting self-made religion and asceticism and severity to the body, but they are of no value in stopping the indulgence of the flesh. (Col. 2:20–23)

God doesn't condemn the proper use of food and drink ("things that all perish as they are used"), but the abuse of them. This applies as much to the glutton as it does to the drunkard. Paul pointed out that the just-say-no approach alone isn't an adequate model of sanctification. Total abstinence[15] is not a virtue in the New Testament; moderation is (the old word for this is *temperance*). C. S. Lewis shed much-needed light on the biblical teaching:

Temperance is, unfortunately, one of those words that has changed its meaning. It now usually means teetotalism [or total abstinence]. But in the days when the second Cardinal virtue was christened "Temperance", it meant nothing of the sort. Temperance referred not specially to drink, but to all pleasures; and it meant not abstaining, but going the right length and no further.… Of course it may be the duty of a particular Christian, or of any Christian, at a particular time, to abstain from strong drink, either because he is the sort of man who cannot drink at all without drinking too much, or because he is with people who are inclined to drunkenness and must not encourage them by drinking himself.… One of the marks of a certain type of bad man is that he cannot give up a thing himself without wanting every one else to give it up. That is not the Christian way. An individual Christian may see fit to give up all sorts of things for special reasons—marriage, or meat, or beer, or the cinema; but the moment he starts saying the things are bad in themselves, or looking down his nose at other people who do use them, he has taken the wrong turning.…

A man who makes his golf or his motor-bicycle the centre of his life, or a woman who devotes

> all her thoughts to clothes or bridge or her dog, is being just as "intemperate" as someone who gets drunk every evening. Of course, it does not show on the outside so easily: bridge-mania or golf-mania do not make you fall down in the middle of the road. But God is not deceived by externals.[16]

While Christians are often content with cleaning up the outward appearance, God is not. He is after a renovation of the heart. A heart filled with the Holy Spirit is able to exert self-control from the inside out. In turn, self-control allows us to live in God's good world while *properly* enjoying God's good things: "You cause the grass to grow for the livestock and plants for man to cultivate, that he may bring forth food from the earth and wine to gladden the heart of man, oil to make his face shine and bread to strengthen man's heart" (Ps. 104:14–15). Self-control is a mark of maturity in the believer's life and characteristic of godliness (2 Pet. 1:3–7). This is the new kind of Spirit-empowered life that Jesus made possible.

Of course, the question of drugs is another matter. It's possible to use alcohol without the intent to become intoxicated. Most of us can enjoy a glass of wine without giving over any control of ourselves to the alcohol. However, the very intent of using recreational marijuana,[17] cocaine, heroin, or other illicit substances is to become intoxicated. Partaking, in and of itself, is an attempt to get high and give control of oneself to the drug. Therefore, drugs cannot be used in moderation because of their inherently intoxicating nature, which directly opposes the biblical teaching on self-control. Thus, Scripture prohibits drug use.

While a life of Spirit-empowered self-control is our ultimate aim, this doesn't preclude careful conduct along the way. Shunning a legalistic approach to sanctification doesn't mean running headlong into licentiousness. Freedom in Christ cannot be a pretense for sin. That's why the Bible, while elevating the virtue of self-control, still offers plenty of warnings and instruction about drunkenness and sobriety:

> Wine is a mocker, strong drink a brawler,
>   and whoever is led astray by it is not wise.
>   (Prov. 20:1)

> Be not among drunkards
>   or among gluttonous eaters of meat,
> for the drunkard and the glutton will come to
>   poverty,
>   and slumber will clothe them with rags....
> Who has woe? Who has sorrow?
>   Who has strife? Who has complaining?
> Who has wounds without cause?
>   Who has redness of eyes?
> Those who tarry long over wine;
>   those who go to try mixed wine.
> Do not look at wine when it is red,
>   when it sparkles in the cup
>   and goes down smoothly.

In the end it bites like a serpent
    and stings like an adder.
Your eyes will see strange things,
    and your heart utter perverse things.
You will be like one who lies down in the midst
        of the sea,
    like one who lies on the top of a mast.
"They struck me," you will say, "but I was not
        hurt;
    they beat me, but I did not feel it.
When shall I awake?
    I must have another drink." (23:20–21,
        29–35)

Woe to those who rise early in the morning,
    that they may run after strong drink,
who tarry late into the evening
    as wine inflames them! (Isa. 5:11)

Now the works of the flesh are evident: sexual immorality, impurity, sensuality, idolatry, sorcery, enmity, strife, jealousy, fits of anger, rivalries, dissensions, divisions, envy, drunkenness, orgies, and things like these. I warn you, as I warned you before, that those who do such things will not inherit the kingdom of God. (Gal. 5:19–21)

Sanctification is a lifelong process with many ups and downs. We must honestly assess our growth, seek the counsel of more mature brothers and sisters in Christ, and act accordingly. Thankfully, God's Story can catch us in the midst of the messiness and brokenness of life and move us toward the health and wholeness only the gospel of Jesus brings.

Action Steps

1. Open your eyes to the real threat substance abuse is to your kids. The world is a different place today than it was when we were growing up. If you think drug and alcohol abuse cannot touch your family, you're wrong. Ask your kids if they know of or have seen their friends using drugs or alcohol. Ask honest but gentle questions and allow your kids the space to share freely without condemning them. Their answers will help you assess how close the threat is to your own kids.

2. Model self-control. From restaurant meal orders to department-store purchases to enjoying a glass of wine, model a self-controlled life for your kids. Just by watching you, they'll learn the proper or improper use of God's good gifts. If you abuse substances, there is a much greater risk your kids will too.

3. Make family dinners an essential part of your routine. Kids who have dinner frequently with their families are less likely to drink or use drugs. Teens who had infrequent family dinners (two or fewer per week) were more than twice as likely to use alcohol and marijuana than kids who regularly ate dinner with their families (five to seven times per week).[18] Of course, it's not the mere act of eating together that has a powerful impact on our kids. The shared time of relationship building is what connects kids and parents.

4. Go beyond the just-say-no model of sanctification. Christian parents must ask themselves if they truly believe in the power of the gospel to change lives. If so, we should also recognize that while rules are important, our emphasis is on the power of the Holy Spirit to sanctify our kids. Clear boundaries play a vital role when our kids our young, but as they mature into the middle-school years and beyond, our focus should be on the gospel and the spiritual disciplines essential to their growth in Christ. Maintain boundaries but also mentor your kids in the cultivation of habits like Bible study, prayer, worship, fasting, and service.

5. Explain the why. Our kids are bombarded with messages connecting alcohol to the good life. They're constantly told recreational marijuana is harmless. In light of this, it's not enough to simply assert that these things are wrong and harmful. Our kids want to know why they are. Think through the issues carefully and be prepared to provide your kids with thoughtful reasons.

6. Regularly host your kids' friends at your home. As a general rule, if John and I, or our wives, don't know the families of our kids' friends, we don't allow them to spend time in those homes.

We need information to make wise decisions. However, we know the rules in our own homes. We know there will be adequate parental supervision. Therefore, we know our kids won't have the opportunity to be tempted with drugs, alcohol, or other vices. We try to make our homes as warm and friendly as possible so that our kids and their friends would rather hang out with us than elsewhere.

7. Teach from real-life examples. If you know a recovering drug addict, have this person sit down with your children and share his or her story. Point to a friend's alcoholism and the consequences it has had on his or her family, not in judgment but to demonstrate the harsh reality of substitute saviors. When a Hollywood celebrity (who allegedly has it all) checks into a drug-rehab facility and makes news headlines, discuss it with your kids. You can powerfully illustrate biblical truth with real-world examples.

8. Confront your kids' problems quickly. If you see signs that your child is struggling, address the issue immediately. If he or she is suffering from depression, confront it and don't let it go unaddressed. Emptiness often results in depression and anxiety, and then kids are tempted to self-medicate with drugs and alcohol. Act fast before your child begins to travel down the road toward substance abuse.

9. Get professional help when needed. Christians must shed the shame associated with getting professional assistance. Christian therapists and counselors can be a tremendous help to our families. Prescription drugs can also help with a real chemical imbalance. Drug-rehab centers can help rescue those in serious crisis. Don't let unbiblical views about psychology be an obstacle to getting professional help for your child. At the same time, keep pointing to Christ as the first and foremost source of help.

10. Be wise with your freedom in Christ. Your Christian freedom to enjoy a cold beer or a nice glass of wine isn't the only consideration. Be wise around your older kids, who may be experiencing regular temptation to drink with their friends. Don't let your freedom weaken their resolve. If a friend or family member has struggled with drunkenness or alcoholism, don't "put a stumbling block or hindrance" in the way by drinking in front of that person (Rom. 14:13). There are serious personal and social costs of drug and alcohol abuse, so we must walk carefully.

At the same time, if you use your freedom to abstain from alcohol, don't "pass judgment" when others exercise their freedom (v. 13). Always remember, "the kingdom of God is not a matter of eating and drinking but of righteousness and peace and joy in the Holy Spirit" (v. 17).

Further Resources

- *The Heart of Addiction: A Biblical Perspective* by Mark E. Shaw (Bemidji, MN: Focus Publishing, 2008)

- *Shepherding a Child's Heart* by Tedd Tripp (Wapwallopen, PA: Shepherd Press, 1995)

Hopecasting

I Am Second is a nonprofit organization and multimedia movement that seeks to proclaim the power of the gospel. Film actors, athletes, musicians, business leaders, drug addicts, and next-door neighbors tell their stories of the redemption and restoration found in Jesus Christ. These YouTube testimonial videos get hundreds of thousands of views online.

One of the most powerful I Am Second stories is the testimony of Brian "Head" Welch, the lead guitarist for the highly successful nu-metal band Korn. Watch it![19] Brian, tatted up from head to toe, shares his dark journey from being a successful rock star to becoming a full-on addict. He was addicted to cocaine, alcohol, pills, and, finally, to the drug that nearly destroyed his life: methamphetamines. His life was spinning out of control. In the midst of Welch's personal destruction and despair, Jesus Christ rescued him. It's an amazing account of the power of the gospel.[20]

Stories like Welch's help us believe that the power of God's Story can transform our own stories, no matter how broken we are.

Discussion Questions

1. What personal experiences have you had with addiction? What were the short- and long-term consequences?

2. How are alcohol and drug use portrayed in media? In what ways are these portrayals incomplete?

3. Which addictive substances are most prevalent in your community? What effects do you see?

Chapter Fourteen

Entertainment

It is not any ism but entertainment that is arguably the most pervasive, powerful and ineluctable force of our time—a force so overwhelming that it has finally metastasized into life.

Neal Gabler, *Life: The Movie*

Most parents are serious about what their kids eat. We know plenty who buy only organic, fair-trade, non-GMO, free-range, cage-free, grass-fed, shade-grown, 100 percent–natural, dolphin-safe food items at the local Whole Foods Market. And they're junk-food Nazis too. They won't let their kids within one hundred yards of high-fructose corn syrup or trans fats. John and I don't blame them. We want our kids to be healthy too.

Ironically, many of those same parents will take the polar-opposite approach when it comes to their kids' entertainment diets. They hand over the remote, tablet, or smartphone and let their kids dive unfettered into a smorgasbord of entertainment options. Instead of filling their stomachs with food, kids fill their hearts and minds with Marvel's *Deadpool* on the big screen or *Neighbors 2: Sorority Rising*, starring heartthrob Zac Efron. On television, they tune in to watch *Pretty Little Liars* and *Family Guy*. Or they can't miss their favorite reality-TV show *Keeping Up with the Kardashians*. Next, they throw on headphones for some music and listen to DNCE's song "Cake by the Ocean" or "Work from Home" by Fifth Harmony.

Many parents are unaware of these artists or titles. They carefully track their kids' dietary habits, but their entertainment habits? Not so much.

Every movie, TV show, and song listed here won a Fox Teen Choice Award in 2016. Thirteen- to nineteen-year-olds vote on these annual awards, which means these entertainment choices were among the most popular among adolescents last year. If you want to stay somewhat in touch with what American youth are listening to and watching, look up a list of Teen Choice Award winners for each year. Doing so will sober you up about entertainment.

DNCE's "Cake by the Ocean" won the award for Teen Choice Party Song. Here is a sampling of the lyrics:

You're a real-life fantasy, you're a real-life fantasy
But you're moving so carefully; let's start living dangerously
Let's lose our minds and go … crazy
Ah ya ya ya ya I keep on hoping
we'll eat cake by the ocean[1]

Obviously, the song is *not* about cake. DNCE's lead man, Joe Jonas, explained: "Working on the record, these Swedish producers that we were working with, they kept confusing 'sex on the beach' with 'cake by the ocean,' so that's how the song started."[2] So, thirteen- to nineteen-year-olds chose a song about having sex on the beach as their favorite party song.

That's *one* piece of entertainment out of thousands that vie for the souls of our kids every single day. Entertainment has become an overwhelming cultural force. There's nothing in Western civilization that rivals the power of entertainment to shape what we think and how we think. "In the past, heroes made history. Today, they make music, movies, and TV shows," culture expert Bill Brown is fond of saying. Only in America could a reality-TV star run for president—and win.

As the title of Neil Postman's book highlights, we're "amusing ourselves to death."[3] If we don't help our kids navigate this entertainment tsunami, the ideas and values of our culture will take many of them captive.

Don't Buy the Cultural Lies

Lie #1: Relax! It's just entertainment.

"Taken captive?" Whenever John and I talk about entertainment, students accuse us of going off the rails. The purpose of music, movies, and TV shows is to deliver fun, enjoyment, and leisure. Entertainers entertain; they don't try to change the world. Or so the cultural lie goes. But the danger here is a half truth masquerading as the complete story.

Certainly we agree that a lot of entertainment is made for our pleasure and enjoyment. However, it does more than that, and entertainers themselves realize it. Musician and actress Courtney Love, wife of the late Kurt Cobain of Nirvana, rose to prominence in the 1990s and continues to produce music and act today. In an interview with *Spin* magazine, Courtney was clear: "I feel like I have a duty. I as an architect have a need to impose my worldview on the culture. I was born with that need."[4]

George Lucas, a movie producer who needs no introduction, recognized the *Star Wars* movies as more than mere entertainment: "[*Star Wars* is] designed *primarily to make young people think about the mystery*. Not to say, 'Here's the answer.' It's to say, 'Think about this for a second. Is there a God? What does God look like? What does God sound like? What does God feel like? How do we relate to God?'"[5] (emphasis added).

These entertainers understand the power of their medium to deliver ideas.

As a result, entertainment, loaded with ideas, shapes culture. Worldviews are expressed in music, movies, TV shows, video games, and YouTube videos. Sometimes a worldview is explicitly stated. For example, on Cartoon Network's animated children's show *The Amazing World of Gumball*, Gumball (a twelve-year-old cat) looks up to the sky and asks, "Tell me, universe, what is the meaning of life?" In response, the planets sing a catchy tune. And it's completely atheistic. Here's an excerpt:

When you think you've got a problem
And your life is full of doubt
Remember in the scheme of things
Your puny, little, tiny, weeny, meager, futile, worthless,...
gloomy, bleak, and pitiful Life just does not count![6]

However, this kind of straightforward message is rare. The vast majority of the time, worldviews are embedded within entertainment. The ideas aren't explicitly stated or argued; they're assumed. This happens when a movie portrays a particular character as a hero that we should cheer or a villain we should despise. For instance, the movie *Ocean's Eleven* paints the professional criminals played by George Clooney and Brad Pitt as heroes, and by the end of the movie, you're cheering for them to steal millions of dollars. Or take the hit TV show *Modern Family*. Alongside a traditional family, there are a divorce/remarriage/trophy-wife family and a gay couple. Take your pick. Any of these is a "modern family." Neil Postman highlighted the problem:

> Television is our culture's principal mode of knowing about itself. Therefore—and this is the critical point—how television stages the world becomes the model for how the world is properly to be staged. It is not merely that on the television screen entertainment is the metaphor for all discourse. It is that off the screen the same metaphor prevails.[7]

Over time, these ideas trickle into the conscience of the culture, slowly shaping our conceptions of the world, norms of acceptable behavior, and our very identities. "We become what we behold. We shape our tools and thereafter our tools shape us."[8] We created entertainment, and now entertainment is recreating us.

Even our politicians understand the powerful influence of entertainment on culture. Speaking about LGBT issues, Vice President Joe Biden recognized the impact of an NBC sitcom: "Things really begin to change … when the social culture changes.… I think *Will and Grace* probably did more to educate the American public than almost anything anybody's ever done so far."[9] President Barack Obama praised gay comedian and talk-show host Ellen DeGeneres, saying, "Changing hearts and minds, I don't think anyone has been as influential as you on that. I really mean it."[10] A president and vice president recognize it's not *just* entertainment.

Lie #2: The medium is neutral.

No R-rated movies. No explicit lyrics. As long as we avoid sex, drugs, and violence, screen time is largely innocuous. So watch, listen, tweet, and post away! However, this approach underestimates the nature of technology. Entertainment isn't neutral.

What's the primary medium through which entertainment is delivered? The screen. It accomplishes its task through images (pictures and video). Images even accompany songs in the form of music videos. Images allow the mind to become passive. We implicitly express this when we characterize watching TV as "vegging out." Why would we describe it that way? Because watching flickering images on a screen doesn't require much mental effort: we simply passively absorb what is presented. Thus, screens change us from participants into spectators. The screen comes on, and our minds turn off. Images come fast and furious, so we tend not to think carefully about what we're viewing, if we think at all. Yes, screens can literally make us dumber.[11]

Contrast the medium of the screen with the medium of the printed word. A book accomplishes its task not through images but by language. The words in a book force the human mind to work harder. Your mind is active, not passive, as it translates the words into concepts and ideas. For this reason, if you haven't developed a habit of reading, it's hard work to get started. Just as an out-of-shape person struggles the first few times back at the gym, an underactive mind needs time to get back in shape.

Often, entertainment is used to cure boredom, avoid responsibility, or anesthetize the pain of our inner emptiness. Through entertainment, we divert our attention from reality and escape into the triviality and voyeurism of music, movies, and TV. As Aldous Huxley noted, our appetite for distraction is nearly infinite.[12]

Also, in a world with so many entertainment options, we're easily addicted. We come home and instinctively flip on the TV. We get in the car and immediately put a smartphone or tablet in our kids' hands. We can't go to a restaurant anymore without a multitude of video monitors vying for our attention. It's almost impossible to escape the omnipresent screen.

The concern John and I have with entertainment goes beyond the sex and violence to the very medium of the screen itself. After all, as Marshall McLuhan noted, "the medium *is* the message" and exerts its influence over us.[13] Neil Postman addressed the seriousness of the situation:

> When a population becomes distracted by trivia, when cultural life is redefined as a perpetual round of entertainments, when serious public conversation becomes a form of baby-talk, when, in short, a people become an audience and their public business a vaudeville act, then a nation finds itself at risk; culture-death is a clear possibility.[14]

Recapture the Wonder of God's Story

Jesus said, "Man shall not live by bread alone, but by every word that comes from the mouth of God" (Matt. 4:4). If our most important nourishment is found not in physical food but in God and His Word, what does that imply about the entertainment culture?

First, we must return to the grounding of human identity. We are made in the image of God (Gen. 1:26). Like God Himself, image bearers were made to create, not just consume. Entertainment conditions us to orient our lives around constant consumption, but we were made for something richer, deeper, and more fulfilling. We were designed to cultivate God's good world. We're made to work and toil and, from our efforts, to create good things. We're to "subdue" the earth and have "dominion" over it (v. 28). When we overconsume entertainment, we allow the things of this earth to have dominion over us. But when we create, we bear God's image well.

That isn't to say all entertainment is bad. Indeed, creating art is the activity of image bearers, and art can be entertaining. However, art's true power is neutered in an entertainment-driven culture. We weren't made for a life of distraction.

The world needs good art to stir and shape the imagination. A good song can move our emotions. A well-done film can produce moments of joy or preserve essential cultural memories. We properly delight in such things. Solomon declared, "I commend joy, for man has nothing better under the sun but to eat and drink and be joyful, for this will go with him in his toil through the days of his life that God has given him under the sun" (Eccles. 8:15).

Producing a film, writing a musical score, or painting aren't divorced from our life in Christ, but can be done with and for Christ, as the apostle Paul reminded us: "Whatever you do, in word or deed, do everything in the name of the Lord Jesus, giving thanks to God the Father through him" (Col. 3:17). Our good creations point us back to a good God and bring Him glory. "So, whether you eat or drink, or whatever you do, do all to the glory of God" (1 Cor. 10:31).

Our minds play a central role in our sanctification. Paul told us that we're "transformed by the renewal of [our minds]" (Rom. 12:2). The question isn't *if* our minds are being renewed; it's by what? As we consume entertainment, our minds are being renewed. Yet as we've seen, much of what our entertainment culture produces actually harms our sanctification. Instead, God calls us to think about "whatever is true, whatever is honorable, whatever is just, whatever is pure, whatever is lovely, whatever is commendable, … [whatever is excellent and] worthy of praise" (Phil. 4:8).

As we engage an entertainment culture, we can look to the apostle Paul as a role model. In Acts 17, he observed the culture of Athens, and "his spirit was provoked within him as he saw that the city was full of idols" (v. 16). Likewise, the idols of entertainment pervade our culture. What was Paul's response to the idols in his day? Did he wring his hands over how bad the culture had become? Did he condemn the Athenians and then abandon them to their idols? No. He began to reason with them (v. 17). And when the opportunity presented itself, he used their culture as a launching point to proclaim the truth:

> Men of Athens, I perceive that in every way you are very religious. For as I passed along and observed the objects of your worship, I found also an altar with this inscription: "To the unknown god." What therefore you worship as unknown, this I proclaim to you. (vv. 22–23)

Paul understood that human beings are worshippers by nature, and that the Athenians were worshipping false gods. He then proclaimed to them the one true God and the resurrected Jesus. Like the idols of the Athenians, our altars of entertainment advance the false gods of our culture and demand our loyalty and devotion. Yet in the midst of this, we can proclaim the only God worthy of our allegiance and point people to the source of true hope in the resurrected Jesus. Only He can satisfy the longings of our hearts.

Action Steps

1. Take regular breaks from entertainment. One day a week, turn off all screens and establish a rhythm of withdrawal. Create sacred spaces in your home that are screen-free. Make your kitchen table, your living room, or the kids' bedroom a space where screens aren't allowed. Instead, make them places for conversation, reading, writing, thinking, or praying. Vacations are also opportune times to unplug and leave the screens at home. If your kids respond poorly to screen-time breaks, that's an indication of their level of addiction to entertainment *and* a good sign that you're doing the right thing. Be persistent. It may take time to wean your kids off their screens.

2. Become aware of your kids' entertainment diet. Most parents know what their kids are eating and won't allow them to eat whatever food they want. In the same way, find out what your kids are listening to and watching and don't give them free rein. Ask them about their favorite songs and shows and evaluate the content. The first step to helping them navigate entertainment is to know what's entertaining them.

3. Teach your kids how to actively engage entertainment rather than passively absorb it. Don't allow the culture to think for them.

Help your kids evaluate the medium and the message. Messages are everywhere, and our kids need to learn how to identify them.

For instance, watch a movie or TV show together, but hit the pause button at various intervals and discuss what you just viewed. Use this list of questions to guide the conversation:

- What is the main story line and/or overarching theme?
- How are the characters portrayed? Who are the good guys? Who are the villains?
- How are the visuals used to illustrate and accentuate the story line?
- What's the central conflict? Whom does it involve? Is it resolved and how?
- What values are promoted directly or indirectly?
- What is the good life according to the movie?
- Are there any religious references? If so, what is said and how is religion portrayed?
- What worldviews are explored in the movie? How are they portrayed?
- Are there any historical references? Are they accurate or inaccurate?
- How do the messages match up with Scripture?

In the same way, review song lyrics with your kids. Before you let them purchase that song on iTunes, look up the words online *together*. Ask your kids what the song communicates and contrast it with Scripture. Help them see the corrosive messages of bad songs and the life-giving messages of good songs. The goal isn't merely to stop your kids from listening to junk; it's also to help them understand why it's junk so they can stop themselves.

4. Redeem screen time. There are certainly entertainment choices we need to say no to, but we also need to seek out music, movies, and TV shows we can say yes to. We don't have to throw out the baby with the bathwater.

For younger children, replace some of those Disney Channel cartoons with Phil Vischer's excellent series *What's in the Bible?* Substitute that mindless animated feature with a thoughtful, virtue-filled Pixar production.[15]

For teens, celebrate movies that promote virtue and heroism, such as The Lord of the Rings trilogy or a host of other good movies. Watch a classic movie together. View some of the stunning videos by Illustra Media or Exploration Films on God's design in the natural world. Or turn on a well-crafted documentary.

Brett and I can't give you a comprehensive list of titles, so you'll have to do some homework. However, the goal is to become more thoughtful in the entertainment choices you provide your kids. Don't settle for distraction, voyeurism, and triviality.

5. Create alternatives to entertainment consumption. Move your kids beyond the screen. Suggest activities that encourage creativity, not just consumption:

- Buy an art easel and keep an abundant supply of butcher paper, paint, and brushes on hand.
- Designate part of an evening to reading through a literary classic with your kids.
- Get some music lessons for your kids and regularly have them play their instruments for the family. Create music together.
- Keep a good supply of educational games, chess, checkers, board games, card games, trivia games, and puzzles in your home.
- Create films; don't just watch them. Have your kids write a script and then produce a film on a video camera or smartphone.

6. Get your kids outside. Most kids suffer from NDD—nature deficit disorder. They spend too much time indoors. Take your kids to the park, the mountains, or the beach. Go on a family walk, hike, or bike ride. Give them a bunch of cardboard and let them build a fort in the backyard. You may have to push them out the door, and they may complain at first, but eventually their imagination and creativity will take over.

7. For younger kids, don't let the screen become a babysitter. The American Academy of Pediatrics recommends that parents avoid screen time (with the exception of video chatting) for children eighteen months and under and allow no more than one hour of screen time per day for children two to five.[16] The younger children are when they establish unhealthy entertainment habits, the harder it is to break them. Condition their expectations (and their minds) from an early age.

8. Help your kids develop a reading habit. One way to mitigate against an entertainment-oriented culture is to cultivate a love for reading in your kids. First, read to them when they're babies. Do it before they go to bed and throughout the day. Read to them as much as you can. Continue reading to them as they're learning, but let them read to you as well. Finally, they should eventually read books on their own.

Through it all, you're not just helping them establish a reading habit; you're also developing a love for it. As we mentioned earlier, reading will grow and structure their minds in a way images can't. There's a reason God's Word was delivered to us in written form and not on a DVD!

Here's one idea my (Brett's) kids really enjoyed. One night a week, we held what we called Reader's Theater. We'd all dress up in overcoats, sweaters, scarves, and hats and prepare some delicious snacks. Then we'd sit together in the living room, and my wife or I would read as dramatically as we could from a great work of fiction. Each week we'd read a chapter or two until we finished the book. It became a highly anticipated weekly family event. Use our idea or create your own family reading traditions.

9. Practice what you preach. You can't be an entertainment hypocrite, telling your kids one thing while you do another. There may be music, movies, or television shows you need to give up first. You may have to cut down on your own screen time before you ask your kids to reduce theirs. You may need to remove the TV from your bedroom before you take their TVs out. Let them see you model a healthy relationship with entertainment. That will go a long way toward helping them establish one as well.

Further Resources

- *Amusing Ourselves to Death: Public Discourse in the Age of Show Business* by Neil Postman (New York: Penguin, 2005)
- *Hollywood Worldviews: Watching Films with Wisdom and Discernment* by Brian Godawa (Downers Grove, IL: InterVarsity, 2009)
- *The Wisdom of Pixar: An Animated Look at Virtue* by Robert Velarde (Downers Grove, IL: InterVarsity, 2010)
- Axis.org—www.axis.org
- Center for Parent/Youth Understanding—www.CPYU.org
- Plugged In—www.pluggedin.com

Hopecasting

Remember, followers of Jesus are to be in the world but not of it. It's tempting to take the easy path of condemning all modern entertainment and advocating a complete withdrawal from the culture. However, that strategy won't help our kids navigate the cultural waters.

This is true not just of entertainment consumers but of creators as well. Being in the world but not of it means we're agents of redemption. The church desperately needs more Christians redeeming entertainment by creating beautiful art to the glory of God. And that does *not* mean slapping Bible verses on a film or merely inserting "Jesus" into song lyrics. Thankfully, there are artists we can hold up to our kids as models of cultural engagement in the twenty-first century.

Lecrae is a multi-award-winning hip-hop artist, the cofounder of Reach Records, and a devoted follower of Jesus Christ. His 2014 album *Anomaly* debuted at number one on the Billboard 200. His songs depart from the money-sex-violence formula that typifies many of today's hip-hop lyrics. Instead, he expresses gratitude for the Redeemer, discusses social issues like adultery and abortion, and warns about sin, all without "explicit content" warning labels.

Twenty One Pilots is a top-notch, commercially successful rock band with hit songs like "Stressed Out" and "Heathens." Singer Tyler Joseph and drummer Josh Dun are committed Christians who have avoided the "Christian band" label and the mainstream marginalization that comes with it. However, their songs are filled with truth, and they open up about fear, doubt, anxiety, and insecurity and reveal human brokenness in songs like "Screen," where they confess, "We're broken people."[17] Their hit album *Blurryface* is all about the human condition.

Yet Twenty One Pilots subtly encourages their listeners to go deeper in songs like "Car Radio":

Faith is to be awake
And to be awake is for us to think
And for us to think is to be alive[18]

In the end, their albums offer glimpses of hope while avoiding the simplistic statements and Christian platitudes that characterize much of today's "Christian" artistry.

Lecrae, Tyler Joseph, and Josh Dun are artists doing excellent work *as Christians*. They haven't bought into the false dichotomy of secular versus sacred music. Lecrae explains:

> We've limited Christianity to salvation and sanctification.... Christianity is the truth about everything. If you say you have a Christian worldview, that means you see the world through that lens—not just how people get saved and what to stay away from.... Christians need to embrace that there need to be believers talking about love and social issues and all other aspects of life.[19]

Driven by the truth of the Christian worldview, these artists are engaging and redeeming our entertainment culture with exceptional art. At the same time, they're telling God's Story from a huge mainstream platform. May more of our kids follow in their footsteps.

Discussion Questions

1. Pick a song on the Billboard chart or from your kids' playlists. Look up the lyrics and analyze the song together. What messages are found in the lyrics?

2. Revisit the last movie you watched as a family. Who were the heroes? Who were the villains? What messages were embedded in the movie?

3. How much time do you spend on screens each day? Is it too much? How might you reach a healthy balance?

Chapter Fifteen

Racial Tension

There are no ordinary people. You have never talked to a mere mortal. Nations, cultures, arts, civilisations—these are mortal, and their life is to ours as the life of a gnat. But it is immortals whom we joke with, work with, marry, snub, and exploit—immortal horrors or everlasting splendours.

C. S. Lewis, *The Weight of Glory and Other Addresses*

Many Americans hoped the election of our first African American president in 2008 would finally close the book on a part of our dark, divided history and bring racial reconciliation. It clearly didn't. The subsequent protests and riots in the wake of high-profile police shootings of African Americans reveal that our country is still very much divided on the issue of race.

However, such a divide isn't unique to the United States. The modern world is filled with strife between people groups, from the streets of Palestine to the tensions between North and South Korea to the conflict between the Kurds and the Turks. In the recent past, racial conflict in Rwanda, Bosnia, and Darfur (Sudan) resulted in unspeakable violence and genocide. Chechnya. France. India. Sri Lanka. Russia. Bolivia. Belgium. Great Britain. Racial strife is found in nearly every country on earth.

I (Brett) have experienced it firsthand. I remember tense moments as a young elementary-school kid at a local public pool in a Maryland suburb when my four-foot-nine-inch Vietnamese mother stepped in to defend my younger brother and me from a group of African American boys who were taunting us relentlessly because of our Asian background. No ethnicity, socioeconomic status, or cultural environment makes us immune to ethnic strife.

Racism isn't an American problem; it's a human problem. How do we navigate this minefield with our kids?

Don't Buy the Cultural Lies

Lie #1: You are your ethnicity.

Culture tells us that our identity is inextricably linked to our racial classifications. We are Chinese, Mexican, Egyptian, Russian, Swedish, African, and so on. Racial identity is innate and unalterable because race is in the genes. Therefore, a primary part of our identity is found in our ethnicity.

However, the biological differences between ethnic groups—the ones that account for shared characteristics among members of a race—are minuscule. Researchers involved with the Human Genome Project have stated, "If you ask what percentage of your genes is reflected in your external appearance, the basis by which we talk about race, the answer seems to be in the range of .01 percent."[1] Thus, "the concept of race has no genetic or scientific basis."[2] There is no deep unchanging essence that every member of an ethnic group shares. After putting together "a draft of the entire sequence of the human genome, … researchers … unanimously declared, there is only one race—the human race."[3] An overidentification with ethnic identity can unnecessarily exacerbate racial divisions.

Lie #2: Racism is nonexistent, so people need to get over it.

In the view of some, the era of civil rights reformed our nation. We've rooted out all racism in our country, they claim, and have moved past our history of racial discrimination. It's time for people to get over it and quit playing the race card. With beliefs like those, some Americans simply dismiss racism altogether.

However, if racism is discrimination against someone of a different race based on a belief in one's own racial superiority, how can anyone deny that racism still exists? There are plenty of examples:

- Police officials in the city of Ferguson, Missouri, circulating racially charged emails.[4]
- University of Oklahoma fraternity students chanting, "There will never be a ni**** SAE [Sigma Alpha Epsilon]. You can hang him from a tree, but he can never sign with me."[5]

- A man screaming "Go back to Africa" at a black protestor.[6]

Simply peruse social-media channels, and you'll quickly discover blatant racism being spewed from the anonymity of computer screens. Ask ethnic neighbors if they've experienced racism, and they'll likely have a story to share of both personal and systemic discrimination. Or ask yourself how you would respond if your son or daughter brought home a date with a different skin color than yours. There may even be seeds of racism in our own hearts.

Racial divisions are hardly behind us, and it does no good to pretend they are. Racism is detestable. Racism is sin. And racism is a reality. Only by acknowledging it can we confront it.

Lie #3: Racism in the United States is happening everywhere all the time.

From conflicts with police to campus protests to violent riots, the media paints a picture of the entire country engulfed in racial strife. Of course, no one can deny the incidents of racial tension. However, is the portrayal of America as an overtly racist nation accurate? The facts suggest it isn't.

For example, in 1958, only 37 percent of Americans expressed willingness to vote for a black person for president. By 1999, that percentage had risen to 95 percent.[7] In 2008, American voters elected Barack Obama to the White House and reelected him for a second term four years later.

Even more significant, in 1958, only 4 percent of Americans approved of interracial marriage between blacks and whites. In 2013, 87 percent of Americans approved, representing "one of the largest shifts of public opinion in Gallup history."[8] William H. Frey, one of the nation's leading demographers, noted the significance of this shift: "Sociologists have viewed multiracial marriage as a benchmark for the ultimate stage of assimilation of a particular group into society."[9]

There are signs that racism in the United States isn't the ubiquitous problem it's made out to be. While racial tensions continue to flare up, and there is an ongoing need for constructive conversations on race relations, America has made significant progress over the past fifty years. In 1991, Harvard sociologist Orlando Patterson, an African American, declared in the pages of the *New York Times*, "America, while still flawed in its race relations ... is now the least racist white-majority society in the world" and "has a better record of legal protection of minorities than any other society."[10] Certainly not everyone would agree, but it's noteworthy that immigrants from other nations still flock to the United States—and prosper here.

While recognizing contemporary race-relation problems, we also ought to acknowledge cultural progress. Refusing to buy into a false narrative helps prevent Americans from descending into despair as we struggle to overcome racial strife.

Recapture the Wonder of God's Story

Christians must be vigilant not to absorb racialized views of the culture. To accomplish this, our perspectives on race relations must start and end with God's Word. What we discover there is the beautiful unfolding of God's Story, beginning with human oneness and ending with gospel oneness.

Addressing the unbelievers in Athens, Greece, the apostle Paul highlighted God's sovereign plan with the Story of humanity's origin: "[God] made from one man every nation of mankind to live on all the face of the earth, having determined allotted periods and the boundaries of their dwelling place.... 'For we are indeed his offspring'" (Acts 17:26, 28). According to Scripture, God started with the creation of one man, Adam, and from him descended "every nation of mankind." In God's Story, there is one human race. C. S. Lewis paid tribute to this biblical truth, addressing the Pevensie children as the "sons of Adam" and "daughters of Eve" in The Chronicles of Narnia. These dignified titles acknowledge our shared humanity as descendants of the original image bearers.

Our origin as God's image bearers overrides our ethnic origins. From it derives the inherent dignity of every ethnic group. God's Story begins not with the racial superiority of some and the inferiority of others but with the value and equality of all humanity. People of color—all colors!—are precious in His sight.

However, we not only share Adam's origin; we've also inherited his fallenness: "Sin came into the world through one man, and death through sin, and so death spread to all men because all sinned" (Rom. 5:12). As a result, humanity began to fracture, and the depth of our brokenness played out in the alienation, estrangement, and hostility of human relationships. From the beginning, the history of humanity's fallen state has been filled with ethnic divisions, animosity, and bloodshed. Every generation since Adam has needed racial reconciliation.

Where do followers of Christ find their model for such a tall order? In Luke's compelling two-volume work, Luke–Acts. Since first-century Palestine, the world has never seen a more powerful tool for overcoming ethnic barriers as the gospel of Jesus Christ. In the drama of Acts, we see the beautiful transformation of Jewish ethnic particularism into Jesus-centered ethnic universalism within a single generation. Through Christ, "Jews, Gentiles and Samaritans could become a part of God's people without losing their cultural identity."[11]

Remember, first-century Judaism necessitated a radical division between Jew and Gentile, as Yahweh first covenanted with Israel as His primary vehicle to reach the world. However, even within the Abrahamic covenant, we see the seeds of gospel universalism:

> Now the LORD said to Abram, "Go from your country and your kindred and your father's house to the land that I will show you. And I will make of you a great nation, and I will bless you and make your name great, so that you will be a blessing. I will bless those who bless you, and him who dishonors you I will curse, and in you *all the families of the earth shall be blessed*." (Gen. 12:1–3)

In this first covenant with Abraham, we see God's heart for all nations.

The rest of the Old Testament records Israel's failure to become the vehicle God promised to use to bless all the people groups of the world, necessitating the coming of Christ. Luke picked up this story in his gospel, recording the life, death, and resurrection of Jesus and His inauguration of a new kingdom.

Interestingly, Luke, more than any of the gospel writers, took special notice of the oft-despised Samaritans. The embittered relationship between Jews and Samaritans in the first century is clear. Jews saw their Samaritan neighbors as third-class citizens, lower in status than even the Gentiles. But in the book of Luke, Jesus shattered this Jewish paradigm (Luke 9:51–56; 10:26–37; 17:11–19), setting the stage for the radical movement of the gospel in Acts that advanced from "Jerusalem and in all Judea and Samaria, and to the end of the earth" (1:8).

As God's Story unfolds in Acts, the incredible power of the gospel transcends deep ethnic barriers. The gospel pushes beyond ethnic Israel with the explicit inclusion of the Gentiles (Acts 8–13), an unexpected development for the Jewish believers and leaders of the early church (Acts 10–11). Eventually the gospel breaks down Jewish, Samaritan, Roman, Greek, and Ethiopian barriers—and beyond. In Ephesians 2, Paul described how "the dividing wall of [ethnic] hostility" was broken down "by the blood of Christ," resulting in peace as we become "fellow citizens with the saints and members of the household of God" (vv. 13, 14, 19). Only the power of the gospel of Jesus Christ can create one "chosen race, a royal priesthood, a holy nation" (1 Pet. 2:9) from among all the ethnic divisions of this world.

Notice something very important. Luke and Paul didn't focus on creating diversity or sharing privilege and power. The early church didn't have a formal plan to build multiethnic churches. The only plan was to proclaim the gospel. And as people pledged their allegiance to Jesus, they subordinated ethnic and cultural loyalty to Christ and His mission.

The contemporary evangelical church finds itself in a very similar situation as the first-century church, where believers draw lines based on social, cultural, and ethnic differences. We have Caucasian, African American, Hispanic, and Asian congregations, dividing ourselves along humanly constructed lines. This ethnic and cultural particularism ultimately runs contrary to the ethnic and cultural transcendence of the gospel that tells us, "There is neither Jew nor Greek, there is neither slave nor free, there is no male and female, for you are all one in Christ Jesus" (Gal. 3:28). In Christ, we have the one tool that can ultimately overcome racial strife and tear down ethnic barriers. Imagine what a witness we would be to a racially divided world if the church recaptured that first-century, gospel-centered unity once again.

Action Steps

1. Develop deep friendships with those of other ethnicities, and listen carefully to them. Instead of viewing people of different ethnicities as projects to work on, cultivate friendships with them. Invite your Caucasian, black, Hispanic, or Asian neighbors over for dinner. Having people in your home and fellowshipping over food is an invitation to deeper friendship. Afterward, let your kids play together while the adults share conversation. Through mutual relationship, you'll develop a greater appreciation for differences and similarities. And you'll model grace and hospitality for your kids.

2. Examine your own views. Because our kids learn their views on other racial and ethnic groups from us,[12] we ought to first examine our own hearts. How does skin color or ethnicity shape our assumptions about others? Do we find our identity in the gospel of Jesus Christ? Have we cultivated a posture of forgiveness and reconciliation or of hostility and bitterness? Do we simply dismiss all concerns about racism without listening carefully to others?

Followers of Jesus don't have the option of tolerating racial or ethnic barriers. It's sin. We take cues from Scripture, not culture. And yet we don't downplay ethnicity. We can be thankful for our unique ethnic identities while recognizing that the gospel has deeper, broader aims.

3. Expose your kids to other cultures and celebrate God-given diversity. This could be as simple as pointing out for your kids the racial diversity in your family, neighborhood, and church. Take the family to an ethnic restaurant and chat with the owner or attend an ethnic church and talk with the pastor. Or you could take your family on a missions trip to another culture. Exposure to other cultures helps break down barriers and cultivate love and appreciation for those who don't share your ethnic background.

4. Don't let the culture control the conversation on race. The Scriptures must do that. Evaluate everything you hear from politicians, news commentators, and social activists regarding race relations in light of God's Story. Reject cultural values like self-segregation, hostility, resentment, bitterness, victimhood, and entitlement. Instead, go back to your Bible. It has the resources the world needs for racial reconciliation: proper diagnosis of the human condition, confession, forgiveness, redemption, unity, the power of the Holy Spirit, and more. So give God's Word precedence over the current cultural word. Then you'll be able to effectively direct your kids to Scripture as well.

5. Be "quick to hear" and "slow to speak" (James 1:19). Listen to other voices and perspectives on race. Ask about an individual's personal experience with racism and listen carefully. In addition, acknowledge there are different racial experiences. There may be black, Asian, Hispanic, or Caucasian experiences you don't share. You may not agree with other people's perspectives, but their inherent dignity as God's image bearers demands the hard work of listening and trying to understand.

6. Treat individuals as individuals. Fight racial stereotypes. All ethnicities are tempted to dismiss entire groups of people based on generalizations or personal experiences. Give individuals the benefit of the doubt and get to know them personally.

7. Avoid slogans and clichés. Here are some examples:

- We should be color-blind.
- Black lives matter.
- All lives matter.

These phrases are unhelpful not only because they are politicized and can be misunderstood but because they're often used to shut down debate and conversation. The goal for Christians isn't to be blind to color but to embrace the distinctive qualities and uniqueness of God's image bearers. Absolutely, black lives matter, but the slogan today is also the name of an organization with problematic beliefs about human sexuality and the family. And, yes, all lives matter—including preborn ones—but we ought not give the impression that we aren't carefully listening to the concerns of those specific fellow image bearers who believe their value is being dismissed.

8. Hold up heroes of the faith who were of different ethnicities or who championed the rights of others. Read the stories of Christian social reformers like Dietrich Bonhoeffer, William Wilberforce, Martin Luther King Jr., or Frederick Douglass to your kids. Read about missionaries like Amy Carmichael or Eric Liddell. Read stories from a recent Voice of the Martyrs newsletter.

Talk about Christian role models with your kids, especially those from different countries and cultures.

9. Share the gospel with all ethnicities. The only path to true racial reconciliation is redemption through Christ, but Christians must model this truth for the culture. As the world observes our lives, it should be asking, "Why is there racial harmony within Christian churches? Why are there no racial divisions among Christians?" Live your life as a missionary for the gospel of Jesus Christ, and let your kids see it.

10. Be on the lookout for other expressions of discrimination besides race. Race is the most obvious area of discrimination in our culture, but there are others. America has problems with classism (looking down on others of lower socioeconomic status), political division (especially after the 2016 election), and sexism (discrimination of men or women). We must address all discrimination. Start by taking one of the previous action steps and apply it to the other areas of discrimination you discover in your own life, family, church, or community.

Further Resources

- *Divided by Faith: Evangelical Religion and the Problem of Race in America* by Michael O. Emerson and Christian Smith (New York: Oxford University Press, 2001)

- "Letter from Birmingham Jail" by Martin Luther King Jr.—http://kingencyclopedia.stanford.edu/kingweb/popular_requests/frequentdocs/birmingham.pdf
- *United: Captured by God's Vision for Diversity* by Trillia J. Newbell (Chicago, IL: Moody, 2014)

Hopecasting

Is there hope for a racially divided world? Absolutely. It's the hope of the new heavens and new earth:

> [The living creatures and twenty-four elders] sang a new song, saying,
>
> "Worthy are you to take the scroll
> and to open its seals,
> for you were slain, and by your blood you
> ransomed people for God
> from every tribe and language and people
> and nation,
> and you have made them a kingdom and priests
> to our God,
> and they shall reign on the earth." (Rev. 5:9–10)

> I looked, and behold, a great multitude that no one could number, from every nation, from all tribes and peoples and languages, standing before the throne

> and before the Lamb, clothed in white robes, with palm branches in their hands, and crying out with a loud voice, "Salvation belongs to our God who sits on the throne, and to the Lamb!" (7:9–10)

In Revelation, we're given a glimpse of wrongs made right and lies undone. The beautiful vision of the multiethnic hereafter is a reversal of Babel, where language and ethnicity divided the human race. The bride of Christ, the church, which belongs to and is called to advance the already-not-yet kingdom of God, can bring the Bible's vision of reconciliation into the here and now.

No kind of "other-ism," including racism, can be defeated without the power of the gospel. Thus, the church should lead in exposing, confronting, and condemning any and all acts of discrimination and dehumanization. And we must show a better way.

Discussion Questions

1. When you were growing up, did your family interact with those of different races? How were they most commonly perceived or characterized in your home?

2. Is racism a problem in your community? In what ways? Ask someone of a different race these same questions. How does this person's answer compare to yours?

3. What cultural slogans about race are most unhelpful? Why?

Part Four

Christian Worldview Essentials

Chapter Sixteen

How to Read the Bible

It seems puzzling to me how greatly attached to the Bible you seem to be and yet how much like pagans you handle it. The great challenge to those of us who wish to take the Bible seriously is to let it teach us its own essential categories; and then for us to think with them, instead of just about them.

Abraham Joshua Heschel, speaking to a group of Christians

The Bible, like the uniqueness of Christ, sets Christianity apart from all other worldviews and religions. Christianity is a *revealed* worldview. In other words, Christianity's source of authority was established by God, who has revealed Himself in creation, in the Old and New Testaments, and ultimately in Jesus Christ.

The idea of Christian revelation affirms the following:

- God exists, contrary to atheistic or secular worldviews.
- God is personal, contrary to Eastern religions and New Age pantheism.
- God has spoken, contrary to postmodern skepticism.
- God has spoken by Jesus Christ, who is revealed in the Old and New Testaments, contrary to Judaism and Islam.

The Scriptures, then, are no incidental part of the Christian religion. They're essential if we're to know what God has revealed. No new discovery or cultural trend will preempt its authority. Most important, *we* aren't the authority for determining the contours of the Christian faith. The Scriptures are.

Although most Christians confess the Bible as the authoritative Word of God, they read it as if their private interpretations are more important than the Bible as it was given to us. Christians *mis*read the Bible in the following ways:

We don't really read it. We read books about the Bible. We read books about God and the Christian life. We read books that quote a single verse at the top of the page and offer three pages of devotional meditation. But many Christians read very little of the Bible itself. We'll never have a Christian worldview unless we're immersed in the Scriptures.

We read the Bible without recognizing context. "The practice of dividing the Bible in numbered chapters and verses … gives the impression that the Bible is a collection of thousands of self-contained sentences and phrases that can be picked out or combined arbitrarily," writes Eugene Peterson.[1] It's important to know that chapter and verse divisions were added to the Bible much later to help readers find particular sections. They were never intended to break up the Bible into smaller, more readable parts, nor is this helpful. When we approach the Bible this way, we very often miss the meaning both the human author and the divine Author intended. Consider the following examples:

> ***Verses.*** We may find a single verse, like Jeremiah 29:11, inspirational—"'For I know the plans I have for you,' declares the LORD, 'plans for welfare and not for evil, to give you a future and a hope.'" But that verse, like every verse in the Bible, has a context. Sometimes the context is the preceding or following verse. At other times, it's found in another book of the Bible (for example, the gospel writers often referred to Old Testament prophecies or narratives). Eugene Peterson likens taking a verse out of context because it means something to us to treating "Bible verses [as] fortune cookies."[2]

Stories. David and Goliath. Jonah and the big fish. Jesus feeding the five thousand. We often treat these as stand-alone stories that provide us with a "moral McNugget" to apply to our lives. But every story in the Bible is part of a larger story, which is ultimately part of the Story of redemption. Kids often get the impression that Bible stories are *Aesop's Fables*, or even worse, fairy tales—that is, interesting stories we can apply to our lives. Bible stories often have moral applications, but they offer so much more. The Scriptures are given to frame our lives, to tell us who we are in light of God's overarching purposes for the world He created.

Books. Even entire books of the Bible have a context within the larger Story of redemption. If a book is a letter, the context involves discovering who wrote it and to whom it was written. If a book is historical, then we should understand it for what it is. If a book was written to a particular group of people—for example, Leviticus—we must first understand its purpose in that context before we can correctly apply it to ours.

We read the Bible selectively. If we're in the habit of ignoring the context of Scripture, we'll tend to avoid those parts that don't have an obvious moralistic or therapeutic application to our lives. For example, we skip over much of the Old Testament because we don't want to do the hard work of understanding the historical context, and we fail to see its application to twenty-first-century life. Instead, we select the more straightforward and easier parts of Scripture to read. As a result, many Christians simply ignore much of the Bible. But God gave us all of Scripture. As Paul told Timothy, "All Scripture is breathed out by God and profitable for teaching, for reproof, for correction, and for training in righteousness, that the man of God may be complete, equipped for every good work" (2 Tim. 3:16–17). If we aren't learning from all of Scripture, we won't be fully equipped.

We fall for "magic" innovations. Many fall prey to "secret" truths or hidden meanings from popular teachers who claim the Bible promises things it simply doesn't. For example, some turn single verses, taken out of context, into mantras to woo God's private blessings. Others look for numerical codes behind the text that predict the future. This is theologically irresponsible and dangerous to the health of the church, especially if, in our search for hidden meanings, we neglect to understand the obvious, full counsel of God as it has been given to us in the Scriptures.

We overpersonalize texts. A popular childhood song said, "Every promise in the Book is mine," but that's not true. Promises to Israel or Abraham may not be applicable to us. The only way to know what applies to us and what doesn't is by understanding the Bible as it was given to us. Also, radically personalizing the text makes the Bible about us rather than about God. We tend to look for answers to our questions when, in reality, God often wants to reframe our questions by sweeping us into His Story for the world.

Tips for Reading the Bible on Its Own Terms

First, as you read the Bible, remember these things:

Remember to pray. God has given us the Holy Spirit to guide us and reveal His truth to us. As the third person of the Trinity, the Spirit's purposes are fully aligned with God the Father and God the Son. In prayer, we invite the Spirit to open our eyes to the truth God intends for us.

Remember the purpose of the Bible. The Bible is the Story of the world. It exists to frame all of reality for us, God's image bearers, who are redeemed in Christ to join His work in the world. Keep this is mind as you read and teach the Bible, especially to the next generation.

Remember the Story. Wherever we are in the biblical text, we should locate where it is in the overall Story the Bible tells, from the creation of the heavens and the earth to the new creation of the new heavens and the new earth.

Remember that the Story culminates in the person and work of Jesus the Christ. *The Jesus Storybook Bible*, by Sally Lloyd-Jones, does a marvelous job of showing children how the stories of Scripture point to Christ. Many Christian adults would learn a lot about the Bible by reading this children's book!

The apostle Paul offered an incredible description of Jesus in Colossians:

> [Jesus] is the image of the invisible God, the firstborn of all creation. For by him all things were created, in heaven and on earth, visible and invisible, whether thrones or dominions or rulers or authorities—all things were created through him and for him. And he is before all things, and in him all things hold together. And he is the head of the body, the church. He is the beginning, the firstborn from the dead, that in everything he might be preeminent. For in him all the fullness of God was pleased to dwell, and through him to reconcile to himself all things, whether on earth or in heaven, making peace by the blood of his cross. (1:15–20)

Second, as you read the Bible, do the following:

Ignore the chapter and verse divisions. Use these as tools to locate parts of the text, but read the Bible as if they aren't there. Find the transitions that are in the text itself, just as you would any other piece of literature.

Read the Bible as it was written. As we noted earlier, if you're reading a letter, read it like a letter. Ask, "Who wrote this and why? To whom was the author writing?" If it's a poem, read it as poetry. If it's a historical book, read it as history. Ask, "Who is this account about? When did it happen? What was the historical situation behind the book? How does it fit in the overall history of God's redemptive purposes?" Remember, if God inspired this book of books, He not only intended *what* was written; He also intended *how* it was written.

Third, as you read the Bible, avoid the following:

Avoid forced moral and therapeutic applications not explicitly stated in the text. Remember, the Bible is inviting you into God's Story. Where a moral or therapeutic point is being made by the text, hear it and take it seriously. However, do not superimpose an application when it is not there.

Avoid reading any study notes or commentaries until you've actually read the text itself. God has raised up teachers and preachers to help us, and we should hear what those leaders have to say. When reading, however, let the text speak to you before turning to the notes and observations of others.

Avoid reading small bits of Scripture. For bite-size daily readings, read the Psalms and Proverbs or books that can be read in one sitting. Budget longer periods of time each week to read larger portions of Scripture.

Avoid turning Bible characters into superheroes. The only superhero in the Bible is Jesus Christ. While many Bible characters do heroic things, they were always presented as fallen, finite human beings because they were, just as we are. So be careful not to overemphasize the actions of individuals at the expense of making Christ central. The stories of each individual Bible character must be understood in light of the larger Story of Scripture.

One final thought as you read the Bible:

Read in community, with others, as much as or more than you read by yourself. The Bible is given to His people, not to individuals. Both the Old and New Testament books were given to communities and were intended to be read aloud. Personal reading is important, but don't neglect reading the Bible with others.

There is no substitute for reading the Bible, so get started! There are many helpful Bible resources available, but this list includes those Brett and I have found particularly helpful.

For Reading the Bible with Young Children

- *The Big Picture Story Bible* by David R. Helm (Wheaton, IL: Crossway Books, 2004). This children's Bible marvelously tells the biblical Story as one story from the creation to the new creation.
- *The Jesus Storybook Bible: Every Story Whispers His Name* by Sally Lloyd-Jones (Grand Rapids: ZonderKidz, 2007). This children's book tells many of the stories of Scripture, describing how they ultimately point to Jesus Christ.

- *Psalms for Young Children* by Marie-Hélène Delval (Grand Rapids: Eerdmans, 2008). This is a children's version of the Psalms, wonderfully illustrated and written so a child can read and understand each psalm.

For Reading the Bible as It Was Written

- *The Books of the Bible* by Biblica (www.biblica.com/bible/resources/the-books-of-the-bible/). In this publication, the original text of the Bible has been compiled to eliminate the distractions of what's been added to the text and to present the Bible in the way it was originally written, with natural section breaks and a single-column format. Editions include the complete text as well as multivolume texts that reflect the sections of the Old and New Testaments.

For Studying the Bible

- BibleMesh.com. An innovative and interactive online Bible-study course that guides readers through the text and the context of Scripture.
- *Eat This Book: A Conversation in the Art of Spiritual Reading* by Eugene H. Peterson (Grand Rapids: Eerdmans, 2009). A challenge and a guide to reading the Scripture in light of its ultimate purpose for our lives.

- *How to Read the Bible for All Its Worth* by Gordon D. Fee and Douglas Stuart (Grand Rapids: Zondervan, 2003). A classic guide for reading and studying the Scriptures in context.
- *Saving the Bible from Ourselves: Learning to Read and Live the Bible Well* by Glenn R. Paauw (Downers Grove, IL: InterVarsity, 2016). A masterful description of how we misread the Bible, how our attempts to "help" the Bible have hurt, and how to read the Bible on its own terms.

Discussion Questions

1. How were you taught to read the Bible?

2. Which of the wrong Bible reading methods have you been guilty of? Which have you seen others employ?

3. What is your Bible-reading plan? Do you have one?

Chapter Seventeen

Why to Trust the Bible

Always it is stressed that the claim of the word of God upon us is absolute: the word is to be received, trusted and obeyed, because it is the word of God the King.

J. I. Packer, *Knowing God*

Christian parents and leaders have a dilemma. We tell kids that the Bible reveals God's Story, the true Story of reality. However, they hear countless others online, in media, and in school questioning the Bible's authority and relevance. This is a serious matter.

Challenges that undermine the authority of God's Word cannot go unanswered. And we cannot merely assert that the Bible is *the* authoritative book from God and hope kids will simply take our word on the matter. Young people must understand the nature of biblical authority. They must have good reasons to trust the Bible as God's Word.

Clarification

First, we must clarify: the key to understanding how the authority of God is exercised through Scripture is knowing what sort of thing the Bible is. The Bible isn't merely a list of rules or a compilation of doctrines, even though it contains both. We've described the Bible as a story (the Story), but we have to be careful what we communicate when we use story language. "Once upon a time" doesn't demand respect and obedience. "In the beginning" might, but we need to say more.

Ultimately, the authority of the Bible rests in the God whose Word it is. That's why words like *inspiration*, *infallibility*, and *inerrancy* have long been important parts of this conversation for Christians. Those words help us get at the nature of the book itself. If the Bible is just another man-made religious text like the Qur'an or the Book of Mormon, then it doesn't hold any authority over us.

John and I are convinced that the Bible is different from all other sacred religious texts and is the authoritative source of truth for all humanity because it is the inspired Word of God. The God of the universe speaks to us through the Christian Bible—not the Qur'an, not the Bhagavad Gita, not the Mormon scriptures, or any other religious text. God spoke His Word through human authors, using their own individual personalities, to write and compose His unique revelation to humankind in the sixty-six books of the Bible. Thus, the inspired Word of God holds authority over you, me, and our kids.

An Argument for the Authority of the Bible

Let's walk through a three-step argument for the authority of the Bible. First, let's take the claim that the Bible is divine revelation from God. Certainly, all worldviews cannot generate such a claim. For instance, claims of divine revelation don't fit in an atheistic worldview, which holds that there are no divine beings. A theistic worldview is necessary. This seems obvious enough, but the observation surfaces an important step in our argument. If there are things we would come to expect in a theistic worldview, additional evidence for theism will strengthen our overall case. Therefore, before we argue that the Bible is the authoritative Word of God, our first step is to look to natural theology (also called *general revelation*) to provide good reasons for thinking that God exists in the first place. In addition, through the arguments for God's existence, we can also gain insights into His nature and character.

Step 1: God's Existence

Over the past thirty years, the significant contributions of Christian philosophers and scientists have strengthened the arguments for God's existence.[1] We'll briefly highlight three particular arguments that not only offer powerful evidence that God exists but also provide clues to His identity.

The *cosmological argument* points to the beginning of the universe as evidence for a First Cause or Great Beginner. In the words of Maria from *The Sound of Music*, "Nothing comes from nothing. Nothing ever could."[2] Even the dominant view of origins in secular science claims the universe had a beginning. Whoever began the universe must be all-powerful because He was able to create the universe *ex nihilo* (out of nothing). He must possess exceedingly great intelligence, knowing all the laws of physics and chemistry in order to arrange all the constituent parts of the universe. Lastly, the Beginner must be timeless and immaterial if He existed prior to the creation of time and matter. Already, the Beginner sounds like God.

The *fine-tuning argument* points to more information about this Beginner. The universe is incredibly fine tuned. This simply means there are certain conditions in the universe that had to be "just right" to produce life. For example, the gravitational force and expansion rate of the universe had to be constant, and a life-sustaining solar system could have only one star. Scientists tell us there are a multitude of "just right" cosmological constants in the universe that make life on planet Earth possible. If these constants didn't lie within a very narrow range, the universe would be uninhabitable. No fine tuning *of* the universe means no life existing *in* the universe. Therefore, not only does a finely tuned universe point to the existence of a Fine Tuner, but it also suggests that the Fine Tuner has some care and concern for the inhabitants of the universe.

The *moral argument* points to the character and social nature of this Being, the One who began and finely tuned the universe, as the best explanation for the existence of moral values. Love and kindness are virtues because they're grounded in God's loving and kind character. In addition, moral obligations make sense only in the context of a relationship between two persons. The mindless processes of evolution cannot create moral obligations. We have no obligations to inanimate matter. However, we do have obligations to a person, a moral Law Giver, who created and rules over the world.

These three arguments not only give us powerful evidence that God must exist, but they tell us He is a transcendent, intelligent, powerful, personal, and moral being. The universe points us to Him. As the apostle Paul said in Romans 1:20: "[God's] invisible attributes, namely, his eternal power and divine nature, have been clearly perceived, ever since the creation of the world, in the things that have been made." When we give our kids independent arguments for God's existence (notice we didn't offer "The Bible tells me so" reasoning), we strengthen their faith that God is actually real. And we create a solid foundation to build divine revelation upon.

Step 2: Expectations of Divine Revelation

The payoff of starting with the arguments for God's existence in step 1 is the confidence it gives us that we inhabit a theistic universe. And if we have good reasons to think that God is not only real but also powerful, intelligent, moral, and personal, these beliefs will generate other rational expectations. In particular, given the existence of God and what He is like, we can reasonably expect that He would reveal more about Himself to His creatures. It would be quite strange that a personal God who seems interested in our well-being would simply spin the universe into existence and then leave us alone. Instead, it's much more plausible to think He would provide some kind of additional information about who He is and what His purposes are. We would expect Him to shed some light on humanity's big questions.

Furthermore, human beings find themselves in a predicament. The evidence points to a hospitable world that has also been severely corrupted. Pain, suffering, natural disasters, and other sorts of evils and catastrophes make it clear that something has gone terribly wrong. Indeed, the corruption isn't just "out there" in the world; we also discover it "in here," in our very own human hearts. The human condition seems to indicate that we're in some serious trouble, and we need help.

Given the nature of God as an intelligent, personal, and moral being, it also seems very likely He would be concerned about the predicament of His creatures in a corrupted world. Interestingly, every major world religion acknowledges there is a problem and offers an assessment of the human condition as well as a proposal to remedy the situation. If God really has provided a cure for what ails humanity, we would certainly need further guidance to understand our circumstances properly and determine the appropriate actions to take. Therefore, we have an additional reason to expect divine revelation. We might anticipate that a caring creator who knows our trouble may come to our rescue. Thus, God's good character and the world's corruption generate an expectation of additional divine revelation. These proper expectations give us good reason to examine specific claims of divine revelation, to test them, and to assess their authenticity.

Step 3: The Bible Is God's Divine Revelation

There are a number of ways we could test the trustworthiness of the Bible, but we'll highlight three tests in this chapter:

1. Transmission: Is what we have today what was originally written?
2. Historicity: Is what was written what really happened?
3. Inspiration: Is what was written really from God Himself?

First, when we examine how the Bible has been transmitted (or passed along) through the ages, we discover that no other ancient document comes close to the accurate transmission of the biblical text. The thousands upon thousands of manuscript copies we possess of the Old and New Testaments verify this.[3] Therefore, we can conclude that what Matthew, Mark, Luke, John, Paul, Peter, and the rest of the biblical authors originally wrote is what we're actually reading today.

Second, when we look at the historical details, we have good reason to conclude that what was written in the pages of the Bible is accurate and reliable history. For example, archaeological discoveries like the Dead Sea Scrolls or the Caiaphas ossuary are just a couple of examples among thousands of extrabiblical artifacts that support the historicity of the Bible.[4] Therefore, we conclude that the Bible is a reliable historical source containing facts about the history of Israel and the life, death, and resurrection of Jesus of Nazareth.

Third, when we look at the nature of the Bible, we discover divine fingerprints all over it. For instance, what best explains how a collection of books written by approximately forty different authors on three different continents over a period of more than fifteen hundred years can record one unified, coherent story and message? A divine author working through human authors. Or what explains dozens and dozens of fulfilled biblical prophecies about the person and work of Jesus Christ? A divine mind who knows the future. This kind of evidence *and* the transforming power of this book in countless lives over the past two millennia provide compelling evidence that the Bible is no ordinary book but the inspired Word of God.

And because it's inspired by God, it is also inerrant:

> Inerrancy means that when all facts are known, the Scriptures in their original autographs and properly interpreted will be shown to be wholly true in everything that they affirm, whether that has to do with doctrine or morality or with social, physical, or life sciences.[5]

Inerrancy is important because it draws our attention to the primary issue, the nature of the biblical text itself. John and I believe that the "original autographs" of the Old and New Testaments are without error because they are God's Word. Here is a simple, straightforward argument for the inerrancy of Scripture:

1. The Bible is God's Word.
2. God cannot err.
3. Therefore, God's Word cannot err.

If claims 1 and 2 are true, then the conclusion set out in claim 3 necessarily follows. In addition, our earlier arguments from natural theology greatly strengthen the plausibility of this argument by providing an a priori (formed beforehand) belief in inerrancy. From God's character, we infer the character of Scripture. As the Word of God, the Bible is as trustworthy and authoritative as the God who spoke through it.

In Summary

Beginning with natural theology, we have good grounds for believing God exists. In addition, we have rational expectations for divine revelation because of who God is and the predicament we find ourselves in. Finally, the evidence demonstrates that God has indeed spoken and revealed Himself most fully in the Bible.

Because God is the highest authority, the Bible is authoritative. Because He is true and good, so is the Bible. Therefore, we have proper confidence in the Bible as the authoritative Word of God. Because of this, the Bible is also our ultimate source of knowledge on which to base our most important beliefs about the world and from which to test all other knowledge claims. This is vital because the Bible tells the Story of the world and puts incredible demands on human beings, which none of the world's other major religions can rival.

Don't fear diving into the case for the reliability and trustworthiness of the Bible. There's no other book like it in the world.

Further Resources

- *Cold-Case Christianity: A Homicide Detective Investigates the Claims of the Gospels* by J. Warner Wallace (Colorado Springs: David C Cook, 2013)
- *How We Got the Bible*, rev. ed., by Neil R. Lightfoot (Grand Rapids: Baker, 2010)
- *Questioning the Bible: 11 Major Challenges to the Bible's Authority* by Jonathan Morrow (Chicago: Moody, 2014)
- Stand to Reason—www.str.org

Discussion Questions

1. How is the Bible different from other books?

2. Based on the content of this chapter, summarize the reasons why we can trust the Bible.

3. If the Bible is indeed authoritative, what are the implications for your life?

Chapter Eighteen

The Right Kind of Pluralism

We believe that all religions are basically the same.... They only differ on matters of creation, sin, heaven, hell, God, and salvation.

Steve Turner, "Creed"

Today you can proclaim your worldview with a bumper sticker.

Often, it's on the back of a 1980s Volvo or a 1990s Subaru. With various religious symbols arranged like letters, it tells us to "COEXIST." Of course, there's no further information as to how we might go about this. Instead, in our post-Christian, multicultural context, we're expected to know the culprit preventing the sort of peaceful world the bumper sticker calls for: exclusivist religions.

Even within the church, many are uncomfortable asserting that other religions are wrong. When asked whether they affirm that there is only one true religion, only 46 percent of conservative Protestant teenagers and 26 percent of mainline Protestant teenagers did.[1] Adults are in the same boat. Only 36 percent of evangelical Protestants affirmed the statement "My religion is the one, true faith leading to eternal life," and a mere 12 percent of mainline Protestants did. Instead, 57 percent of evangelical Protestants and 83 percent of mainline Protestants agreed that "many religions can lead to eternal life."[2]

So is Christianity exclusively true, or is it just one religious option among many? Are Christians pluralists? Should they be?

It depends on what *pluralism* means. "We live in a pluralist society" is a true statement if the word is being used in a *descriptive* sense. To meet a Hindu or a Muslim these days, one only needs to go across the street, not across the ocean. In this sense, Christians can and should be pluralists, aware that we live in a religiously diverse culture and ready to make a case for the Christian worldview while recognizing the inherent dignity of all people.

Unfortunately, pluralism is more commonly used today in a *prescriptive* sense. "We live in a pluralist society" often means that because we live in a religiously diverse culture, no religion can claim to be true over and above another. To do so, we're told, is the height of intolerance.

What the Culture Teaches about Religion and Truth

1. All religions are equally true and legitimate paths to God.

All religions—Christianity, Judaism, Islam, Hinduism, and Buddhism—lead to the same place. They just take different paths to get there. This is our culture's pluralistic vision.

Simple logic refutes this view. One of the fundamental laws of logic, the law of noncontradiction, says that opposite ideas cannot both be true at the same time and in the same way. The particular claims of different religions are contradictory. For example, Islam teaches that God is a unitarian being, while Christianity teaches that God is Trinitarian. Hinduism and Buddhism say we are reincarnated after death, while Islam and Christianity teach that heaven or hell is our final destination. To say these views are all true at the same time is as wrongheaded as affirming two plus two equals four *and* five. The answers are mutually exclusive. It's possible they are both false, but it's not possible that both are true.

Furthermore, there is a presumption within pluralism that undermines its own claims. Exclusivism affirms the possibility that one religion is objectively true; therefore, contradictory religious claims are false. Pluralism says we must reject exclusivist truth claims about religion and instead embrace all religious views as equally true. Do you see the problem? In an attempt to repudiate exclusivism, pluralism turns out to be exclusivist too—by excluding exclusivism.

2. Religion is a matter of preference, not objective truth.

Personal preferences are subjective. They are grounded in the likes and dislikes of an individual (a subject). For instance, you might like chocolate ice cream, while I like vanilla, but neither of us would claim we have the one true flavor. What you prefer may not be what I prefer, and vice versa. Many people think about religious claims the way they think about ice cream. Christians have their truth, Muslims have their truth, and so on.

However, this misconstrues the nature of religious claims, which are grounded not in individual preferences but in the nature of reality. Religions make objective claims about the nature of God, humanity, salvation, the afterlife, and more. When Christians or Muslims say, "God exists," they make an objective claim about the existence of God, and its truth value is independent from what they think or say. Objective claims aren't true because someone believes them. They're either true or false whether anyone believes them or not. Each religion has its stock of beliefs about reality. Each has its take on the true Story of the world. Each is either objectively right or objectively wrong.

3. If you were born in Saudi Arabia, you would be a Muslim, not a Christian. Religious views are merely the result of sociological conditioning.

While it's true that people are more likely to identify with the dominant religion of their country or culture, that tells us nothing about the truth or falsity of the worldview in question. Again, religions make objective claims about reality that are either true or false, regardless of whether people believe them. The sociology of religious belief, which is what this myth explores, speaks only to the *development* of religious belief. It doesn't address whether the religious claims in question are true or false. To dismiss religion as merely the product of culture commits the genetic fallacy.[3]

4. If you think your religion is the one true religion, you are intolerant.

If you have the audacity to think Christianity is true and other religions are false, you're considered intolerant. Or a bigot. Or narrow minded.

This is nothing more than name calling. In logical terms, this is known as an *ad hominem fallacy*, where the person is attacked rather than the argument. What we think about people personally is entirely irrelevant when it comes to the truth or falsity of their claims. Perhaps they're the biggest jerks in the world, but their religious views may still be true.

If someone calls you intolerant for making a religious-truth claim, simply respond with a nondefensive question: "What do you mean by that?"

In contemporary culture, to be intolerant means you think you're right and other people are wrong. However, such a view is self-contradictory. If someone thinks we're wrong to claim that Christianity is true, then they think they are *right* and we are *wrong*. But according to their definition, they would be intolerant too!

Classical tolerance actually entails disagreement about important matters, but we "tolerate" those who hold differing opinions, treating one another with respect even while disagreeing.

The Christian Vision of Religions and Truth

The Christian Story starts out not with "once upon a time" but "in the beginning, God." The God of the Bible is real and true, and He spoke everything into existence (Ps. 33:6). After the fall of humanity, God covenanted with Abraham to redeem and restore humankind by building a great nation, Israel, and blessing all the families of the earth through His chosen people (Gen. 12). The first and greatest commandment given to the Jews was to worship the one true God (Exod. 20:3–6; Deut. 6:1–5). Whenever they were unfaithful to Him, He sent His prophets to remind Israel, "Thus says the LORD, the King of Israel and his Redeemer, the LORD of hosts: 'I am the first and I am the last; besides me there is no god'" (Isa. 44:6).

Time and time again, Israel's leaders abandoned Yahweh, the only true God, ultimately dividing the nation and ushering it into ruin. Through Israel, God demonstrated the inadequacy of fallen humankind to save ourselves, but He never forgot His covenant to Abraham. Instead, God Himself did for us what we couldn't do for ourselves: Jesus, the second person of the triune Godhead, "emptied himself, by taking the form of a servant, being born in the likeness of men. And being found in human form, he humbled himself by becoming obedient to the point of death, even death on a cross" (Phil. 2:7–8). "[Jesus] himself bore our sins in his body on the tree, that we might die to sin and live to righteousness. By his wounds you have been healed" (1 Pet. 2:24).

In other words, the entire Christian Story takes place in the real world. It is objective history, not a matter of preference. Christian claims are either true or false.

Within this historically verifiable Story, Jesus boldly declared, "I am the way, and the truth, and the life. No one comes to the Father except through me" (John 14:6). His closest followers, from the very beginning, repeated His exclusivist message: "There is salvation in no one else, for there is no other name under heaven given among men by which we must be saved" (Acts 4:12).

We can understand why Jesus is the sole path to God only when we locate His person and work within the entirety of God's Story. Why is Jesus the exclusive means of salvation? Because of the fall. Because of sin. Sin separated us from our holy God, and divine justice required punishment. Jesus is the only way because He is the only one who solved the problem of sin. No other religious leader did, or could do, what Jesus, the sinless lamb of God, did. He paid the penalty for sin and satisfied God's justice. That is why Jesus could say, "Unless you believe that I am he you will die in your sins" (John 8:24).

Rather than reject God's exclusive plan, we should be grateful in the way a diseased patient rejoices when a cure is found. The redemption and restoration we have through the exclusive means of Jesus' death and resurrection are cause for celebration. That's why it's called the gospel—it's good news.

Helping Kids Navigate the New Kind of Pluralism

1. Teach your kids that Christianity is objectively true. Emphasize truth first and then experience. God isn't real simply because we feel Him. He is real even if we don't feel Him. When Israel strayed in its affections for Him, God didn't stop being God. He continued to be the sovereign Lord of all, whether Israel believed it or not. For our kids, we need to primarily frame the Christian faith in terms of its truthfulness. As J. Warner Wallace says, "I'm not a Christian because it 'works' for me.... I'm a Christian because it is true. I'm a Christian because I want to live in a way that reflects the truth. I'm a Christian because my high regard for the truth leaves me no alternative."[4]

2. Teach your kids *why* Christianity is objectively true. It's not enough to teach our kids the "what"; we must also teach them the "why." Thus, apologetics—defending the Christian faith and providing reasons and evidence for its truthfulness—is an essential part of our kids' discipleship (1 Pet. 3:15). We must go beyond "The Bible tells me so" answers and equip them with the rational arguments and historical evidence for God, Jesus, and Scripture. By the time they're in middle school and throughout their high school years, we should be providing them with a regular dose of apologetics. Here are four essential questions our kids must be able to answer before they graduate from our homes:

1. Does truth exist, and can we know it?
2. Does God exist, and what's the evidence?
3. Did Jesus rise from the dead, and what's the evidence?
4. Is the Bible trustworthy, and what's the evidence?

Thankfully, there are a multitude of Christian apologetics and worldview books, websites, and curriculum resources available to help answer these questions. Start with Stand to Reason at www.str.org and the Colson Center for Christian Worldview at www.colsoncenter.org.

3. Teach your kids other religious views. Isolating our kids from false ideas isn't a good strategy. Inoculating them is. Unless we lock them in the basement for the duration of their lives, our kids *will* be exposed to the false ideas of other worldviews. They'll have Muslim classmates, Buddhist bosses, atheist professors, and Mormon neighbors. To be effective ambassadors for Christ in this pluralistic world, our kids need to be equipped to examine and challenge those worldviews.

The most effective way John and I have found to teach alternative religions and worldviews is to get the teaching out of the classroom and into real life. Here are some practical ideas:

- Visit www.mormon.org/missionaries and schedule Mormon missionaries to visit your home or youth group. Beforehand, visit www.mrm.org

(Mormon Research Ministry) and do some homework *with* your kids. Meet the missionaries with them present, and dialogue about the mutually exclusive claims of Mormonism and Christianity. Debrief your kids afterward.

- Visit a local religious site with your kids, like a mosque or temple, and dialogue with a representative. Be friendly and ask lots of questions about what this person believes and why he or she believes it. Debrief your kids afterward.
- Invite a non-Christian neighbor over for dinner and ask this person to share with your family his or her answers to the five big worldview questions in chapter 4 (origin, identity, meaning, morality, and destiny). Ask questions. Debrief your kids afterward.

4. Teach your kids how to question well. Christians aren't the only ones who need to give reasons for what they believe. Every worldview should be able to provide justification for its claims. Teach your kids to ask two questions over and over again: (1) What do you mean by that? and (2) How do you know that's true? They can ask these questions of anyone they encounter. In our experience, John and I have discovered that most people don't know what they believe about spiritual matters or why they believe it. When kids discover that *and* are equipped with apologetics themselves, they'll grow in their own confidence to engage a pluralistic world.

5. Model truth and grace in every conversation. Remember, our goal in conversations with non-Christians is not to win an argument but to win the person. If you aren't kind and gracious, you'll be dismissed as an arrogant jerk. But if you don't have some knowledge of the truth either, you'll be dismissed as ignorant and uneducated. Like Jesus, bring truth and grace together (John 1:14). We must treat people with dignity and respect because they're made in God's image, and yet we must never compromise the exclusive message of the gospel.

6. Prepare your kids for pushback. Proclaiming Jesus as the exclusive path to God won't win any popularity contests these days, so kids must develop biblical expectations regarding the world's response to the gospel. The world is going to take offense. Peter identified Jesus as "a stone of stumbling, and a rock of offense" (1 Pet. 2:8). Think about how the apostles were treated when they proclaimed Jesus in first-century Palestine. They were arrested, brought before the authorities, ordered to stop preaching the good news, and then beaten before they were released. Their response? "They left the presence of the council, rejoicing that they were counted worthy to suffer dishonor for the name. And every day, in the temple and from house to house, they did not cease teaching and preaching that the Christ is Jesus" (Acts 5:41–42). This should be our response as well.

The Right Kind of Pluralist

Shane was thrilled. He and his girlfriend, Francesca, had just finished hours of conversation with their skeptical friends at a local restaurant. They kicked off the conversation by presenting philosophical arguments for God, eventually convincing their skeptical friends to acknowledge that God must exist.

Next, they moved into a conversation about Christianity while their friends raised objections to Christian exclusivism with the all-religions-are-basically-the-same argument. Shane and Francesca discussed the clear differences among various religious views, arguing that the varying claims about God, salvation, and the afterlife are mutually exclusive. Then they offered some of the evidence for the truthfulness of Christianity. Eventually the conversation came to an end, but only after they had covered a tremendous amount of ground about God and religion.

Who exactly are Shane and Francesca? High school students I (Brett) met while speaking at a summer camp in Missouri. In a message sent to me the week after camp, Shane divulged all the details about their conversation. Often John and I cringe when Christian students talk with skeptical friends about Christianity. Sometimes the conversation ends with the Christian kids doubting what they believe. By the time we learn what happened to them, they're pleading with us to help them pick up the pieces of a fractured faith.

Not this time.

After the encounter, Shane said he felt confident *during* the conversation, even in the face of his friends' serious objections. He shared that his faith in Christ felt "a lot stronger" *after* the conversation too. Francesca said the conversation made her "think even harder" about her Christianity, but she also expressed a newfound confidence in Christ.

What's the difference between Shane and Francesca and the typical Christian student whose faith gets challenged? Training *before* the encounter. After spending five days learning worldview and apologetics at summer camp, Shane and Francesca were equipped to engage. Instead of helping them pick up the pieces in the aftermath of a skeptical challenge, we built a solid foundation of faith before the encounter.

Francesca told me, "Before camp, my heart was won over by the amazing experiences I had at church, but Christianity never made sense in my mind. All of the messages at camp helped me to understand that Christianity is also true rationally, bringing my head and heart together. Thank you!"

When we equip our youth with the truth of Christ, they develop courage and confidence for every encounter. And when you help them build that foundation in a pluralistic world, they'll thank you too.

Further Resources

- *I Don't Have Enough Faith to Be an Atheist* by Norman L. Geisler and Frank Turek (Wheaton, IL: Crossway Books, 2004)

- *Seeking Allah, Finding Jesus: A Devout Muslim Encounters Christianity* by Nabeel Qureshi (Grand Rapids: Zondervan, 2014)
- Impact 360 Institute's Gap Year and Student Conferences—www.impact360institute.org
- Summit Ministries Student Conferences—www.summit.org

Discussion Questions

1. Describe an interaction you've had with someone who holds a different worldview. Was it productive or frustrating? How?

2. How does our culture currently define *truth*? What is a better definition?

3. How would you respond to someone who says, "It's intolerant to believe any religion is better than another."

Chapter Nineteen

Taking the Gospel to the Culture

The Gospel is like a caged lion. It does not need to be defended; it simply needs to be let out of its cage.

Unknown

Throughout this book Brett and I have been talking mostly about defense. Indeed, the goal of this book, as the subtitle says, is to help students successfully navigate the culture without drowning in it. Surviving the cultural moment isn't the totality of what we're called to do. We're also called to be faithful ambassadors to the culture.

In Jeremiah 28, God told Jeremiah to oppose the false prophet Hananiah, who was misleading the people of Israel regarding their time of exile in Babylon. In a very public display, Hananiah proclaimed that within two years, God would defeat the Babylonians and bring His people back to Jerusalem. He was wrong.

God wanted His people to live fully in the midst of their exile rather than hunker down and wait for rescue. Through Jeremiah, God instructed His people,

> Build houses and live in them; plant gardens and eat their produce. Take wives and have sons and daughters; take wives for your sons, and give your daughters in marriage, that they may bear sons and daughters; multiply there, and do not decrease. But seek the welfare of the city where I have sent you into exile, and pray to the LORD on its behalf, for in its welfare you will find your welfare. (Jer. 29:5–7)

Like the people of Israel, Christians today can mistakenly place our hope in a short-term fix—like an election or predicting the rapture—especially when the culture around us seems out of control. But any hope placed in a change of circumstance isn't biblical hope. Biblical hope rests squarely on the fact that the biblical Story of the world, from creation to new creation, is our true Story, secured by the resurrection of Jesus Christ.

Like the exiles, we must learn to live well in this cultural moment. The following four questions are shaped by the Story and can help us confront the challenges of the culture around us.[1]

Question 1: What good can we celebrate, protect, promote, and preserve? Because God created His world good, there is beauty even in the darkest times. Even when lies dominate, truth still exists.

Christians should *celebrate* those aspects of culture that reflect God's character and nature. Technology can be used for good. True stories can be told. Beautiful art can be made and celebrated.

In fact, non-Christians often produce cultural goods worthy of praise. We need not shy away from this truth as long as we exercise appropriate caution. After all, "every good gift and every perfect gift is from above, coming down from the Father of lights" (James 1:17). Theologians call this *common grace*. God still blesses His world—often using His fallen image bearers—with goodness, truth, and beauty.

Question 2: What is missing that we can contribute? Christians should *create* culture.[2] As Jeremiah told the Israelites, building houses, having babies, growing crops, and marrying bring good even to a pagan society. In Israel's time of exile, Daniel offered wisdom and understanding to the government. In just the past few decades, abject poverty around the world has been dramatically reduced, often because Christians have been among those providing access to resources for wealth creation. A new generation of Christian storytellers, like S. D. Smith, the author of *The Green Ember*, are bringing children the kinds of good stories that shape the imagination.

Question 3: What evil can we stop? Christians must at times *confront* culture. God hates evil. As His people, we can do no less. If we love Him, we'll be—like Paul in Athens—distressed when idols are offered His adulation, and lust or violence violate His image. Throughout history, from the British abolitionists to modern-day pro-lifers, Christians have honored God by opposing evil.

But I'm no William Wilberforce, many think. *What influence do I have? I don't have the platform or abilities that famous Christian activists do.* Perhaps, but we do have the power to stop porn from infiltrating our smartphones. We can vote and voice alarm over the slaughter of the innocent. We can confront the racism in our own hearts. Whatever evil we can stop, we should.

Question 4: What brokenness can we restore? Many aspects of our culture are redeemable. Whenever possible, Christians should co-opt and correct culture, redirecting it to its God-given potential. Broken relationships can be reconciled. Family members affected by crime and incarceration can be restored to one another and their communities. Fashion can be reimagined so that the dignity inherent in each human being is respected.

In these four questions we see five legitimate ways Christians can deal with the ideas, institutions, trends, fashions, and habits of our culture: *celebrate, create, confront, co-opt, or correct.* Beautiful art, brilliant ideas, and compelling stories should be celebrated. New policy solutions and clever inventions should be created to solve contemporary problems. Lies, slander, and false religions should be confronted. New technologies can be co-opted for kingdom use. False information and misperceptions about others should be corrected and replaced with truth.

Discerning which approach is appropriate for specific situations isn't always easy, but Christians ought never be passive consumers of culture. Instead, we need to sharpen one another in the body of Christ so we can make wise decisions.

Aim for the Middle

Some Christians mistakenly think that change will come only when we acquire the levers of cultural power. God has called some to high places, but He's called all of us to be faithful right where we are, in our own spheres of influence.

We all have, as theologian T. M. Moore describes it, "a personal mission field."[3] There is culture to be celebrated, created, confronted, co-opted, and corrected all around us as we relate to the people in our families, neighborhoods, communities, churches, and social circles. As Brett and I said in chapter 3, we're called to these places for the sake of these people.

As kids mature and begin thinking about their future, we need to help them see they're on mission precisely where they're placed. God gifts them with abilities, experiences, and relationships and has placed them in the world as His ambassadors. It is at this intersection, suggests Frederick Buechner, that they find their calling:

> There are all different kinds of voices calling you to all different kinds of work, and the problem is to find out which is the voice of God.... By and large a good rule for finding out is this. The kind of work God usually calls you to is the kind of work (a) *that you need most to do* and (b) *that the world most needs to have done.*
>
> If you really get a kick out of your work, you've presumably met requirement (a), but if

> your work is writing TV deodorant commercials, the chances are you've missed requirement (b). On the other hand, if your work is being a doctor in a leper colony, you have probably met requirement (b), but if most of the time you're bored or depressed by it, the chances are you have not only bypassed (a), but probably aren't helping your patients much either....
>
> *The place God calls you to is the place where your deep gladness and the world's deep hunger meet.*[4] (emphasis added)

Amen.

Discussion Questions

1. What good in your sphere of influence can you celebrate, protect, promote, and preserve?

2. What is missing in your sphere of influence that you can contribute?

3. What is evil in your sphere of influence that must stop?

4. What is broken in your sphere of influence that you can help restore?

Notes

Chapter 1

1. Attributed to C. S. Lewis in Brian Godawa, "Postmodern Movies: The Good, the Bad, and the Relative, Part 1," *Spiritual Counterfeits Project Newsletter* 23, no. 3 (Spring 1999), www.scp-inc.org/publications/newsletters/N2303/index.php.
2. C. S. Lewis, in Colin Duriez, *The A–Z of C. S. Lewis: An Encyclopedia of His Life, Thought, and Writing* (Oxford: Lion Books, 2013), 69.
3. For this section, we rely heavily on Kevin J. Vanhoozer, Charles A. Anderson, and Michael J. Sleasman, eds., "Introduction: Toward a Theory of Cultural Interpretation," in *Everyday Theology: How to Read Cultural Texts and Interpret Trends* (Grand Rapids: Baker, 2007), 15–60.
4. Andy Crouch, *Culture Making: Recovering Our Creative Calling* (Downers Grove, IL: InterVarsity Books, 2008), 37.
5. A terrific summary of this vision can be found in Crouch, *Culture Making*, 20–24.
6. See, for example, "Chuck Colson's Final Speech" (speech, "Breaking the Spiral of Silence Conference," Chuck Colson Center for Christian Worldview, Lansdowne, VA, March 30, 2012), in *BreakPoint*, April 20, 2015, www.breakpoint.org/bpcommentaries/entry/12/27228.
7. John Calvin, *Institutes of the Christian Religion*, ed. John T. McNeill, trans. Ford Lewis Battles (Philadelphia: Westminster, 1960), 1.11.8.
8. Ken Myers, *All God's Children and Blue Suede Shoes: Christians and Popular Culture,* 2nd ed. (Wheaton, IL: Crossway, 2012), 34.

9. Peter L. Berger, *The Sacred Canopy: Elements of a Sociological Theory of Religion* (New York: Anchor Books, 1967), 3. Much of the discussion that follows is our attempt to simplify Berger's description of society found in the first chapter of his book.

10. Vanhoozer et al., *Everyday Theology*.

11. Vanhoozer et al., *Everyday Theology*.

Chapter 2

1. Francis A. Schaeffer, *Whatever Happened to the Human Race?* (Wheaton, IL: Crossway, 1983), 93.

2. Rodney Stark, *The Rise of Christianity: How the Obscure, Marginal Jesus Movement Became the Dominant Religious Force in the Western World in a Few Centuries* (San Francisco: HarperSanFrancisco, 1997), chap. 5.

3. See, for example, the stories Warren Cole Smith and John Stonestreet tell in *Restoring All Things: God's Audacious Plan to Change the World through Everyday People* (Grand Rapids: Baker, 2015).

4. Evangelist Dwight L. Moody and radio preacher J. Vernon McGee each used versions of this line to communicate their chagrin over social efforts that, they thought, got in the way of sharing the message of personal salvation.

5. Some scholars doubt the apostle Peter was the author of this epistle, claiming it was written after his death and posthumously attributed to him. There are good reasons, however, to believe the consistent witness of the church that Peter was indeed the author. Dr. David Malick offers a good summary of these arguments in "An Introduction to the Book of 1 Peter," Bible.org, accessed December 27, 2016, bible.org/article/introduction-book-1-peter.

6. Francis A. Schaeffer, *A Christian Manifesto* (Wheaton, IL: Crossway Books, 1982), 17.

7. Lesslie Newbigin, *A Walk through the Bible*, 2nd ed. (Louisville, KY: Westminster John Knox, 1999), 4.

8. Smith and Stonestreet, *Restoring All Things*, 20. Internal citations omitted.

9. For a thorough discussion of the four-chapter summary of Scripture, see Cornelius Plantinga Jr., *Engaging God's World: A Christian Vision of Faith, Learning, and Living* (Grand Rapids: Eerdmans, 2002). See also Charles

W. Colson and Nancy Pearcey, *How Now Shall We Live?* (Wheaton, IL: Tyndale, 1999).

10. Lecrae, "Race, Righteous Anger, and Resolution," Q Commons, Denver, Colorado, October 13, 2016; see video at *Artists and Poets*, QIdeas.org, accessed December 27, 2016, http://qideas.org/videos/artists-and-poets/.

11. For a thorough description of structure versus direction, see Albert M. Wolters, *Creation Regained: Biblical Basics for a Reformational Worldview*, 2nd ed. (Grand Rapids: Eerdmans, 2005), chap. 5.

12. C. S. Lewis, *The Lion, the Witch and the Wardrobe* (New York: Collier Books, 1970), 159–60.

13. We owe the wording of this question to the excellent film series *For the Life of the World: Letters to the Exiles*, directed by Eric Johnson and David Michael Phelps (Acton Institute/Gorilla Pictures, 2014).

Chapter 3

1. Sophie Scholl, quoted in Steven Garber, *The Fabric of Faithfulness: Weaving Together Belief and Behavior*, rev. ed. (Downers Grove, IL: InterVarsity, 2007), 188.

2. Steven Garber uses the phrase "I am Christian and I am German, therefore I am responsible for Germany" to describe the Scholls' approach to culture, but we think it also reflects Bonhoeffer's approach. See Garber, *Fabric of Faithfulness*, 180.

3. Garber, *Fabric of Faithfulness,* 176.

4. Thomas Howard, *Evangelical Is Not Enough: Worship of God in Liturgy and Sacrament* (Nashville: Thomas Nelson, 1984), 36–37.

5. Dietrich Bonhoeffer, *Dietrich Bonhoeffer: Witness to Jesus Christ*, ed. John de Gruchy (Minneapolis: Augsburg Fortress, 1991), 293–94.

6. The Epicureans believed the gods were remote and detached and had lost interest in humanity. They could, therefore, live however they pleased. Unsurprisingly, Epicureanism often took the form of hedonism. The Stoics, on the other hand, were fatalists. They believed the gods determined just about every detail of human life. The apostle Paul confronted both worldviews in the Mars Hill sermon.

7. Rod Dreher, *The Benedict Option: A Strategy for Christians in a Post-Christian Nation* (New York: Penguin, 2017).

8. Christian Smith and Melinda Lundquist Denton, *Soul Searching: The Religious and Spiritual Lives of American Teenagers* (New York: Oxford University Press, 2009); see also Kenda Creasy Dean, *Almost Christian: What the Faith of Our Teenagers Is Telling the American Church* (New York: Oxford University Press, 2010).

Chapter 4

1. Wikipedia, s.v. "Information Age," https://en.wikipedia.org/wiki/Information_Age.

2. Team Gwava, "How Much Data Is Created on the Internet Each Day?," *Gwava* (blog), September 8, 2016, www.gwava.com/blog/internet-data-created-daily.

3. Thomas L. Friedman, *The World Is Flat: A Brief History of the Twenty-First Century* (New York: Farrar, Straus, and Giroux, 2006).

4. T. S. Eliot, *The Rock: A Pageant Play* (New York: Harcourt, Brace, 1934), pt. 1, lines 15–16.

5. Richard M. Weaver, *Ideas Have Consequences* (Chicago: University of Chicago Press, 1984).

6. Nancy Pearcey, *Total Truth: Liberating Christianity from Its Cultural Captivity* (Wheaton, IL: Crossway Books, 2008), 165.

7. Danielle Kreutter, "UCCS Professors' Email: No Debating Class Topic Will Be Allowed," *Gazette*, September 1, 2016, http://gazette.com/uccs-professors-email-no-debating-class-topic-will-be-allowed/article/1584615.

8. A good discussion of the difference between true tolerance and fake tolerance can be found in David Kinnaman and Gabe Lyons, *Good Faith: Being a Christian When Society Thinks You're Irrelevant and Extreme* (Grand Rapids: Baker, 2016).

9. Aldous Huxley, *Brave New World Revisited* (New York: RosettaBooks, 2010), 35.

10. Neil Postman, *Amusing Ourselves to Death: Public Discourse in the Age of Show Business* (New York: Penguin, 1985).

11. James Boswell, *Boswell's Life of Johnson,* ed. Charles Grosvenor Osgood (New York: Charles Scribner's Sons, 1917), xviii.

12. W. Gary Phillips, William E. Brown, and John Stonestreet, *Making Sense of Your World: A Biblical Worldview*, 2nd ed. (Salem, WI: Sheffield, 2008), 86.

13. Ernest Nagel, "Naturalism Reconsidered," *Proceedings and Addresses of the American Philosophical Association* 28 (1954–55), 5–17.

14. Bill is a friend, former college president, and current Senior Fellow of Worldview and Culture at the Chuck Colson Center for Christian Worldview and dean of the Colson Fellows Program. See www.colsonfellows.org.

15. Email to John Stonestreet, cited in Chuck Colson, "Can't Turn This Worldview Thing Off: Send Your Kid to Summit," *BreakPoint Commentaries*, April 6, 2015, www.breakpoint.org/bpcommentaries/entry/13/27139.

16. See Sean McDowell and John Stonestreet, *Same-Sex Marriage: A Thoughtful Approach to God's Design for Marriage* (Grand Rapids: Baker, 2014).

17. See C. S. Lewis, *The Four Loves* (Orlando, FL: Harcourt, 1988).

18. Judith S. Wallerstein, Julia M. Lewis, and Sandra Blakeslee, *The Unexpected Legacy of Divorce: The 25 Year Landmark Study* (New York: Hyperion, 2000), xiii.

Chapter 5

1. Chris Broussard, *Outside the Lines*, ESPN, April 29, 2013; see Chris Greenberg, "Chris Broussard, ESPN Reporter, Calls Being Gay an 'Open Rebellion to God,'" *Huffington Post*, April 30, 2013, www.huffingtonpost.com/2013/04/29/chris-broussard-espn-nba-gay-reaction_n_3180080.html.

2. Conor Friedersdorf, "Refusing to Photograph a Gay Wedding Isn't Hateful," *Atlantic*, March 5, 2014, www.theatlantic.com/politics/archive/2014/03/refusing-to-photograph-a-gay-wedding-isnt-hateful/284224/.

3. Elane Photography, LLC, Plaintiff-Petitioner, v. Vanessa Willock, Defendant-Respondent, 309 P.3d 53 (N. M. 2013), http://web.law.columbia.edu/sites/default/files/microsites/gender-sexuality/elane_photography_nm_sct_opinion.pdf.

4. Elane Photography v. Willock.

5. Rod Dreher, in a must-read article written the same year as these two events, correctly identified this new vision of human identity as the result of a "cosmological shift." See Rod Dreher, "Sex after Christianity," *American Conservative*, April 11, 2013, www.theamericanconservative .com/articles/sex-after-christianity/. The title of this chapter echoes the the title of his article.

6. Two very helpful books on sexuality in modern culture, both of which include discussions on identity and sexuality are Dale S. Kuehne, *Sex and the iWorld: Rethinking Relationships beyond an Age of Individualism* (Grand Rapids: Baker, 2009); and Jonathan Grant, *Divine Sex: A Compelling Vision for Christian Relationships in a Hypersexualized Age* (Grand Rapids: Brazos, 2015). The best book, in our view, for those struggling with identity because of same-sex attraction is Wesley Hill, *Washed and Waiting: Reflections on Christian Faithfulness and Homosexuality* (Grand Rapids: Zondervan, 2010).

7. Peter L. Berger, "Modern Identity: Crisis and Continuity," in Wilton S. Dillon, ed., *The Cultural Drama: Modern Identities and Social Ferment* (Washington, DC: Smithsonian Institution Press, 1974), 176.

8. Quoted in Steven Garber, *The Fabric of Faithfulness: Weaving Together Belief and Behavior*, rev. ed. (Downers Grove, IL: InterVarsity, 2007), 93.

9. Luc Ferry, *Learning to Live: A Young Person's Guide*, trans. Theo Cuffe (Edinburgh, Scotland: Canongate Books, 2006), 72.

10. Friedrich Nietzsche, *The Will to Power*, ed. and trans. Walter Kaufmann and trans. R. J. Hollingdale (New York: Vintage Books, 1968), 401.

11. No one tells this story better than Rodney Stark in his book *The Rise of Christianity: How the Obscure, Marginal Jesus Movement Became the Dominant Religious Force in the Western World in a Few Centuries* (San Francisco: HarperSanFrancisco, 1997).

12. Henry Grunwald, "The Year 2000: Is It the End—or Just the Beginning?," *Time*, March 30, 1992, http://content.time.com/time/magazine/article /0,9171,975194,00.html.

13. Grunwald, "The Year 2000."

14. Blaise Pascal, *Pensées*, trans. A. J. Krailsheimer (New York: Penguin, 1995), 45.

15. For a helpful description of the postmodern worldview, see W. Gary Phillips, William E. Brown, and John Stonestreet, *Making Sense of Your World: A Biblical Worldview*, 2nd ed. (Salem, WI: Sheffield, 2008), 48–58.

16. James E. Marcia et al., *Ego Identity: A Handbook for Psychosocial Research* (New York: Springer, 1993). For a helpful summary, see "Marcia's States of Adolescent Identity Development," YouTube video, posted by Tiffany Dickie, January 31, 2014, www.youtube.com/watch?v=a8HIY_bqrVo. Only a portion of Marcia's theory is discussed here. We're indebted to Dr. Peter Cha, my (John's) seminary professor at Trinity International University, who first pointed me to Marcia's theory and applied it to the context of the church and home.

17. This is our paraphrase of Steven Garber, who rightly points out that for a worldview to last, it must be "sufficient for the questions and crises ..., particularly the challenge of modern and postmodern consciousness with its implicit secularization and pluralization." See Steven Garber, *Fabric of Faithfulness*, 51, 122–32.

18. A terrific resource on how and why to walk *with* kids is Jeff Myers, *Grow Together: The Forgotten Story of How Uniting Generations Unleashes Epic Spiritual Potential* (Colorado Springs: Summit Ministries, 2014). See also the accompanying film, available at www.growtogether.org.

19. Garber, *Fabric of Faithfulness,* 51.

Chapter 6

1. Sherry Turkle, *Alone Together: Why We Expect More from Technology and Less from Each Other* (New York: Basic Books, 2011). Her February 2012 TED talk "Connected, but Alone?" offers a helpful summary of the book, as well as many of the points we discuss in this chapter. See www.ted.com/talks/sherry_turkle_alone_together?language=en.

2. Sherry Turkle, "Alone Together" (speech, TEDxUIUC, Champaign, IL, February 2011), www.youtube.com/watch?v=MtLVCpZIiNs.

3. Sherry Turkle, *The Second Self: Computers and the Human Spirit* (New York: Simon and Schuster, 1984).

4. Sherry Turkle, *Life on the Screen: Identity in the Age of the Internet* (New York: Simon and Schuster, 1997).

5. Turkle, "Connected, but Alone?"

6. Henry David Thoreau, "Where I Lived and What I Lived For," in *Walden: An Annotated Edition*, ed. Walter Harding (New York: Houghton Mifflin, 1995), 89.

7. See Sally Andrews et al., "Beyond Self-Report: Tools to Compare Estimated and Real-World Smartphone Use," *PLOS One* 10, no. 10 (October 2015), journals.plos.org/plosone/article?id=10.1371/journal.pone.0139004.

8. Bureau of Labor Statistics, American Time Use Survey, 2004–2009, cited in Eleanor Krause and Isabel V. Sawhill, "How Free Time Became Screen Time," Brookings Institution, September 13, 2016, www.brookings.edu/blog/social-mobility-memos/2016/09/13/how-free-time-became-screen-time/.

9. Glenn Enoch et al., *The Nielson Total Audience Report: Q1 2016* (New York: Nielson, 2016), 4, cited in Jacqueline Howard, "Americans Devote More Than 10 Hours a Day to Screen Time, and Growing," CNN, July 29, 2016, www.cnn.com/2016/06/30/health/americans-screen-time-nielsen/.

10. We're grateful to John's colleague Shane Morris for articulating these consequences in this very helpful format. Shane has been thinking and writing about technology for some time, and these thoughts were communicated to John in an email, October 5, 2016.

11. See Julie Hiramine's terrific work at Generations of Virtue, www.generationsofvirtue.org.

12. For a full description of each of these lies, and to read the single best book available for parents on helping kids navigate the digital age, see Kathy Koch, *Screens and Teens: Connecting with Our Kids in a Wireless World* (Chicago: Moody, 2015).

13. See Centers for Disease Control and Prevention, "Suicide Trends among Persons Aged 10–24 Years—United States 1994–2012," *Morbidity and Mortality Weekly Report* 64, no. 8 (March 2015): 201–5, www.cdc.gov/mmwr/preview/mmwrhtml/mm6408a1.htm.

14. See Craig M. Gay, introduction, in *The Way of the (Modern) World: Or, Why It's Tempting to Live as If God Doesn't Exist* (Grand Rapids: Eerdmans, 1998), 1–28.

15. See Gay, *Way of the (Modern) World*, 2.

16. Research cited in Anne Fishel, "The Most Important Thing You Can Do with Your Kids? Eat Dinner with Them," *Washington Post*, January 12, 2015, www.washingtonpost.com/posteverything/wp/2015/01/12/the-most-important-thing-you-can-do-with-your-kids-eat-dinner-with-them/?utm_term=.b61005c506d0.

Chapter 7

1. Diana West, *The Death of the Grown-up: How America's Arrested Development is Bringing Down Western Civilization* (New York: St. Martin's Press, 2007), 1.
2. This is a very brief summary of the story West tells. We've left out a lot of details, but the main point is that adolescence as a stage of life is fabricated and recent. See West, *Death of the Grown-up*, chaps. 1–2.
3. West, *Death of the Grown-up*, 6.
4. Mark Regnerus, "Sex Is Cheap: Why Young Men Have the Upper Hand in Bed, Even When They're Failing in Life," *Slate*, February 25, 2011, www.slate.com/articles/double_x/doublex/2011/02/sex_is_cheap.single.html. See also Austin Institute for the Study of Family and Culture, "The Economics of Sex: It's a Tough Market out There," accessed March 2014, www.austin-institute.org/wp-content/uploads/2014/02/V10-Resource-Guide.pdf. Though Regnerus didn't invent the phrase "the economics of sex," he has offered the most accessible explanation. This description of the idea first appeared in John Stonestreet and Sean McDowell, *Same-Sex Marriage: A Thoughtful Approach to God's Design for Marriage* (Grand Rapids: Baker, 2014), 114.
5. Regnerus, "Sex Is Cheap."
6. Pope Benedict XVI, *Light of the World: The Pope, the Church, and the Signs of the Times; A Conversation with Peter Seewald*, trans. Michael J. Miller and Adrian J. Walker (San Francisco: Ignatius Press, 2010), chap. 5.
7. Del Tackett, founder of *The Truth Project*, said this in a speech given at a private gathering of leaders in January 2009.
8. David Brooks, *The Road to Character* (New York: Random House, 2015), 54.
9. C. S. Lewis, *The Abolition of Man* (New York: HarperOne, 2001), 26.

10. Dallas Willard, *Renovation of the Heart: Putting on the Character of Christ* (Colorado Springs: NavPress, 2002), 29.

11. Michael Miller, in "If We Know What's Right, Can We Do It?," *Doing the Right Thing: Making Moral Choices in a World Full of Options*, session 3, hosted by Brit Hume (Grand Rapids: Zondervan, 2009), DVD series.

12. Edmund Burke, "Letter from Mr. Burke to a Member of the National Assembly in Answer to Some Objections to His Book on French Affairs—1791," in *The Works of Edmund Burke*, 9 vols. (Boston: Charles C. Little and James Brown, 1839), 3:326.

13. Aristotle, *Nicomachean Ethics,* trans. W. D. Ross (350 BCE), http://classics.mit.edu/Aristotle/nicomachaen.html.

14. For a helpful introduction to the church calendar, see Mark D. Roberts, "Introduction to the Christian Year: What Is the Liturgical Year or Church Year? How Can It Make a Difference in Your Relationship with God?," *Reflections on Christ, Church, and Culture* (blog), 2011, www.patheos.com /blogs/markdroberts/series/introduction-to-the-christian-year/.

15. Lewis, *Abolition of Man*, chap. 1. Full text available online at https://archive .org/stream/TheAbolitionOfMan_229/C.s.Lewis-TheAbolitionOfMan _djvu.txt.

16. Lewis, *Abolition of Man*, 25.

17. C. S. Lewis, *The Voyage of the Dawn Treader* (New York: Collier Books, 1970), 1.

18. Eugene H. Peterson, *A Long Obedience in the Same Direction: Discipleship in an Instant Society*, 2nd ed. (Downers Grove, IL: InterVarsity, 2000). Peterson borrowed this quote from, of all people, the atheist Friedrich Nietzsche but properly sanctified it in this terrific book.

19. Lewis, *Voyage of the Dawn Treader*, 89–91.

20. Frederica Mathewes-Green, *First Fruits of Prayer: A Forty-Day Journey through the Canon of St. Andrew* (Brewster, MA: Paraclete Press, 2006), 12.

Chapter 8

1. Data from multiple sources cited in Covenant Eyes, "Pornography Statistics: Annual Report 2015," www.covenanteyes.com/pornstats/. For full report with original sources, download the report from the website: Covenant

Eyes, *Pornography Statistics: 250+ Facts, Quotes, and Statistics about Pornography Use* (Owosso, MI: Covenant Eyes, 2015).

2. The Barna Group, *The Porn Phenomenon: The Explosive Growth of Pornography and How Its Impacting Your Church, Life, and Ministry* (Ventura, CA: Barna Group, 2016), cited in Chrissy Gordon, "Josh McDowell Ministry and Barna Group Unveil Key Findings for *The Porn Phenomenon*," Josh McDowell Ministry, January 19, 2016, www.josh.org/news-release/key-findings-for-the-porn-phenomenon-unveiled/.

3. Joe S. McIlhaney Jr. and Freda McKissic Bush, *Hooked: New Science on How Casual Sex Is Affecting Our Children* (Chicago: Northfield Publishing, 2008).

4. Dr. Victor B. Cline, *Pornography's Effects on Adults and Children* (New York: Morality in Media, 1999), http://66.210.33.157/mim/full_article.php?article_no=323.

5. Fight the New Drug, *Harmful Effects of Pornography: 2016 Reference Guide* (San Francisco: Fight the New Drug, 2016), http://store.fightthenewdrug.org/collections/books/products/harmful-effects-of-pornography-2016-reference-guide.

6. *The Porn Phenomenon* can be purchased at https://barna-resources.myshopify.com/products/porn-phenomenon.

7. Exercise great caution here. First, if you struggle with porn, skip this step. It's better to simply flee from any possible temptation. Second, the truth about the porn industry is deeply disturbing and may be hard to stomach. Here are two honest yet somewhat filtered accounts: (1) Shelley Lubben, "Ex-Porn Star Tells the Truth about the Porn Industry," *Covenant Eyes* (blog), October 28, 2008, www.covenanteyes.com/2008/10/28/ex-porn-star-tells-the-truth-about-the-porn-industry/; and (2) "How to Identify (and Rescue) a Victim of Sex Trafficking," *Fight the New Drug* (blog), June 21, 2016, http://fightthenewdrug.org/how-to-spot-and-rescue-a-sex-trafficking-victim/.

8. "Hilton Announces Removal of All Porn Channels from Hotels," LifeSiteNews.com, August 20, 2015, www.lifesitenews.com/news/public-blitz-forces-hilton-hotels-to-drop-porn.

9. "Russell Brand Talks Sex, Softcore & Hardcore Porn," YouTube video, posted by Fight the New Drug, February 23, 2015, www.youtube.com/watch?v=5kvzamjQW9M.

10. Terry Crews's Facebook page, accessed December 30, 2016, www.facebook.com/realterrycrews/videos/1083942814959410/.

11. Shmuley Boteach and Pamela Anderson, "Take the Pledge: No More Indulging Porn," *Wall Street Journal*, August 31, 2016, www.wsj.com/articles/take-the-pledge-no-more-indulging-porn-1472684658.

Chapter 9

1. Arielle Kuperberg and Joseph E. Padgett, "Dating and Hooking Up in College: Meeting Contexts, Sex, and Variation by Gender, Partner's Gender, and Class Standing," *Journal of Sex Research* 52, no. 5 (2015): 525, www.tandfonline.com/doi/full/10.1080/00224499.2014.901284?scroll=top&needAccess=true.

2. Jean M. Twenge, Ryne A. Sherman, and Brooke E. Wells, "Sexual Inactivity during Young Adulthood Is More Common among U.S. Millennials and iGen: Age, Period, and Cohort Effects on Having No Sexual Partners after Age 18," *Archives of Sexual Behavior* (August 2016): 1–8, http://link.springer.com/article/10.1007/s10508-016-0798-z.

3. Centers for Disease Control and Prevention, "Youth Risk Behavior Surveillance—United States, 2015," *Morbidity and Mortality Weekly Report (MMWR)* 65, no. 6 (June 2016): 27, www.cdc.gov/healthyyouth/data/yrbs/pdf/2015/ss6506_updated.pdf.

4. Data from National Survey of Family Growth, 1982–2002, analysis in Lawrence B. Finer, "Trends in Premarital Sex in the United States, 1954–2003," *Public Health Reports* 122, no. 1 (January–February 2007), www.guttmacher.org/sites/default/files/pdfs/pubs/journals/2007/01/29/PRH-Vol-122-Finer.pdf.

5. Centers for Disease Control and Prevention, "Sexually Transmitted Disease Surveillance, 2014," cited in Centers for Disease Control and Prevention, "CDC Fact Sheet: Reported STDs in the United States; 2014 National Data for Chlamydia, Gonorrhea, and Syphilis," November 2015, www.cdc.gov/std/stats14/std-trends-508.pdf.

6. Centers for Disease Control, "CDC Fact Sheet."

7. Centers for Disease Control and Prevention, "CDC Fact Sheet: Incidence, Prevalence, and Cost of Sexually Transmitted Infections in the United

States," February 2013, www.cdc.gov/std/stats/sti-estimates-fact-sheet -feb-2013.pdf.

8. Robyn L. Fielder et al., "Sexual Hookups and Adverse Health Outcomes: A Longitudinal Study of First-Year College Women," *Journal of Sex Research* 51, no. 2 (2014): 131–44, www.ncbi.nlm.nih.gov/pmc/articles /PMC3946692/.

9. Sara E. Sandberg-Thoma and Claire M. Kamp Dush, "Casual Sexual Relationships and Mental Health in Adolescence and Emerging Adulthood," *Journal of Sex Research* 51, no. 2 (2014): 121–30, www.tandfonline.com/doi/abs/10.1080/00224499.2013.821440.

10. Melina M. Bersamin et al., "Risky Business: Is There an Association between Casual Sex and Mental Health among Emerging Adults?," *Journal of Sex Research* 51, no. 1 (2014): 43–51, www.tandfonline.com/doi/abs/10 .1080/00224499.2013.772088.

11. Jennifer L. Walsh et al., "Do Alcohol and Marijuana Use Decrease the Probability of Condom Use for College Women?," *Journal of Sex Research* 51, no. 2 (2014): 145–58, www.tandfonline.com/doi/abs/10.1080/00224499 .2013.821442.

12. Kay Hymowitz et al., *Knot Yet: The Benefits and Costs of Delayed Marriage in America* (Charlottesville, VA: National Marriage Project, 2013), 14, http://nationalmarriageproject.org/wp-content/uploads/2013/03 /KnotYet-FinalForWeb.pdf.

13. Galena K. Rhoades and Scott M. Stanley, *Before "I Do": What Do Premarital Experiences Have to Do with Marital Quality among Today's Young Adults?* (Charlottesville, VA: National Marriage Project, 2014), 5, http://nationalmarriageproject.org/wordpress/wp-content/uploads/2014 /08/NMP-BeforeIDoReport-Final.pdf.

14. Rhoades and Stanley, *Before "I Do,"* 9.

15. William G. Axinn and Arland Thornton, "The Relationship between Cohabitation and Divorce: Selectivity or Causal Influence?," *Demography* 29, no. 3 (August 1992): 357–74, cited in Glenn T. Stanton, *The Ring Makes All the Difference: The Hidden Consequence of Cohabitation and the Strong Benefits of Marriage* (Chicago: Moody, 2011), 60.

16. Michael D. Newcomb and P. M. Bentler, "Assessment of Personality and Demographic Aspects of Cohabitation and Marital Success," *Journal of Personality Assessment* 44, no. 1 (1980): 16.

17. Sade Patterson, "Campus Sex Week: Abortion Is Healthy, Bible Supports Homosexual Sex, Orgies Are Fun," College Fix, November 24, 2015, www.thecollegefix.com/post/25234/.

18. Sade Patterson, "This College Student Taught Campus Feminists What a Real 'Sex Week' Looks Like," College Fix, April 5, 2016, www.thecollegefix.com /post/26884/.

Chapter 10

1. David Kinnaman and Gabe Lyons, *unChristian: What a New Generation Really Thinks about Christianity … and Why It Matters* (Grand Rapids: Baker, 2007), 93.

2. Lawrence S. Mayer and Paul R. McHugh, "Sexuality and Gender: Findings from the Biological, Psychological, and Social Sciences," *New Atlantis*, no. 50 (Fall 2016): 14, 31, www.thenewatlantis.com/docLib/20160819 _TNA50SexualityandGender.pdf.

3. For example, see J. Michael Bailey et al., "Genetic and Environmental Influences on Sexual Orientation and Its Correlates in an Australian Twin Sample," *Journal of Personality and Social Psychology* 78, no. 3 (March 2000): 524–36, www.ncbi.nlm.nih.gov/pubmed/10743878.

4. "What Causes a Person to Have a Particular Sexual Orientation?" in American Psychological Association, "Sexual Orientation and Homosexuality: Answers to Your Questions for a Better Understanding," accessed October 4, 2016, www.apa.org/topics/lgbt/orientation.aspx.

5. Martin Duberman, quoted in David Benkof, "Nobody Is 'Born That Way,' Gay Historians Say," Daily Caller, March 19, 2014, http://dailycaller.com/2014 /03/19/nobody-is-born-that-way-gay-historians-say/#ixzz4M3W9sgPQ.

6. See Stanton L. Jones and Mark A. Yarhouse, *Ex-Gays? A Longitudinal Study of Religiously Mediated Change in Sexual Orientation* (Downers Grove, IL: InterVarsity, 2007).

7. Peter Sprigg and Timothy Dailey, eds., "What Causes Homosexuality?," chap. 1 in *Getting It Straight: What the Research Shows about Homosexuality*

(Washington, DC: Family Research Council, 2004), http://downloads.frc.org/EF/EF08L41.pdf.

8. Edward O. Laumann et al., *The Social Organization of Sexuality: Sexual Practices in the United States* (Chicago: University of Chicago Press, 1994), 216.

9. Paul Van de Ven et al., "A Comparative Demographic and Sexual Profile of Older Homosexually Active Men," *Journal of Sex Research* 34, no. 4 (1997), 349–60.

10. James H. Price et al., "Perceptions of Cervical Cancer and Pap Smear Screening Behavior by Women's Sexual Orientation," *Journal of Community Health* 21, no. 2 (April 1996): 89–105; Daron G. Ferris et al., "A Neglected Lesbian Health Concern: Cervical Neoplasia," *Journal of Family Practice* 43, no. 6 (December 1996): 581; C. J. Skinner et al., "A Case-Controlled Study of the Sexual Health Needs of Lesbians," *Genitourinary Medicine* 72, no. 4 (August 1996): 277–80.

11. Katherine Fethers et al., "Sexually Transmitted Infections and Risk Behaviours in Women Who Have Sex with Women," *Sexually Transmitted Infections* 76, no. 5 (October 2000): 347.

12. Centers for Disease Control and Prevention, "Sexually Transmitted Disease Surveillance, 2014," cited in Centers for Disease Control and Prevention, "CDC Fact Sheet: Reported STDs in the United States; 2014 National Data for Chlamydia, Gonorrhea, and Syphilis," November 2015, www.cdc.gov/std/stats14/std-trends-508.pdf.

13. Centers for Disease Control and Prevention, "HIV among Gay and Bisexual Men: Fast Facts," September 30, 2016, www.cdc.gov/hiv/group/msm/index.html.

14. Centers for Disease Control and Prevention, "HIV Testing and Risk Behaviors among Gay, Bisexual, and Other Men Who Have Sex with Men—United States," *Morbidity and Mortality Weekly Report* 62, no. 47 (November 2013): 958–62, www.cdc.gov/mmwr/preview/mmwrhtml/mm6247a4.htm.

15. David Island and Patrick Letellier, *Men Who Beat the Men Who Love Them: Battered Gay Men and Domestic Violence* (New York: Routledge, 2012), 14.

16. Centers for Disease Control and Prevention, "Sexual Identity, Sex of Sexual Contacts, and Health-Related Behaviors among Students in Grades 9–12—United States and Selected Sites, 2015," *Morbidity and Mortality*

Weekly Report (MMWR) Surveillance Summaries 65, no. 9 (August 2016): 1–202, www.cdc.gov/mmwr/volumes/65/ss/ss6509a1.htm.

17. Spartacus International Gay Guide, "Gay Travel Index," May 26, 2016, www.spartacusworld.com/gaytravelindex.pdf.

18. For the Netherlands, see Theo G. M. Sandfort et al., "Same-Sex Sexual Behavior and Psychiatric Disorders: Findings from the Netherlands Mental Health Survey and Incidence Study (NEMESIS)," *Archives of General Psychiatry* 58, no. 1 (January 2001): 88–89. For England, see Apu Chakraborty et al., "Mental Health of the Non-heterosexual Population of England," *British Journal of Psychiatry* 198, no. 2 (February 2011): 143–48. For New Zealand, see David M. Fergusson, L. John Horwood, and Annette L. Beautrais, "Is Sexual Orientation Related to Mental Health Problems and Suicidality in Young People?," *Archives of General Psychiatry* 56, no. 10 (October 1999): 876–80.

19. By the way, know the definition of *discrimination*. It's a contemporary buzzword most people haven't thought about clearly. Simply put, *discrimination* is "the recognition and understanding of the difference between one thing and another." And it's something everyone does. We all believe we should discriminate against certain behaviors, but which behaviors and why are the key questions.

20. See Rosaria Champagne Butterfield, *The Secret Thoughts of an Unlikely Convert: An English Professor's Journey into Christian Faith*, rev. ed. (Pittsburgh, PA: Covenant and Crown, 2014).

21. See Christopher Yuan and Angela Yuan, *Out of a Far Country: A Gay Son's Journey to God; A Broken Mother's Search for Hope* (Colorado Springs: WaterBrook, 2011).

Chapter 11

1. Wikipedia, s.v. "Cisgender," https://en.wikipedia.org/wiki/Cisgender.

2. See John Stonestreet, "Spell-Checking 'Cisgender': Neosexual Propaganda," *BreakPoint Commentaries*, June 21, 2016, www.breakpoint.org/bpcommentaries/entry/13/29453.

3. See Valeriya Safronova, "Meet CoverGirl's New Cover Boy," *New York Times,* October 12, 2016, www.nytimes.com/2016/10/16/fashion/meet-covergirls-new-cover-boy.html.

4. Jessi Hempel, "My Brother's Pregnancy and the Making of a New American Family," *Time*, September 12, 2016, http://time.com/4475634/trans-man-pregnancy-evan/.

5. In an online article the American Psychological Association offered this explanation: "Transgender is an umbrella term for persons whose gender identity, gender expression or behavior does not conform to that typically associated with the sex to which they were assigned at birth. Gender identity refers to a person's internal sense of being male, female or something else." American Psychological Association, "Answers to Your Questions about Transgender People, Gender Identity and Gender Expression," accessed October 6, 2016, www.apa.org/topics/lgbt/transgender.aspx.

6. "Washington Schools to Teach Gender Identity Curriculum in Kindergarten," Family Policy Institute of Washington, June 2, 2016, www.fpiw.org/blog/2016/06/02/washington-schools-to-teach-gender-identity-curriculum-in-kindergarten/.

7. Ariel Levy, "Dolls and Feelings: Jill Soloway's Post-patriarchal Television," *New Yorker*, December 14, 2015, www.newyorker.com/magazine/2015/12/14/dolls-and-feelings.

8. "College Kids Say the Darndest Things: On Identity," video produced by Family Policy Institute of Washington, April 13, 2016, www.youtube.com/watch?v=xfO1veFs6Ho.

9. Susan Donaldson James, "Pittsburgh Man Thinks He's a Dog, Goes by Name 'Boomer,'" ABC News, November 6, 2013, http://abcnews.go.com/Health/pittsburgh-man-thinks-dog-boomer/story?id=20801512.

10. Fox 10 Staff, "From Human to Reptile: Tiamat's Transformation into the Dragon Lady," Fox 10 News, August, 29, 2016, www.fox10phoenix.com/news/arizona-news/197200001-story.

11. Candace Amos, "Transgender Woman Leaves Wife and 7 Kids to Live as a 6-Year-Old Girl," *New York Daily News*, December 12, 2015, accessed October 16, 2016, www.nydailynews.com/news/world/transgender-woman-leaves-wife-7-kids-live-girl-article-1.2463795.

12. Carolyn Moynihan, "Alas, Marrying Oneself Is Now a Thing … Really," *Stream*, September 3, 2016, https://stream.org/marrying-oneself-now-a-thing/.

13. Bradford Richardson, "New York Businesses Face Hefty Penalties for 'Misgendering' Customers," *Washington Times*, May 18, 2016, www.washingtontimes.com/news/2016/may/18/de-blasio-fine-businesses-wrong-gender-pronouns/.

14. Another reason to reject the idea is that it's self-refuting. If everything is merely a social construction and can be changed, doesn't that mean the idea of social construction is a social construction that can be changed as well? Isn't social construction merely a social construction?

15. For an excellent essay on this, read Roberta Green Ahmanson's article, "The New Dignity: Gnostic, Elitist, Self-Destructive Will-to-Power," *Public Discourse*, November 24, 2015, www.thepublicdiscourse.com/2015/11/15948/.

16. Stella Morabito, "Trouble in Transtopia: Murmurs of Sex Change Regret," *Federalist*, November 11, 2014, http://thefederalist.com/2014/11/11/trouble-in-transtopia-murmurs-of-sex-change-regret/.

17. David Batty, "Sex Changes Are Not Effective, Say Researchers," *Guardian,* July 30, 2004, www.theguardian.com/society/2004/jul/30/health.mentalhealth.

18. American Psychiatric Association, "Gender Dysphoria," in *Diagnostic and Statistical Manual of Mental Disorders*, 5th ed. (Arlington, VA: American Psychiatric Publishing, 2013), 302.85.

19. For more information see "Body Integrity Identity Disorder," www.biid.org.

20. Azadeh M. Meybodi, Ahmad Hajebi, and Atefeh G. Jolfaei, "Psychiatric Axis I Comorbidities among Patients with Gender Dysphoria," *Psychiatry Journal* (August 2014), www.ncbi.nlm.nih.gov/pmc/articles/PMC4142737/.

21. Stephanie L. Budge, Jill L. Adelson, and Kimberly A. S. Howard, "Anxiety and Depression in Transgender Individuals: The Roles of Transition Status, Loss, Social Support, and Coping," *Journal of Consulting and Clinical Psychology* 81, no. 3 (June 2013): 545–57, www.ncbi.nlm.nih.gov/pubmed/23398495.

22. Seattle's Children Hospital Gender Clinic, "What Is the Gender Clinic?," accessed December 31, 2016, www.seattlechildrens.org/clinics-programs/gender-clinic/.

23. American College of Pediatricians, "Gender Ideology Harms Children," August 17, 2016, www.acpeds.org/the-college-speaks/position-statements/gender-ideology-harms-children.

24. Walt Heyer, "Bruce Jenner Wants to Change the World When He Should Change His Mind," *Federalist*, April 27, 2015, http://thefederalist.com/2015/04/27/bruce-jenner-wants-to-change-the-world-when-he-should-change-his-mind/.

25. Data from K. D. Kochanek et al., "Deaths: Final Data for 2002," *National Vital Statistics Reports* 53, no. 5 (2002), cited in Jaime M. Grant, Lisa A. Mottet, and Justin Tanis, *Injustice at Every Turn: A Report of the National Transgender Discrimination Survey* (Washington, DC: National Center for Transgender Equality and National Gay and Lesbian Task Force, 2011), 2.

26. For example, you may face severe fines if you don't use transgender pronouns in New York City. See Joe Tacopino, "Not Using Transgender Pronouns Could Get You Fined," *New York Post*, May 19, 2016, http://nypost.com/2016/05/19/city-issues-new-guidelines-on-transgender-pronouns/.

27. You can find many of his articles at the following websites: (1) *Federalist*—http://thefederalist.com/author/walt-heyer/; and (2) *Public Discourse*—www.thepublicdiscourse.com/author/walt-heyer/.

28. Walt Heyer, "I Was a Transgender Woman," *Public Discourse,* April 1, 2015, www.thepublicdiscourse.com/2015/04/14688/.

29. Paul McHugh, "Transgenderism: A Pathogenic Meme," *Public Discourse*, June 10, 2015, www.thepublicdiscourse.com/2015/06/15145/.

Chapter 12

1. Statistics from multiple sources, cited in Joshua Becker, "21 Surprising Statistics That Reveal How Much Stuff We Actually Own," *Becoming Minimalist* (blog), accessed October 7, 2016, www.becomingminimalist.com/clutter-stats/.

2. Data from US Commerce Department, February 2011, cited in Mark Whitehouse, "Number of the Week: Americans Buy More Stuff They Don't Need," *Wall Street Journal*, April 23, 2011, http://blogs.wsj.com/economics/2011/04/23/number-of-the-week-americans-buy-more-stuff-they-dont-need/.

3. Christian Smith, with Patricia Snell, *Souls in Transition: The Religious and Spiritual Lives of Emerging Adults* (New York: Oxford University Press, 2009), 67.

4. Laura A. Pratt, Debra J. Brody, and Quiping Gu, "Antidepressant Use in Persons Aged 12 and Over: United States, 2005–2008," *NCHS Data Brief*, no. 76 (October 2011): 1, www.cdc.gov/nchs/data/databriefs/db76.htm.

5. Centers for Disease Control and Prevention, "Suicide among Adults Aged 35–64 Years—United States, 1999–2010," *Morbidity and Mortality Weekly Report (MMWR)* 62, no. 17 (May 2013): 321–25, www.cdc.gov/mmwr/preview/mmwrhtml/mm6217a1.htm?s_cid=mm6217a1_w.

6. Jean M. Twenge et al., "Birth Cohort Increases in Psychopathology among Young Americans, 1938–2007: A Cross-Temporal Meta-analysis of the MMPI," *Clinical Psychology Review* 30, no. 2 (March 2010): 145–54, www.ncbi.nlm.nih.gov/pubmed/19945203.

7. S. S. Luthar and C. Sexton, "The High Price of Affluence," in R. Kail, ed., *Advances in Child Development* (San Diego: Academic Press, 2005); and M. Csikszentmihalyi and B. Schneider, *Becoming Adult: How Teenagers Prepare for the World of Work* (New York: Basic Books, 2000), cited in Madeline Levine, *The Price of Privilege: How Parental Pressure and Material Advantage Are Creating a Generation of Disconnected and Unhappy Kids* (New York: HarperCollins, 2008), 17.

8. Data analysis from multiple sources, Erin El Issa, "2016 American Household Credit Card Debt Study," *NerdWallet* (blog), www.nerdwallet.com/blog/credit-card-data/average-credit-card-debt-household/.

9. Daniel Kahneman and Angus Deaton, "High Income Improves Evaluation of Life but Not Emotional Well-Being," *Proceedings of the National Academy of Sciences (PNAS)* 107, no. 38 (September 2010), www.pnas.org/content/107/38/16489.full.

10. Ravi Zacharias, *Can Man Live without God* (Nashville: Word, 1994), 320.

11. Charles H. Spurgeon, *Evening by Evening: A New Edition of the Classic Devotional Based on the Holy Bible, English Standard Version*, ed. Alistair Begg (Wheaton, IL: Crossway, 2007), 339.

12. Cornelius Plantinga Jr., *Not the Way It's Supposed to Be: A Breviary of Sin* (Grand Rapids: Eerdmans, 1995), 10.

13. Saint Augustine, *Confessions*, trans. Henry Chadwick (New York: Oxford University Press, 2008), 1.1.3.

14. Liana C. Sayer, Suzanne M. Bianchi, and John P. Robinson, "Are Parents Investing Less in Children? Trends in Mothers' and Fathers' Time with Children," *American Journal of Sociology* 110, no. 1 (July 2004): 2.

15. Derrick Feldmann et al., *Cause, Influence, and the Next Generation: The 2015 Millenial Impact Workforce Report* (West Palm Beach, FL: Achieve/ Millennial Impact Project, 2015), http://fi.fudwaca.com/mi/files/2015 /07/2015-MillennialImpactReport.pdf.

Chapter 13

1. Philip Cushman, "Why the Self Is Empty: Toward a Historically Situated Psychology," *American Psychologist* 45, no. 5 (May 1990): 600, 608.

2. Maggie Fox, "Americans Are Drinking More—a Lot More," NBC News, April 23, 2015, www.nbcnews.com/health/health-news/americans-are -drinking-more-lot-more-n347126.

3. Douglas Main, "30 Percent of Americans Have Had an Alcohol-Use Disorder," *Newsweek*, June 3, 2015, www.newsweek.com/30-percent -americans-have-had-alcohol-use-disorder-339085.

4. Alexandra Sifferlin, "Alcohol Problems Affect about 33 Million U.S. Adults," *Time*, June 3, 2015, http://time.com/3907691/alcohol-problems-study/.

5. HealthDay, "Ten Percent of Americans Admit Illegal Drug Use," CBS News, September 4, 2014, www.cbsnews.com/news/ten-percent-of-americans -admit-illegal-drug-use/.

6. Caleb Diehl and Michael Schramm, "Study: Daily Marijuana Use among College Students at Highest Rate in 35 Years," *USA Today College*, September 1, 2015, http://college.usatoday.com/2015/09/01/study-daily -marijuana-use-among-college-students-at-highest-rate-in-35-years/.

7. "Heroin: The Poisoning of America," CNN, October 17, 2016, www.cnn .com/2016/10/13/health/heroin-poisoning-of-america/.

8. National Institute on Drug Abuse, "Monitoring the Future Survey, Overview of Findings 2015," revised December 2015, https://www .drugabuse.gov/related-topics/trends-statistics/monitoring-future /monitoring-future-survey-overview-findings-2015.

9. Lloyd D. Johnston et al., *Monitoring the Future: National Survey Results on Drug Use, 1975–2014*, vol. 2 (Ann Arbor: University of Michigan Institute for Social Research, 2015), 27.

10. Jeffery M. Jones, "In U.S., 58% Back Legal Marijuana Use," Gallup, October 21, 2015, www.gallup.com/poll/186260/back-legal-marijuana.aspx.

11. Research cited in National Institute on Alcohol Abuse and Alcoholism, "College Drinking," December 2015, http://pubs.niaaa.nih.gov /publications/CollegeFactSheet/CollegeFactSheet.pdf.

12. Sushrut Jangi, "Can We Please Stop Pretending Marijuana Is Harmless?," *Boston Globe*, October 8, 2015, www.bostonglobe.com/magazine /2015/10/08/can-please-stop-pretending-marijuana-harmless /MneQebFPWg79ifTAXc1PkM/story.html. See also National Institute on Drug Abuse, "Want to Know More? Some FAQs about Marijuana," "Marijuana: Facts for Teens," May 2015, www.drugabuse.gov/publications /marijuana-facts-teens/want-to-know-more-some-faqs-about-marijuana.

13. Jennifer Alsever, "Is Pot Losing Its Buzz in Colorado?," *Fortune*, June 29, 2016, http://fortune.com/pot-marijuana-colorado/.

14. Wayne Drash and Max Blau, "In America's Drug Death Capital: How Heroin Is Scarring the Next Generation," CNN, September 16, 2016, www.cnn.com/2016/09/16/health/huntington-heroin/index.html. See also Corky Siemaszko, "Ohio City Releases Shocking Photos to Show Effects of 'Poison Known as Heroin,'" NBC News, September 10, 2016, www .nbcnews.com/news/us-news/ohio-city-releases-shocking-photo-show -effects-poison-known-heroin-n645806.

15. That is *not* to say there is never a time and place for abstaining from certain things that aren't sinful in and of themselves. For instance, it's wise for the recovering addict to avoid addictive substances altogether. In addition, it's right for a more mature Christian to abstain from food or drink when partaking would cause a brother or sister to stumble (Rom. 14:13–23).

16. C. S. Lewis, *Mere Christianity* (New York: HarperCollins, 1980), 78–79.

17. What about medicinal marijuana? We should distinguish the intent to get high (recreational marijuana) from the intent to heal (medical marijuana). A systematic review of the scientific research is inconclusive about the medical benefits. Research should continue *before* we start enacting public policy. See Penny F. Whiting et al., "Cannabinoids for Medical Use: A

Systematic Review and Meta-analysis," *JAMA* 313, no. 24 (June 2015): 2456–73, http://jamanetwork.com/journals/jama/fullarticle/2338251.

18. National Center on Addiction and Substance Abuse at Columbia University, "The Importance of Family Dinners VIII" (September 2012), 7, www.centeronaddiction.org/addiction-research/reports/importance-of-family-dinners-2012.

19. "Brian Welch—White Chair Film—I Am Second," YouTube video, published November 20, 2012, www.youtube.com/watch?v=q6EIhkAyy3s.

20. Brian "Head" Welch, with Carol Traver, *With My Eyes Wide Open: Miracles and Mistakes on My Way Back to Korn* (Nashville: Thomas Nelson, 2016).

Chapter 14

1. DNCE, "Cake by the Ocean," © 2015 Republic Records.

2. Gaby Wilson, "Joe Jonas Finally Explains What 'Cake by the Ocean' Means," MTV News, September 21, 2015, www.mtv.com/news/2277755/joe-jonas-dnce-cake-by-the-ocean-means/.

3. Neil Postman, *Amusing Ourselves to Death: Public Discourse in the Age of Show Business*, 20th anniversary ed. (New York: Penguin, 2005).

4. Courtney Love, interview by Philip Weiss, in "The Love Issue," *Spin*, October 1998, 100.

5. George Lucas, interview by Bill Moyers, in "Of Myth and Men," *Time*, April 18, 1999, http://content.time.com/time/magazine/article/0,9171,23298-3,00.html.

6. You can watch the song for yourself on YouTube: www.youtube.com/watch?v=n-865kufgag.

7. Postman, *Amusing Ourselves to Death*, 92.

8. John M. Culkin, "A Schoolman's Guide to Marshall McLuhan," *Saturday Review*, March 18, 1967, 51–53.

9. Joe Biden, quoted in "May 6: Joe Biden, Kelly Ayotte, Diane Swonk, Tom Brokaw, Chuck Todd," *Meet the Press*, NBC, May 6, 2012, www.nbcnews.com/id/47311900/ns/meet_the_press-transcripts/t/may-joe-biden-kelly-ayotte-diane-swonk-tom-brokaw-chuck-todd/.

10. Barack Obama, quoted in Matt Wilstein, "President Obama Credits Ellen DeGeneres with Turning the Tide on LGBT Equality," *Daily Beast*, February 12, 2016, www.thedailybeast.com/articles/2016/02/12/president-obama-credits-ellen-degeneres-with-turning-the-tide-on-lgbt-equality.html.

11. Kirsten Corder et al., "Revising on the Run or Studying on the Sofa: Prospective Associations between Physical Activity, Sedentary Behaviour, and Exam Results in British Adolescents," *International Journal of Behavioral Nutrition and Physical Activity* 12, no. 106 (September 2015), http://ijbnpa.biomedcentral.com/articles/10.1186/s12966-015-0269-2.

12. Aldous Huxley, *Brave New World Revisited* (New York: RosettaBooks, 2010), 35.

13. Marshall McLuhan, *Understanding the Media: The Extensions of Man* (Berkeley, CA: Gingko Press, 2003), 25, 555.

14. Postman, *Amusing Ourselves to Death*, 154.

15. For an excellent examination of Pixar films, read Robert Velarde's book *The Wisdom of Pixar: An Animated Look at Virtue* (Downers Grove, IL: InterVarsity, 2010).

16. Anya Kamenetz, "Kids and Screen Time: A Peek at Upcoming Guidance," National Public Radio, January 6, 2016, www.npr.org/sections/ed/2016/01/06/461920593/kids-and-screen-time-a-peek-at-upcoming-guidance.

17. Twenty One Pilots, "Screen," *Vessel*, © 2013, Fueled by Ramen.

18. Twenty One Pilots, "Car Radio," *Vessel*, © 2013, Fueled by Ramen.

19. Emma Green, "Lecrae: 'Christians Have Prostituted Art to Give Answers,'" *Atlantic*, October 6, 2014, www.theatlantic.com/entertainment/archive/2014/10/lecrae-christians-have-prostituted-art-to-give-answers/381103/.

Chapter 15

1. Natalie Angier, "Do Races Differ? Not Really, Genes Show," *New York Times*, August 22, 2000, www.nytimes.com/2000/08/22/science/do-races-differ-not-really-genes-show.html.

2. National Human Genome Research Institute, "White House, Office of the Press Secretary," press release, June 26, 2000, www.genome.gov/10001356/june-2000-white-house-event/.

3. Angier, "Do Races Differ?"

4. Wesley Lowery and Kimberly Kindy, "These Are the Racially Charged E-mails That Got 3 Ferguson Police and Court Officials Fired," *Washington Post*, April 3, 2015, www.washingtonpost.com/news/post-nation/wp/2015/04/03/these-are-the-racist-e-mails-that-got-3-ferguson-police-and-court-officials-fired/.

5. Eliott C. McLaughlin, "'Disgraceful' University of Oklahoma Fraternity Shuttered after Racist Chant," CNN, March 10, 2015, www.cnn.com/2015/03/09/us/oklahoma-fraternity-chant/.

6. Daniel Chaitin, "Trump Supporter Yells 'Go Back to Africa' to Black Woman," *Washington Examiner*, March 12, 2016, www.washingtonexaminer.com/watch-trump-supporter-yells-go-back-to-africa-to-black-woman/article/2585671.

7. Frank Newport, "Americans Today Much More Accepting of a Woman, Black, Catholic, or Jew as President," Gallup, March 29, 1999, www.gallup.com/poll/3979/americans-today-much-more-accepting-woman-black-catholic.aspx.

8. Frank Newport, "In U.S., 87% Approve of Black-White Marriage, vs. 4% in 1958," Gallup, July 25, 2013, www.gallup.com/poll/163697/approve-marriage-blacks-whites.aspx.

9. William H. Frey, *Diversity Explosion: How New Racial Demographics Are Remaking America* (Washington, DC: Brookings Institution Press, 2014), 193.

10. Orlando Patterson, "Race, Gender, and Liberal Fallacies," Opinion, *New York Times*, October 20, 1991, www.nytimes.com/1991/10/20/opinion/op-ed-race-gender-and-liberal-fallacies.html.

11. Harold Dollar, *St. Luke's Missiology: A Cross-Cultural Challenge* (Pasadena, CA: William Carey Library, 1996), 22.

12. See, for example, Eli Saslow, "The White Flight of Derek Black," *Washington Post*, October 15, 2016, www.washingtonpost.com/national/the-white-flight-of-derek-black/2016/10/15/ed5f906a-8f3b-11e6-a6a3-d50061aa9fae_story.html.

Chapter 16

1. Eugene H. Peterson, *Eat This Book: A Conversation in the Art of Spiritual Reading* (Grand Rapids: Eerdmans, 2006), 101.
2. Peterson, *Eat This Book*, 101.

Chapter 17

1. William Lane Craig, "God Is Not Dead Yet: How Current Philosophers Argue for His Existence," *Christianity Today*, July 3, 2008, www.christianitytoday.com/ct/2008/july/13.22.html.
2. Richard Rodgers, "Something Good," © 1965, performed by Julie Andrews and Christopher Plummer in *The Sound of Music*, directed by Robert Wise (Twentieth Century Fox, 1965).
3. For an excellent video introduction to the transmission of the New Testament, watch Dr. Daniel Wallace's presentation "Did Copyists Copy the New Testament Correctly?," YouTube video, published April 1, 2015, www.youtube.com/watch?v=AklwfTtAFoM.
4. For an excellent introduction to the reliability of the New Testament, read J. Warner Wallace's book *Cold-Case Christianity: A Homicide Detective Investigates the Claims of the Gospels* (Colorado Springs: David C Cook, 2013).
5. Paul D. Feinberg, "The Meaning of Inerrancy," chap. 9 in *Inerrancy*, ed. Norman L. Geisler (Grand Rapids: Zondervan, 1980), 294.

Chapter 18

1. Christian Smith, with Melinda Lundquist Denton, *Soul Searching: The Religious and Spiritual Lives of American Teenagers* (New York: Oxford University Press, 2005), 74–75, table 24.
2. Pew Forum on Religion and Public Life, "U.S. Religious Landscape Survey," 2008, http://assets.pewresearch.org/wp-content/uploads/sites/11/2015/01/comparison-Views-of-Ones-Religion-as-the-One-True-Faith.pdf.
3. People commit the genetic fallacy when they attempt to show that a claim is false simply based on its origin rather than on the soundness of its argument. For example, "You can't believe two plus two equals four because Miss

Crabapple taught you that, and she doesn't even have a college degree." The correct answer to the mathematical equation two plus two is independent of the origin or source of our belief (Miss Crabapple).

4. J. Warner Wallace, "I'm Not a Christian Because It Works for Me," *Cold-Case Christianity* (blog), April 5, 2013, http://coldcasechristianity.com/2013/im-not-a-christian-because-it-works-for-me/.

Chapter 19

1. See Warren Cole Smith and John Stonestreet, *Restoring All Things: God's Audacious Plan to Change the World through Everyday People* (Grand Rapids: Baker, 2015), 25–26. See also David Kinnaman and Gabe Lyons, *Good Faith: Being a Christian When Society Thinks You're Irrelevant and Extreme* (Grand Rapids: Baker, 2016), 79–91.

2. See Andy Crouch, *Culture Making: Recovering Our Creative Calling* (Downers Grove, IL: InterVarsity, 2013).

3. See T. M. Moore, *Ready. Set. Go!* A ViewPoint Study (Lansdowne, VA: Colson Center for Christian Worldview, 2013), 13, https://colsoncenter.org/images/content/wilberforce/ViewPoint_Studies/VPReadySetGo.pdf.

4. Frederick Buechner, "Vocation," in *Wishful Thinking: A Theological ABC* (New York: Harper and Row, 1973), 95. For a thorough description of the idea of calling, see Smith and Stonestreet, "Conclusion: Two Personal Stories," in *Restoring All Things,* 203–8.